EMERGING INNOVATION:
Business Transformation in the New Normal
111 COMPACT CASE STUDIES

Muhammad Usman Tariq, Ph.D.
Rommel Pilapil Sergio, Ph.D.

Copyright © Muhammad Usman Tariq and
Rommel Pilapil Sergio 2023
All Rights Reserved.

ISBN 979-8-89067-778-5

Table of Contents

Case Study 1: Unveiling the Secrets of Operational
Excellence at UAE's King's Hospital 31

> **Themes:** Operations management, Business research, Quality improvement tools, Quality management & improvement, Quality system, Continuous improvement Programme

Case Study 2: Al Ain's Winning Formula: Promoting
Vitamin D Water in the Middle East 36

> **Themes:** Marketing advertising, Marketing mix, Product (and packaging), Promotion activities, Distribution, Retailing and distribution, social media/social networking, Brand management

Case Study 3: Abu Dhabi Uncovered: A New Tourist
Hotspot on the Horizon 41

> **Themes:** Marketing advertising, Communication strategies, Destination branding, Place marketing, Tourism, Marketing mix, Service marketing, Service marketing strategies

About the Editors

Muhammad Usman Tariq, PhD, is a distinguished professional with over fifteen years of experience in both academia and industry, focusing on the integration of artificial intelligence (AI) and emerging technologies in higher education. As a leading expert in research and case studies, Dr. Tariq has worked in private and public sectors across the United States, Asia, and the Middle East, serving as a practitioner, facilitator, trainer, supervisor, consultant, researcher, assessor, online tutor, and counselor. His first inventor status on four scientific patents showcases his dedication to research and innovation. His intellectual contributions include more than 200+ research articles, case studies, and book chapters.

Dr. Tariq is an advocate for the transformative potential of AI in higher education, having published numerous research articles, reviews, and book chapters exploring AI applications and implications in teaching, learning, and administration. His research interests encompass AI-driven personalization, online and self-paced learning, student, and faculty engagement, and the ethical considerations of AI in education. He is a Chartered Fellow at the Chartered Institute of Personnel and Development (CIPD).

In addition to his academic contributions, Dr. Tariq has worked as a standards consultant and trainer for industries representing Six Sigma, quality, health and safety, environmental systems, project management, and information security standards. He has collaborated with several international accreditation agencies, such as NQF, ENQF, CAA, CEA, ABET, ACBSP, AACSB, WASC, and NCEAC, at both the institute and program levels. He is a certified organizational change leader and assessor, playing a pivotal role in developing and implementing change initiatives across various sectors, including aviation, manufacturing, food, hospitality, education, finance, research, software, and transportation.

Dr. Tariq holds the degrees Doctor of Business Administration (With Distinction) from California Southern University, Master of Science in Computing Science with a specialization in Software Engineering from Shaheed Zulfikar Ali Bhutto Institute of Science and Technology, and Bachelor of Science in Computing from Bahria University. He is a certified Organisational change leader and assessor, playing a pivotal role in developing and implementing change initiatives across various sectors, including aviation, manufacturing, food, hospitality, education, finance, research, software, and transportation.

With a passion for learning and development, project management, and training, Dr. Tariq is a member of several doctoral advisory committees at numerous universities and serves on the Harvard Business Review Advisory Council. His extensive experience, research, and commitment to advancing the field of AI in higher education make him uniquely positioned to provide valuable insights and guidance through this book.

Rommel Pilapil Sergio, PhD, is a community leader, multi-awarded educator, an Amazon best-selling author, an academic researcher, and a philanthropist.

Dr. Sergio is a Professor of Management and Associate Dean at the Canadian University Dubai (CUD), United Arab Emirates (UAE). He also served as the Program Director of the Master of Science in Leadership and Organizational Development at the Abu Dhabi School of Management. Before teaching at the CUD, he taught courses at the American University in the Emirates and at De La Salle University-Dasmariñas (DLSU-D) in the Philippines. He also served various institutions as Human Resource and Organizational Development Consultant in the UAE and other countries.

Dr. Sergio has co-authored several management case studies at the UK Case Center. He has presented and published academic research papers and has garnered awards from several international academic conferences, including Harvard University. His current research focus is on human resource management, leadership, organizational behaviour, strategic management, and organizational development and change.

Dr. Sergio holds a Post-Doctoral Bridge to Business and Management at the Tulane University of Louisiana, a private research university in New Orleans, Louisiana, USA. In 2011, the Association to Advance Collegiate Schools of Business (AACSB) in Florida, USA, certified him as "Academically Qualified" to teach business courses. He has earned two doctorate degrees: PhD in Management with a concentration in Human Resource Management (With High-Level Distinction) at the University of Liverpool, UK, and a PhD in Counseling Psychology (With Highest Distinction) at DLSU-D, the Philippines.

He is a humanitarian at heart, spearheading pro bono counseling programs for distressed overseas workers. Moreover, he has extended free educational consulting in selected schools in Dubai, UAE, through psychosocial services, organizational development, and human resource initiatives. This spurred him to write the book, **Unbroken: Trials to Triumph, The Making of a Community Leader.**

His over thirty years of experience as a community leader has prompted him to establish numerous mental health programs in various schools and community organizations in the UAE and the Philippines. As a philanthropist, he has established the Dr. Rommel Pilapil Sergio Scholarship Foundation which envisions honoring and fostering outstanding achievement, helping academically qualified but financially needful students, and encouraging enrolment in particular academic programs needed in the Philippines. His ground-breaking research on happiness, organizational and personal wellness, leadership, and mental health made him write his first best-selling book on Amazon, **Management Cases: Thriving Organizations in the New Normal.**

A Note to the Reader

In an increasingly dynamic and interconnected world, the business landscape continues to evolve at a dizzyingly rapid pace. As a result, organizations, educators, and professionals must continually adapt and innovate to stay ahead of the curve. With this in mind, we have developed a compendium of case studies designed to provide valuable insights, stimulate critical thinking, and inspire new approaches to tackling contemporary challenges. This book, **Emerging Innovation: Business Transformation in the New Normal, 111 Compact Case Studies**, brings together a diverse collection of case studies spanning various countries, industries, and disciplines, offering readers an opportunity to explore the depth and breadth of modern business practices. Each case study has been carefully selected to showcase unique challenges faced by organizations and to highlight the innovative strategies employed to overcome these obstacles.

The book aims to provide a valuable learning resource for undergraduate, graduate, executive, and professional courses alike. Each case study is structured in a concise and accessible format, complete with a synopsis, teaching objectives, challenges, questions, alignment with the United Nations Sustainable Development Goals (SDGs), and references. This approach ensures that readers can efficiently navigate and engage with the content, maximizing the educational value of each case study.

Instructors are encouraged to use the proposed questions as a foundation for classroom discussions and assessments, tailoring them to the specific requirements of their courses. The diverse range of case studies allows for flexibility in their application across various programs and disciplines, ensuring a rich and engaging learning experience for all.

Beyond the classroom, this book serves as a valuable resource for professionals seeking to broaden their understanding of contemporary business challenges and best practices. By examining real-world scenarios and exploring the strategies employed by organizations, readers will be better equipped in steering through the ever-changing business landscape and in developing unique innovative solutions in their workplaces.

As readers delve into the pages of this book, we hope they will find them all enlightening and inspiring. Through the exploration of these case studies, valuable insights will be gained; analytical skills sharpened; and an understanding of the complexities of modern business platforms, enhanced. Embracing the learning journey ahead and, ultimately, applying the lessons learned to the readers' own academic or professional endeavors, will truly make this book one for happy reading and learning!. Lastly, Readers can visit **www.thecasehq.com** for various case studies available with teaching notes to use in the classroom environment.

Acknowledgments

Writing a book is a collaborative effort that involves the contributions and support of many people. We would like to express our gratitude to the individuals and organizations who have played significant roles in the creation of **Emerging Innovation: Business Transformation in the New Normal, 111 Compact Case Studies.**

First and foremost, we would like to thank our family and friends for their unwavering support and encouragement throughout the writing process. Their love and patience have been invaluable.

We are thankful to Abu Dhabi University and the Canadian University Dubai for their support.

We are grateful to the students who have taken relevant courses, and who have challenged us to think critically and creatively about the subject matter.

We would like to extend our thanks to the reviewers who provided constructive feedback and suggestions that have helped improve the quality of the book.

Finally, we would like to express our appreciation to the team at Notion Press who has been supportive and professional throughout the publishing process.

Thank you to all who have contributed to this book. Your support has been immeasurable and we could not have done this without you.

Case Studies Commonalities and Guidance

The case studies presented within this book adhere to a consistent methodology designed to cater to a diverse target audience and customizable session plans.

TARGET AUDIENCE

These case studies are versatile and suitable for undergraduate, graduate, executive, or professional-level courses, serving as concise explorations with thought-provoking questions for students and professionals to delve deeper into the subject matter. Instructors have the flexibility to tailor additional questions based on the specific needs and objectives of their courses, ensuring these case studies remain relevant and applicable across a broad range of disciplines and programs.

PROPOSED SESSION PLAN

This session plan can be adapted to accommodate different teaching techniques, such as role-plays, simulations, debates, or expert guest lectures, to enhance the learning experience and better suit the case study's content and context. One important point to mention is that these are compact case studies and students need to delve deeper into these case studies using discussion questions. Instructors can use the below guidelines to ask students for detailed perspectives.

1. Introduction (10 minutes)

   - Briefly introduce the case study topic and its relevance to the course.
   - Provide an overview of the learning objectives and expected outcomes.

2. Pre-discussion Individual Work (15 minutes)

   - Distribute the case study materials to participants and allow them to read and analyze the content individually.
   - Encourage students to take notes and formulate their thoughts and questions.

3. Small Group Discussions (20 minutes)

   - Divide participants into small groups of 3-5 members.
   - Instruct each group to discuss the case study, focusing on the key issues, challenges, and possible solutions.
   - Encourage groups to consider the provided questions as well as any additional questions generated during the individual work phase.

4. Whole Class Discussion (20 minutes)

   - Reconvene the entire class and invite representatives from each group to present their findings and insights.
   - Encourage an open exchange of ideas and engage in critical discussions, comparing and contrasting various perspectives.

5. Instructor-Led Analysis (15 minutes)

   - Summarize the key takeaways and offer expert insights into the case study.
   - Provide additional context and real-world examples to solidify understanding.
   - Address any misconceptions or misunderstandings that may have arisen during the discussions.

6. Reflection and Application (10 minutes)

    - Guide participants in reflecting on the case study and discussing its implications for their own professional or academic pursuits.
    - Encourage students to consider how the concepts and lessons learned can be applied to real-world situations and challenges.

7. Conclusion (5 minutes)

    - Recap the main points and lessons of the case study.
    - Reiterate the relevance of the case study to the course objectives and broader themes.
    - Assign any follow-up tasks or readings, if applicable.

Unveiling the Secrets of Operational Excellence at UAE's King's Hospital

Themes: Operations management, Business research, Quality improvement tools, Quality management & improvement, Quality system, Continuous improvement Programme

TEACHING OBJECTIVES

The case study is intended to qualify students to:

- Evaluate the healthcare industry landscape in the UAE and identify current trends.
- Analyze the challenges faced by hospitals in the UAE, including King's Hospital
- Evaluate the existing performance management structure and patient experience level prevalent in the UAE healthcare system.

SYNOPSIS

King's Hospital is a leading healthcare institution in the UAE, known for its high-quality medical care and educational services. However, with the growth of the healthcare industry in the UAE, the hospital has faced numerous challenges, including intense market competition, variability in performance management, substandard patient experience, and lack of motivational infrastructure and culture. This case study discusses the operational excellence strategy adopted by King's Hospital to overcome these challenges and achieve sustainability in the competitive healthcare landscape of the UAE.

Healthcare Industry Landscape in the UAE: The healthcare industry in the UAE is growing rapidly, driven by factors such as population growth, increasing prevalence of chronic diseases, and government initiatives to improve healthcare services. The sector is highly competitive, with the emergence of new hospitals and the inflow of private equity funds. Additionally, the UAE has become a medical tourism hub, with patients from around the world seeking high-quality medical care in the country.

Operational Excellence Strategy

To overcome these challenges, King's Hospital implemented an operational excellence strategy that focuses on patient-centered care and continuous improvement. The hospital adopted a flexible and manageable approach to operations management, aligning its operations with its market strategies. The hospital also implemented quality improvement tools such as Lean Six Sigma to identify and eliminate waste and improve efficiency. Additionally, the hospital established a culture of continuous improvement by providing training and support to staff members and regularly collecting and analyzing patient feedback.

Results

The operational excellence strategy adopted by King's Hospital has yielded significant results. The hospital has improved its patient experience, with increased patient satisfaction and decreased wait times. The hospital has also achieved significant efficiency improvements and reduced its operating costs. Additionally, the hospital has established a culture of continuous improvement, with staff members actively involved in identifying and implementing process improvements.

Conclusion

King's Hospital has successfully implemented an operational excellence strategy that has enabled it to overcome the challenges faced by hospitals in the UAE healthcare industry. The hospital has shifted from a conventional hospital-centered framework to a patient-focused service model, adopting a flexible and manageable approach to operations management and aligning its operations with its market strategies. The hospital has also established a culture of continuous improvement, with staff members actively involved in identifying and implementing process improvements. The success of King's Hospital demonstrates the importance of operational excellence in achieving sustainability in the competitive healthcare landscape of the UAE.

INDUSTRY CONTEXT

The case study is set in the healthcare sector of the United Arab Emirates (UAE), which has become highly competitive due to the emergence of new hospitals and the inflow of private equity funds. Hospitals are facing challenges in terms of providing consistent quality healthcare services, maintaining patient satisfaction, and building a strong reputation in the market.

CHALLENGES

- Intense competition: The healthcare sector in the UAE has become highly competitive, with the emergence of new hospitals and private equity funds inflow, which poses a challenge to the sustainability of existing hospitals like King's Hospital.
- Variability in performance management: The variability in the performance management system of King's Hospital can impact its ability to provide consistent quality healthcare services, leading to patient dissatisfaction and a declining reputation.

- Substandard patient experience: The substandard patient experience at King's Hospital could lead to low patient retention, negative word-of-mouth, and reduced trust in the hospital's ability to provide quality healthcare services.

LESSONS LEARNED

- Shifting from a hospital-centered framework to a patient-focused service model is essential for sustainability in the healthcare industry.
- Implementing quality improvement tools and a continuous improvement program can improve performance management and enhance the patient experience.

QUESTIONS

1. What are some of the key challenges that King's Hospital faces in achieving operational excellence? How might these challenges be addressed?
2. How has the healthcare landscape in the UAE evolved in recent years, and what impact has this had on hospitals like King's Hospital?
3. How can King's Hospital modify its services to shift from a hospital-centered framework?

UN SDGS: Quality Education (4); Sustainable cities and communities (11)

RESOURCES

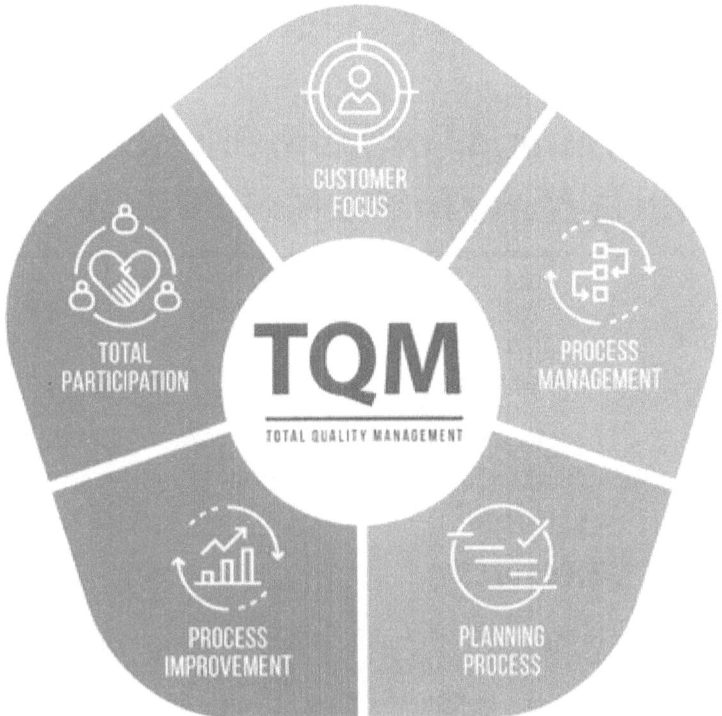

Source: Author

REFERENCES

1. Belrhiti, Z., Giralt, A. N., & Marchal, B. (2018). Complex leadership in healthcare: a scoping review. *International journal of health policy and management, 7*(12), 1073.

2. Bichescu, B. C., Bradley, R. V., Smith, A. L., & Wei, W. (2018). Benefits and implications of competing on process excellence: Evidence from California hospitals. *International Journal of Production Economics, 202*, 59-68.

3. Edelman, E. R., Hamaekers, A. E., Buhre, W. F., & Van Merode, G. G. (2017). The use of operational excellence principles in a university hospital. *Frontiers in medicine, 4*, 107.

Al Ain's Winning Formula: Promoting Vitamin D Water in the Middle East

Themes: Marketing advertising, Marketing mix, Product (and packaging), Promotion activities, Distribution, Retailing and distribution, social media/social networking, Brand management

TEACHING OBJECTIVES

The case study is intended to qualify students to:

- Analyze the marketing mix strategies of Al Ain's Vitaminwater
- Evaluate the distribution and promotion strategies utilized by Al Ain's Vitaminwater
- Identify the key elements that helped Al Ain's Vitaminwater differentiate itself from its competitors and create a unique market position in the UAE and GCC markets

SYNOPSIS

Al Ain's Vitaminwater is a new player in the non-alcoholic beverage industry of the UAE and GCC markets. The brand is produced by the UAE-based Agthia Group company and offers an enhanced water product range enriched with Vitamin D. The market is highly competitive, with established multinational corporations such as PepsiCo and Coca-Cola already having a strong presence. Despite the competition, Al Ain's Vitaminwater has successfully differentiated itself from its competitors by focusing on innovation in packaging, labels, appearance, and components.

Marketing Mix Strategies

Al Ain's Vitaminwater has adopted a unique marketing mix strategy to differentiate itself from its competitors. The brand has focused on the product and packaging element, emphasizing innovation in its product offering and packaging design. The brand's unique packaging, featuring an orange-colored bottle with a distinctive label design, has helped it stand out on store shelves. The product is also enriched with Vitamin D, providing a unique selling point in a market where most bottled water products are not enriched with any additional nutrients.

Distribution and Promotion Strategies

Al Ain's Vitaminwater has utilized a multi-channel advertising strategy that emphasizes social media marketing to amplify the brand personality, while also prioritizing retail and distribution channels. The brand has partnered with major retailers and distributors in the UAE and GCC markets to ensure maximum visibility and accessibility. The brand's social media presence is also strong, with a focus on creating engaging content that highlights the unique features and benefits of the product. The brand has also conducted promotional activities at various events and festivals, increasing its brand visibility among its target audience.

Creating a Unique Market Position

Al Ain's Vitaminwater has differentiated itself from its competitors by creating a unique market position based on innovation, health benefits, and distinctive packaging. The brand's unique selling proposition has helped it gain market share and establish a loyal customer base. In 2018, the brand was recognized for its innovation, winning the 'Best of the Middle East' award at the annual Gamma Innovations Awards in the UK.

Conclusion

Al Ain's Vitaminwater has successfully differentiated itself from its competitors in the highly competitive beverage industry of the UAE and GCC markets. The brand's focus on innovation, health benefits, and distinctive packaging has helped it establish a unique market position and gain market share. The brand's marketing mix strategy, including social media marketing, distribution, and promotion activities, has also contributed to its success. However, the brand must continue to innovate and navigate the complex distribution and retail landscape to maintain its market position and compete against established multinational corporations.

INDUSTRY CONTEXT

The case study is set in the non-alcoholic beverage industry of the United Arab Emirates (UAE) and Gulf Cooperation Council (GCC) markets, which is highly competitive and dominated by multinational corporations such as Coca-Cola and PepsiCo. New players in the market face the challenge of establishing a unique market position through product differentiation and effective distribution and promotion strategies.

CHALLENGES

- Competing against established multinational corporations such as Coca-Cola and PepsiCo in the highly competitive non-alcoholic beverage industry of the UAE and GCC markets.
- Establishing a unique market position for Al Ain's Vitaminwater through product differentiation in packaging, labels, appearance, and components, despite competition from existing market players.
- Implementing effective distribution and promotion strategies to establish a successful market presence and reach a wider audience in the competitive non-alcoholic beverage industry of the UAE and GCC markets.

LESSONS LEARNED

- Innovation and product differentiation are essential to establish a unique market position in a highly competitive industry.
- Effective multi-channel advertising strategies, such as social media marketing, can amplify brand personality and increase brand awareness.

QUESTIONS

1. What specific marketing mix strategies did Al Ain's Vitaminwater adopt to differentiate itself from its competitors in the UAE and GCC markets?
2. How did Al Ain's Vitaminwater utilize social media marketing to amplify its brand personality and increase brand awareness in the target markets?
3. What distribution and promotion strategies did Al Ain's Vitaminwater implement to reach its target audience in the UAE and GCC markets?

UN SDGS Climate action (13); Responsible consumption and production (12)

RESOURCES

Al Ain's Vitaminwater marketing campaign. Source: Aghtia

REFERENCES

1. Agthia. About Agthia. 2021. https://agthia.com/en-us/About-Agthia.

2. Al Ain. *Our Products.* 2021. https://www.alainwater.com/our-products/. —. Our Story. 2021. https://www.alainwater.com/our-story/.

3. Albawaba Signal. *Agthia Partners* With Leo Burnett to Promote Its Water Brands. October 11, 2018. https://www.albawaba.com/business/pr/agthiapartners-leo-burnett-promote-its-water-brands-1198338.

Abu Dhabi Uncovered: A New Tourist Hotspot on the Horizon

Themes: Marketing advertising, Communication strategies, Destination branding, Place marketing, Tourism, Marketing mix, Service marketing, Service marketing strategies

TEACHING OBJECTIVES

The case study is intended to qualify students to:

- Evaluate the concept of destination branding in the context of the tourism industry
- Appraise the significance of destination marketing in promoting tourism destinations
- Analyze the service marketing mix and its role in creating customer value in the tourism industry

SYNOPSIS

The Abu Dhabi Tourism department has embarked on a journey to transform the city into a world-class tourist destination, leveraging the city's heritage, culture, and tourism assets. Despite the challenges posed by the COVID-19 pandemic, Abu Dhabi remains committed to attracting tourists worldwide by prioritizing safety and security measures to instill confidence in visitors. The Department of Tourism collaborates closely with stakeholders to deliver guidance on best practices to exceed global service excellence standards. The case study examines the various strategies adopted by the Abu Dhabi Department of Tourism to position the city as a preferred destination on the world tourism map.

Destination Branding and Marketing

The concept of destination branding is critical in promoting tourism destinations. Destination branding aims to create a positive image of the destination in the minds of potential tourists, emphasizing its unique attributes, attractions, and experiences. The Abu Dhabi Department of Tourism has invested significantly in promoting Abu Dhabi's diverse array of leisure activities, cultural attractions, nature, and entertainment options, in addition to organizing high-profile events in partnership with industry stakeholders.

Service Marketing Mix

The service marketing mix is a critical component of destination marketing. The 7 Ps of service marketing (Product, Price, Place, Promotion, People, Process, and Physical evidence) play a crucial role in creating customer value in the tourism industry. The Abu Dhabi Department of Tourism has focused on developing a comprehensive service marketing mix strategy to attract and retain tourists. The department has implemented various initiatives to improve the quality of its tourism products and services, such as enhancing the accessibility and safety of tourist destinations, providing training to employees to deliver superior customer service, and using technology to enhance the overall customer experience.

Service Marketing Strategies

The Abu Dhabi Department of Tourism has adopted various service marketing strategies to position the city as a preferred destination for tourists worldwide. The department has implemented a customer-centric approach, emphasizing the importance of delivering personalized experiences to meet the diverse needs and preferences of tourists. The department has also focused on building strong relationships with industry stakeholders to create a collaborative and supportive environment for the tourism industry. The department has implemented various marketing and communication strategies to promote Abu Dhabi as a preferred destination, such as social media marketing, influencer marketing, and content marketing.

Conclusion

The Abu Dhabi Department of Tourism has demonstrated a strong commitment to transforming Abu Dhabi into a world-class tourist destination. The department has leveraged the city's heritage, culture, and tourism assets to create a positive image of the destination in the minds of potential tourists. The department has focused on delivering superior customer service by implementing various service marketing strategies, such as enhancing the accessibility and safety of tourist destinations, providing training to employees to deliver superior customer service, and using technology to enhance the overall customer experience. The department's efforts have positioned Abu Dhabi as a preferred destination for tourists worldwide, demonstrating the significance of destination branding and marketing in promoting tourism destinations.

INDUSTRY CONTEXT

The case study is set in the tourism industry of Abu Dhabi, which has evolved into a world-class tourist destination through the Abu Dhabi Tourism department's efforts to conserve, promote, and leverage the city's heritage, culture, and tourism assets. Despite the challenges posed by the COVID-19 pandemic, the department remains committed to attracting tourists worldwide by prioritizing safety and security measures to instill confidence in visitors.

CHALLENGES

- Attracting tourists in a highly competitive global tourism market, with other destinations offering similar experiences and attractions.

- Maintaining a positive destination image and managing the expectations of tourists while delivering quality services and experiences.
- Adapting to changes in the tourism industry, including evolving traveler's preferences, technological advancements, and sustainability concerns, while maintaining a competitive edge.

LESSONS LEARNED

- Effective employee engagement is crucial for achieving operational excellence in the telecommunications industry.
- A reasoned strategical approach and incentives can improve employee motivation and engagement.

QUESTIONS

1. What strategies has the Abu Dhabi Department of Tourism adopted to position Abu Dhabi as a preferred tourist destination on the world tourism map?
2. How has Abu Dhabi successfully positioned itself as a safe and secure destination for tourists during the COVID-19 pandemic, and what impact has this had on visitor confidence and the tourism industry as a whole?
3. What are the key characteristics of service marketing, and how do they apply to the tourism industry?

UN SDGS: Decent work and economic growth (8); Sustainable cities and communities (11)

RESOURCES

Source: Lovin.co

REFERENCES

1. Ben. "When Will Abu Dhabi Airport's New Terminal Open? | One Mile at A Time". One Mile at A Time, 2020. https://onemileatatime.com/new-abu-dhabi-airport-terminal/.

2. Department of Culture and Tourism. "Strategy." Department of Culture and Tourism, 2018. https://tcaabudhabi.ae/en/media.centre/news/strategy.aspx.

3. Giampiccoli, Andrea, and Oliver Mtapuri. "Moving Beyond The 3S'S—Sun, Sea, And Sand: An Interpretation of The Tourism Development Strategy Framework for Abu Dhabi, U.A.E..." *The Arab World Geographer 17*, no. 4 (2014): 339-356.

Etisalat's Game-Changing Approach to Employee Engagement

Themes: Operations management, Employee engagement, Operational excellence, Innovation, Performance management, Strategy, Human resource management

TEACHING OBJECTIVES

The case study is intended to qualify students to:

- Analyze Etisalat's core competencies for operational excellence.
- Evaluate challenges to employee engagement at Etisalat.
- Evaluate Etisalat's strategies for achieving operational excellence through employee engagement.

SYNOPSIS

Etisalat is the largest telecommunications company in the UAE and has received recognition for its employee engagement and operational excellence initiatives. The company has implemented a range of incentives to motivate employees, such as offering an all-expense-paid trip to Japan for "Breakthrough Outstanding Project Contributors." However, the company's strategic approach to employee engagement has been a key factor in increasing engagement levels, tailored to meet its specific requirements. This case study examines Etisalat's strategies for achieving operational excellence through employee engagement.

Core Competencies for Operational Excellence

Etisalat's core competencies for operational excellence include a focus on innovation, customer-centricity, and employee engagement. The company has invested in developing new technologies and services to meet the changing needs of its customers. Etisalat also places a strong emphasis on employee engagement, recognizing the critical role that engaged employees play in achieving operational excellence and delivering superior customer service.

Strategies for Achieving Operational Excellence through Employee Engagement

Etisalat has implemented various strategies for achieving operational excellence through employee engagement. The company has developed a comprehensive employee engagement program that focuses on creating a positive work culture, providing opportunities for employee development and growth, and recognizing and rewarding employee contributions. The company also regularly solicits employee feedback and uses this feedback to drive continuous improvement in its employee engagement initiatives.

Incorporating the "Five Essential Elements of Well-being"

Etisalat has modified its engagement model by incorporating the "Five Essential Elements of Well-being": physical, social, community, financial, and professional. This approach has resulted in a more comprehensive wellness program that caters to employees' needs. The company recognizes that employees who feel supported and fulfilled in these essential areas are more likely to be engaged and productive at work.

Results

Etisalat's strategies for achieving operational excellence through employee engagement have yielded positive results. Recent research indicates that 91% of employees are content working for Etisalat, with 85% reporting increased job satisfaction. The company's focus on employee engagement has also contributed to its success in delivering superior customer service and maintaining its position as the largest telecommunications company in the UAE.

Conclusion

Etisalat's employee engagement and operational excellence initiatives have positioned the company as a leader in the telecommunications industry. The company's focus on innovation, customer-centricity, and employee engagement has enabled it to adapt to changing market conditions and meet the evolving needs of its customers. Etisalat's strategies for achieving operational excellence through employee engagement, including its comprehensive employee engagement program and incorporation of the "Five Essential Elements of Well-being," have yielded positive results and positioned the company for continued success.

INDUSTRY CONTEXT

The telecommunications industry in the UAE is highly competitive, with several established players vying for market share. The industry is subject to rapidly evolving technological advancements, which require companies to continuously adapt their operations to remain competitive.

CHALLENGES

- Maintaining high levels of employee engagement and motivation in a rapidly changing industry.
- Ensuring operational excellence in the face of intense competition and evolving technological advancements.
- Adapting to changing customer preferences and expectations in the telecommunications industry

LESSONS LEARNED

- Effective employee engagement strategies are crucial to maintaining a motivated and skilled workforce, which is necessary for achieving operational excellence.
- To remain competitive in a rapidly changing industry, companies must prioritize innovation and continuously adapt their operations to meet changing customer needs and preferences.

QUESTIONS

1. How Etisalat's employee engagement strategy and its key components will improve operations?
2. What are the potential challenges to maintaining high levels of employee engagement at Etisalat?
3. How Etisalat's focus on employee engagement contributes to operational excellence has established them a leader in the industry?

UN SDGs: Sustainable cities and communities (11); Industry, innovation, and infrastructure (9)

RESOURCES

Source: Etisalat

REFERENCES

1. Al-Jabri, I. M. (2020). Investigating the mediating role of knowledge sharing on employee engagement: Evidence from a developing nation. *International Journal of Human Capital and Information Technology Professionals (IJHCITP)*, *11*(1), 47-63.

2. Chopde, P. T. (2020). A Study of Learning & Development, Team Work, Work Culture & Leadership as well as Demographic Characteristics of Employees on Engagement Level of Employees in a Telecom Organisation in Pune. *PalArch's Journal of Archaeology of Egypt/Egyptology*, *17*(9), 1722-1730.

3. Firdous, T. (2020). The Effects of Employee Engagement on Employee Turnover: A Case Study from the UAE. In *Human Capital in the Middle East* (pp. 93-118). Palgrave Macmillan, Cham.

Sephora's Journey to Unparalleled Customer Experiences

Themes: Customer service, Technology, Technology & innovation management, Augmented and virtual reality, Artificial intelligence, Strategy, Customer experience

TEACHING OBJECTIVES

The case study is intended to qualify students to:

- Analyze Sephora's core competencies in customer service.
- Evaluate Sephora's use of advanced technology and social media to enhance the customer experience.
- Propose strategies to create a seamless shopping experience.

SYNOPSIS

Sephora is an international beauty and cosmetic retailer that has evolved from a French perfume store to a superstore for makeup products. The company has established itself as a competitive brand by prioritizing customer-centric approaches and effectively leveraging social media platforms to enhance the customer experience. This case study examines Sephora's strategies for delivering unparalleled customer experiences through its core competencies in customer service and its use of advanced technology and social media.

Core Competencies in Customer Service

Sephora's core competencies in customer service include a focus on personalization, engagement, and convenience. The company has implemented various initiatives to personalize the shopping experience, such as offering customized product recommendations based on customer preferences and providing personalized beauty consultations. Sephora also places a strong emphasis on engagement, using social media platforms to engage with customers, address their queries, complaints, and suggestions, and build a sense of community around its brand. The company has also prioritized convenience by offering a seamless shopping experience, with features such as buying online and picking up in-store, free shipping, and a mobile app for easy shopping on the go.

Use of Advanced Technology and Social Media

Sephora has effectively leveraged advanced technology and social media to enhance the customer experience. The company uses augmented and virtual reality technology to enable customers to try on products virtually and experiment with new looks before making a purchase. Sephora has also implemented artificial intelligence technology to provide personalized product recommendations and streamline the checkout process. The company's social media strategy focuses on providing customers with detailed product information, engaging with them through community-based platforms, and quickly addressing their queries, complaints, and suggestions.

Importance of Creating a Flawless Shopping Experience

Sephora recognizes the importance of creating a flawless shopping experience for its customers. The company has implemented various strategies to achieve this, such as offering a wide range of products and brands, providing personalized product recommendations, and using advanced technology to enable customers to try on products virtually. Sephora also places a strong emphasis on training its employees to deliver superior customer service, ensuring that every customer interaction is a positive one.

Results

Sephora's strategies for delivering unparalleled customer experiences have yielded positive results. The company has established itself as a leader in the beauty and cosmetic industry, with a loyal customer base and a strong brand reputation. Sephora's focus on personalization, engagement, and convenience, coupled with its use of advanced technology and social media, has enabled the company to deliver superior customer experiences and maintain a competitive edge in the market.

Conclusion

Sephora's journey to unparalleled customer experiences highlights the importance of prioritizing customer-centric approaches, leveraging advanced technology and social media, and creating a flawless shopping experience. Sephora's core competencies in customer service, use of advanced technology and social media, and focus on delivering a superior shopping experience have enabled the company to establish itself as a leader in the beauty and cosmetic industry. Sephora's success demonstrates the significance of customer experience in building brand loyalty and maintaining a competitive edge in the market.

INDUSTRY CONTEXT

The cosmetics industry is highly competitive, with several established players and new entrants continuously emerging in the market. The industry is dynamic, with changing trends and consumer preferences.

CHALLENGES

- Competition from established players in the cosmetics industry makes it challenging for Sephora to maintain its market position and attract new customers.

- Keeping up with changing consumer preferences and market trends, which requires Sephora to be innovative and proactive in introducing new products and services.
- Ensuring consistent and high-quality customer service across all its stores and online platforms is crucial to retaining customer loyalty and attracting new ones.

LESSONS LEARNED

- Customer-centricity and the provision of a seamless shopping experience are critical to the success of a business in the cosmetics industry.
- The use of social media and advanced technology can significantly enhance customer engagement, promote products, and improve the customer experience.

QUESTIONS

1. How does Sephora leverage social media to engage customers and promote products?
2. What advanced technologies does Sephora use to enhance the customer experience, and how do they work?
3. What are Sephora's core competencies for customer service, and how do they drive the company's success?

UN SDGS: Good Health and Well-being (3); Industry, innovation, and infrastructure (9)

RESOURCES

BUSINESS MODEL CANVAS

PARTNERS	PROCESSES	OFFERINGS	RELATIONSHIPS	CUSTOMER
construction contractors	reception	food rooms reception business facilities TV laundry third-party vendors	comfortable hygienic budget-friendly easily accessible	travelers who drive budget-minded travelers
travel organizations	delivery from supplier			
travel agencies	**RESOURCES** location facility physical building reputation brand professional association		**CHANNELS** booking system printed ads email news-feed	reservation websites travel agents
suppliers				

internal / *external*

COST STRUCTURE	REVENUE STREAMS
utility, franchise fee booking service provider public relationship salary	rents upgraded service/items vendors

20

Source: Author

REFERENCES

1. Evelina, L. W., & Safitri, Y. (2019, August). Customer Experience Bali Natural Beauty Care Through Social Media. In *2019 International Conference on Information Management and Technology (ICIMTech)* (Vol. 1, pp. 82-86). IEEE.
2. Koetz, C. (2019). Managing the customer experience: a beauty retailer deploys all tactics. *Journal of Business Strategy*.
3. Leavy, B. (2019). Decoupling: customer-centric perspectives on disruption and competitive advantage. *Strategy & Leadership*.

Carrefour's Supply Chain Mastery: A Behind-the-Scenes Look

Themes: Logistics & supply chain, Supply chain, Supply chain infrastructure, Logistics infrastructure, Retail brand strategy, Hypermarkets

TEACHING OBJECTIVES

The case study is intended to qualify students to:

- Explain the core competencies of Carrefour to support its logistics and distribution system.
- Evaluate possible challenges faced by Carrefour's regarding the distribution system and explore strategies Carrefour uses to handle challenges.
- Propose strategies to balance its distribution system with business continuity.

SYNOPSIS

Carrefour, the largest retail store in the United Arab Emirates, boasts a logistics and distribution system critical to its supply-chain management and development strategy. This case study provides a behind-the-scenes look at Carrefour's supply chain mastery, exploring the core competencies that support its logistics and distribution system, possible challenges faced by Carrefour, and strategies the company uses to handle these challenges.

Core Competencies to Support Logistics and Distribution System

Carrefour's core competencies in logistics and distribution include a focus on operational efficiency, a dedicated truck fleet, and a commitment to quality customer service. The company operates automatic distribution centers 24/7 and hires only experienced drivers with accident-free driving records who provide dedicated customer service. Carrefour's retail stores are significant customers of the distribution units, and drivers receive a "Private Fleet Driver Handbook" emphasizing the importance of politeness when interacting with store crew members and others.

Strategies

Carrefour has implemented several strategies, such as leveraging data analytics to optimize transportation routes and minimize delivery times, implementing an automated warehouse system to increase efficiency and reduce labor costs, and establishing partnerships with local suppliers to minimize lead times and transportation costs. The company also places a strong emphasis on employee training and development, ensuring that its logistics and distribution teams have the skills and knowledge required to execute their functions efficiently.

Importance of Balancing Distribution System with Business Continuity

Balancing Carrefour's distribution system with business continuity is crucial to ensure that the company can continue to deliver goods to customers in the event of disruptions such as natural disasters or supply chain disruptions. Carrefour has implemented several strategies to maintain business continuity, such as establishing backup distribution centers and warehouses, implementing a robust disaster recovery plan, and developing strong relationships with suppliers to ensure a consistent supply of goods.

Results

Carrefour's logistics and distribution system has yielded positive results, enabling the company to maintain a strong position in the retail industry and meet customer expectations for timely delivery and high-quality customer service. The company's focus on operational efficiency, dedicated truck fleet, and commitment to quality customer service has enabled it to optimize its logistics and distribution system and maintain a competitive edge in the market.

Conclusion

Carrefour's supply chain mastery highlights the importance of balancing logistics and distribution with business continuity, implementing strategies to handle potential challenges, and prioritizing operational efficiency and customer service. Carrefour's core competencies in logistics and distribution, commitment to employee training and development, and focus on business continuity have enabled the company to maintain a strong position in the retail industry and continue to meet customer expectations. Carrefour's success demonstrates the significance of logistics and distribution in supply-chain management and development strategy.

INDUSTRY CONTEXT

Carrefour operates in the retail industry, which is highly competitive and dominated by established players such as Walmart and Amazon. Carrefour's logistics and distribution systems are crucial to its success in the highly competitive retail industry.

CHALLENGES

- Ensuring consistent and reliable delivery of products to retail stores across the United Arab Emirates through an efficient distribution system.

- Recruiting and retaining expert drivers who can provide dedicated customer service and drive long distances accident-free.
- Maintaining and upgrading the automated distribution centers to keep up with technological advancements and changing market demands.

LESSONS LEARNED

- A well-designed and executed logistics and distribution system can significantly contribute to the success of a retail store, particularly in a competitive market.
- Recruiting and retaining skilled and experienced drivers can improve the quality of customer service and help build a reliable brand reputation.

QUESTIONS

1. What are Carrefour's core competencies in logistics and distribution management?
2. What distribution challenges may Carrefour encounter and how can they be addressed?
3. How does Carrefour train and recruit its drivers to ensure efficient and high-quality distribution service?

UN SDGS: Decent work and Economic Growth (8); Industry, innovation, and infrastructure (9)

RESOURCES

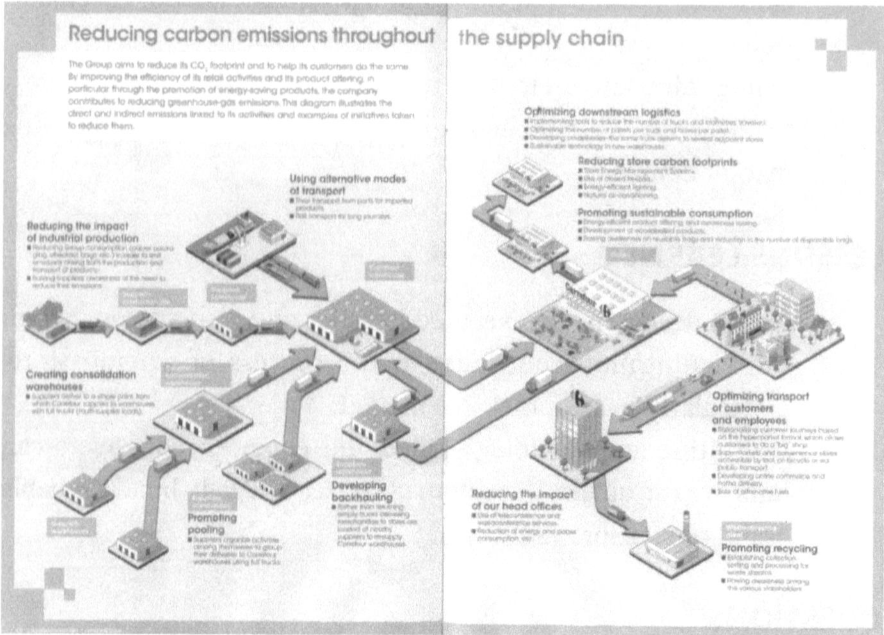

Source: CMUSCM

REFERENCES

1. Ali, O., & Hingst, R. (2018). Improving the retailer industry performance through RFID technology: a case study of Wal-Mart and Metro Group. In *Cases on Quality Initiatives for Organisational Longevity* (pp. 196-220). IGI Global.

2. Amiman, R. J., Lapian, S. J., & Tumewu, F. J. (2018). Evaluating store attributes of transmart Carrefour Manado as a new store using importance and performance analysis. *Jurnal EMBA: Jurnal Riset Ekonomi, Manajemen, Bisnis dan Akuntansi*, 6(1).

3. Beck, M. (2019). *Cost-Benefit Analysis of the Integration of Electric Semi Trucks to the Walmart Distribution Network within the United States* (Doctoral dissertation).

Breaking New Ground in e-Health with Health 4.0 and Industry 4.0

Themes: Industry 4.0, e-Health, Ecosystem, Health care, Industry impact, Health 4.0

TEACHING OBJECTIVES

The case study is intended to qualify students to:

- Explain the concept of Industry 4.0 and its integration with Health 4.0.
- Assess the impact of Health 4.0 on the healthcare sector.
- Develop recommendations for the implementation of Health 4.0 in the healthcare industry.

SYNOPSIS

The case study focuses on the integration of Industry 4.0 with Health 4.0 and its impact on the healthcare sector. Health 4.0 is an emerging concept in the healthcare industry that leverages advanced technologies such as artificial intelligence, 5G, IoT, medical IoT, and blockchain to provide real-time healthcare services to patients. Industry 4.0 provides a range of advanced technologies to overcome complex challenges in the healthcare industry.

Health 4.0 and Industry 4.0

Health 4.0 is an ecosystem that leverages various technologies such as virtualization, service orientation, interoperability, real-time interactions, security, resilience, and modularity to improve healthcare services. Industry 4.0 provides technologies that can automate computing power, and machine communication procedures, and maximize production efficiency while minimizing costs. The integration of Industry 4.0 with Health 4.0 aims to improve healthcare services, enhance relations between healthcare professionals and patients, and overcome complex challenges in the healthcare industry.

Impact of Health 4.0 on the Healthcare Sector

The adoption of Health 4.0 technologies in the healthcare sector has numerous benefits, including enhanced virtualization, real-time healthcare services to patients, automation of data collection, and improved healthcare outcomes. Health 4.0 also allows healthcare professionals to collect and analyze data from patients, enabling them to provide customized and personalized healthcare services.

Recommendations for Implementation

To implement Health 4.0 in the healthcare industry, organizations need to adopt a comprehensive strategy that includes a focus on patient-centric care, investment in advanced technologies, and partnerships with technology providers. The implementation of Health 4.0 also requires the development of a skilled workforce, the adoption of data privacy and security policies, and the establishment of standards for data interoperability.

Conclusion

The integration of Industry 4.0 with Health 4.0 provides a range of advanced technologies that can revolutionize the healthcare industry. The adoption of Health 4.0 technologies can improve healthcare outcomes, enhance patient satisfaction, and reduce costs. To implement Health 4.0, organizations need to develop a comprehensive strategy that includes a focus on patient-centric care, investment in advanced technologies, partnerships with technology providers, and the development of a skilled workforce. The implementation of Health 4.0 has the potential to transform the healthcare industry and improve healthcare services for patients.

INDUSTRY CONTEXT

Health 4.0 is a concept that emerged from Industry 4.0, which refers to the fourth industrial revolution characterized by automation, data exchange, and digital technologies. In the healthcare sector, Health 4.0 involves the integration of digital technologies and data to improve patient care and enhance healthcare services.

CHALLENGES

- Resistance to change and adoption of new technologies by healthcare professionals and patients.
- Ensuring data privacy and security in the digital healthcare ecosystem.
- Addressing the digital divide and ensuring equitable access to healthcare services for all individuals.

LESSONS LEARNED

- The integration of digital technologies and data can lead to significant improvements in patient care and healthcare services.
- Addressing challenges related to data privacy and security, and equitable access to healthcare services are critical for the successful implementation of Health 4.0.

QUESTIONS

1. How can Industry 4.0 be integrated with Health 4.0 to enhance healthcare services and improve patient care?
2. What are some of the challenges in adopting Health 4.0 technologies in the healthcare sector, and how can they be addressed?
3. What are the benefits of digitizing health data and adopting advanced technologies in the healthcare sector, and how have they transformed patient care?

UN SDGS: Decent work and Economic Growth (8); Industry, innovation, and infrastructure (9)

RESOURCES

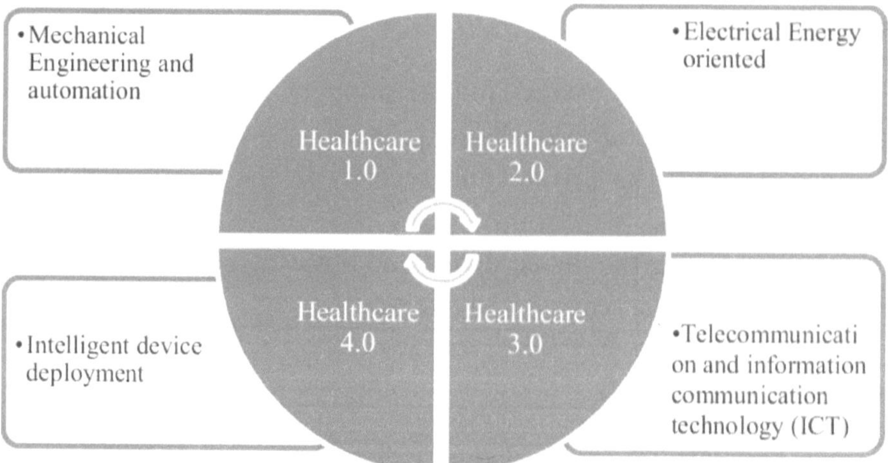

Source: Author

REFERENCES

1. Javaid, M., & Haleem, A. (2019). Industry 4.0 applications in the medical field: a brief review. *Current Medicine Research and Practice, 9*(3), 102-109.

2. Jayaraman, P. P., Forkan, A. R. M., Morshed, A., Haghighi, P. D., & Kang, Y. B. (2020). Healthcare 4.0: A review of frontiers in digital health. *Wiley Interdisciplinary Reviews: Data Mining and Knowledge Discovery, 10*(2), e1350.

3. Khan, M. A., & Salah, K. (2018). IoT security: Review, blockchain solutions, and open challenges. *Future Generation Computer Systems, 82*, 395-411.

Amazon's Trailblazing AI Innovations: A Digital Odyssey

Themes: Digital journey, Artificial Intelligence, Innovation, Intelligence, Digital Innovation

TEACHING OBJECTIVES

The case study is intended to qualify students to:

- Analyze AI's core competencies in organizational development.
- Evaluate challenges and their impact on Amazon regarding AI adoption.
- Evaluate the ROI of AI on Amazon's business.

SYNOPSIS

This case study focuses on the utilization of artificial intelligence by Amazon to enhance its business operations. By leveraging machine learning algorithms, Amazon can collect and analyze consumer data, including purchase history, searches, and GPS-based location, to provide personalized recommendations to customers. This approach has helped Amazon maintain strong relationships with its customers, leading to increased sales and retention rates. Additionally, Amazon offers customized marketing and sales channels to cater to the unique needs of each customer. The company's successful loyalty program, Amazon Prime, has achieved high retention rates in the US and UAE, with millions of subscribers. Despite the potential challenges of adopting artificial intelligence, Amazon has managed to leverage its core competencies to achieve a strong return on investment.

Core Competencies

Amazon's core competencies in innovation and operational excellence have been instrumental in developing an AI-based infrastructure that enables the company to maintain strong customer relationships and increase sales and retention rates. Amazon's ability to constantly experiment and refine its business models, along with its focus on customer obsession, has been the driving force behind its success in AI adoption.

Impact of AI Adoption

The adoption of AI is not without challenges. One of the primary concerns is data privacy, as companies must ensure that data collection and usage adhere to ethical and legal standards. Additionally, the adoption of AI requires significant investment in technology and training, which can be costly for businesses. However, Amazon has managed to overcome these challenges by leveraging its core competencies to achieve a strong return on investment.

ROI of AI on Amazon's Business

The case study delves into the various ways in which Amazon has utilized AI to streamline its business operations, including inventory management, supply chain optimization, and fraud detection. By leveraging AI, Amazon has been able to achieve significant improvements in efficiency and cost savings. The success of Amazon's loyalty program, Amazon Prime, is also attributed to its AI-driven personalized recommendations and customized marketing channels.

Conclusion

The case study highlights the importance of innovation and digital transformation in driving business success, particularly in the era of AI and digital disruption. Amazon's success in AI adoption can be attributed to its core competencies in innovation and operational excellence, as well as its focus on customer obsession. AI adoption is not without challenges, but with the right approach, it can lead to significant improvements in efficiency and cost savings, ultimately driving business growth and success.

INDUSTRY CONTEXT

The case study is set in the e-commerce industry, with Amazon being the focus company. Amazon is a global e-commerce giant, providing a wide range of products and services, from books and electronics to streaming and cloud services.

CHALLENGES

- Integrating and adopting artificial intelligence (AI) into Amazon's business model.
- Ensuring that AI is used ethically and transparently to avoid unintended consequences and negative effects on customers.
- Balancing the use of AI with human involvement to provide a personalized and humanized customer experience.

LESSONS LEARNED

- The use of AI can significantly improve operational efficiency and provide personalized customer experiences.
- However, the ethical and transparent use of AI must be a priority to prevent unintended consequences and negative effects on customers.

QUESTIONS

1. How has Amazon leveraged artificial intelligence to improve customer experience and loyalty?

2. What are some potential challenges that Amazon may face in adopting and investing in artificial intelligence, and how can it address them?

3. How has Amazon's investment in robotics impacted its operations and competitive position, and what are the lessons learned?

UN SDGS: Decent work and Economic Growth (8); Industry, innovation, and infrastructure (9)

RESOURCES

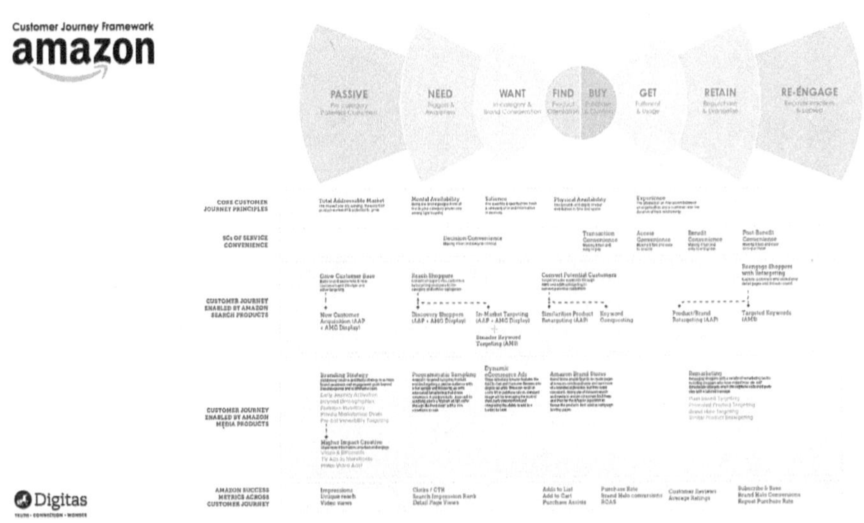

Source: Digitas

REFERENCES

1. AlSheibani, S., Messom, C., & Cheung, Y. (2020, January). Re-thinking the competitive landscape of artificial intelligence. In *Proceedings of the 53rd Hawaii international conference on system sciences.*

2. Dhanabalan, T., & Sathish, A. (2018). Transforming Indian industries through artificial intelligence and robotics in industry 4.0. *International Journal of Mechanical Engineering and Technology, 9*(10), 835-845.

3. Guha, A., Grewal, D., Kopalle, P. K., Haenlein, M., Schneider, M. J., Jung, H., ... & Hawkins, G. (2021). How artificial intelligence will affect the future of retailing. *Journal of Retailing, 97*(1), 28-41.

Charting the Course for SMEs in the Post-COVID Landscape

Themes: SMEs, enterprises, COVID-19, Pandemic impact, SMEs challenges, Economy

TEACHING OBJECTIVES

The case study is intended to qualify students to:

- Analyze the impact of the next phase of COVID-19 on Small and Medium-sized firms.
- Evaluate potential challenges faced by SMEs during the next phase of the COVID-19 pandemic.
- Propose strategies for SMEs to overcome the challenges of COVID-19.

SYNOPSIS

The case study explores the challenges and strategies for small and medium-sized enterprises (SMEs) in the UAE as they prepare for the next phase of the COVID-19 pandemic. The pandemic has forced many SMEs to pivot their business models and adapt to new ways of serving customers, such as takeout and online services. The Targeted Economic Support Scheme (TESS) has provided financial relief to some SMEs, but it remains important for businesses to consider long-term strategies for sustainability. As the economy begins to recover and customer needs continue to evolve, SMEs must be prepared to redesign their business models to stay competitive. The case study emphasizes the need for SMEs to develop strategies for the future and adapt to new challenges to survive and thrive in the post-pandemic business landscape.

Impact of the Next Phase of COVID-19 on SMEs

The next phase of the COVID-19 pandemic is expected to have a significant impact on SMEs, with many businesses facing financial difficulties and uncertainty. SMEs may experience reduced demand for their products or services due to changes in customer preferences, and disruptions in the supply chain may result in inventory shortages. Additionally, changes in regulations and government policies may impact business operations and increase costs.

Strategies for SMEs to Overcome the Challenges of COVID-19

The case study proposes various strategies for SMEs to overcome the challenges of COVID-19. These include developing digital capabilities, diversifying revenue streams, adopting flexible and remote work arrangements, and collaborating with other businesses to share resources and reduce costs. SMEs must also consider long-term strategies for sustainability, such as building resilient supply chains and investing in research and development.

Conclusion

The case study highlights the challenges faced by SMEs in the post-COVID landscape and emphasizes the need for long-term strategies for sustainability. SMEs must adapt to new customer needs and preferences and invest in digital capabilities to remain competitive. Collaboration and innovation can help SMEs navigate the challenges of the pandemic and emerge stronger and more resilient.

INDUSTRY CONTEXT

Small and medium-sized enterprises (SMEs) in the UAE have faced significant challenges due to the COVID-19 pandemic, including business shutdowns and changes in consumer behavior.

CHALLENGES

- Reduced demand for products or services due to economic uncertainty and changing consumer behavior
- Difficulty in accessing financing and managing cash flow
- Adapting to new regulations and health and safety guidelines

LESSONS LEARNED

- The importance of flexibility and agility in adapting to changing circumstances
- The need for strong financial planning and management, including exploring new financing options

QUESTIONS

1. What are the challenges for SMEs during COVID-19, and how can they overcome them?
2. How does TESS support SMEs during the pandemic, and what are its limitations?
3. What key areas do SMEs need to reconsider in their operating models to adapt to changing customer needs during and after the pandemic?

UN SDGS: Decent work and Economic Growth (8); Sustainable cities and communities (11)

RESOURCES

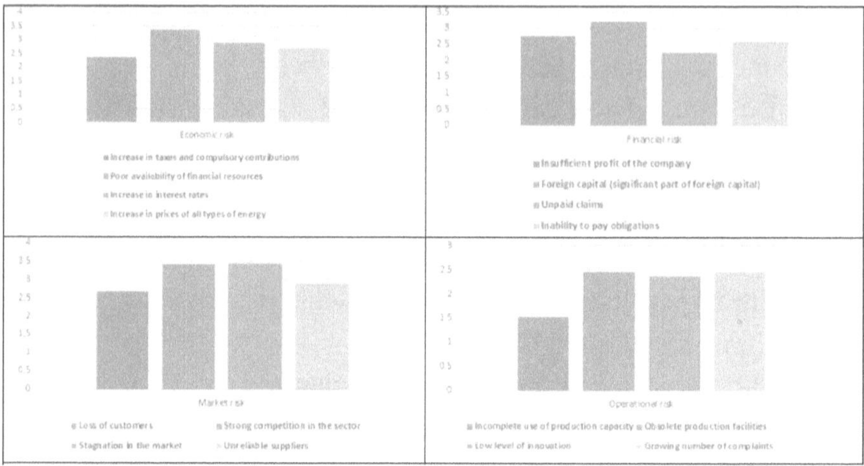

Source: Katarzyna et al., 2021

REFERENCES

1. Alves, J. C., Lok, T. C., Luo, Y., & Hao, W. (2020). Crisis management for small business during the COVID-19 outbreak: Survival, resilience and renewal strategies of firms in Macau.

2. Baker, T., & Judge, K. (2020). How to Help Small Businesses Survive COVID-19. *Columbia Law and Economics Working Paper*, (620).

3. Gregurec, I., Tomičić Furjan, M., & Tomičić-Pupek, K. (2021). The impact of COVID-19 on sustainable business models in SMEs. *Sustainability, 13*(3), 1098.

Lego Serious Play: Igniting Workplace Creativity and Innovation

Themes: Innovation, Lego, Serious Play, Innovative thinking, Work challenges

TEACHING OBJECTIVES

The case study is intended to qualify students to:

- Explain the role of Lego Serious Play in fostering innovative thinking.
- Analyze the process of adopting Lego Serious Play step-by-step.
- Evaluate the key factors that make Lego Serious Play an effective innovation tool.

SYNOPSIS

As technology continues to evolve, computer operators and engineers face more complex challenges in their work. To address these challenges, innovative thinking and collaboration are essential. Lego Serious Play is a methodology that aims to transform team dynamics and encourage communication by ensuring that every member is heard. It provides an alternative to traditional team-building methods, allowing for a broader range of views and perspectives to be considered. Teams work together to achieve shared objectives, with each member contributing their unique skills and experiences. One of the fundamental aspects of a group is the interconnectedness between participants. Lego Serious

Play allows members to express their ideas by building models with their hands, encouraging innovation through acting. The basic idea is that members have knowledge about concepts and solutions to problems that exist in their minds, but they are not always conscious of them. By acting out these solutions, they can be brought to light. The high innovative potential of Lego Serious Play is due to its instinctive character, which allows for the free expression of ideas. The use of story narration is also a key aspect of Lego Serious Play, promoting discussion and exploration rather than mere explanation.

Role of Lego Serious Play

The case study highlights the importance of innovative thinking and collaboration in the workplace. Lego Serious Play provides an alternative to traditional team-building methods by creating a safe space for team members to share their ideas and experiences. The use of Lego bricks allows members to express their ideas tangibly and visually, which can stimulate creative thinking and inspire innovative solutions.

Adopting Lego Serious Play

The case study provides a step-by-step process for adopting Lego Serious Play, including identifying objectives, selecting participants, and creating a model. The process involves a series of exercises designed to promote communication and collaboration among team members, leading to innovative thinking and problem-solving.

Key Factors of Effective Innovation Tool

The case study delves into the key factors that make Lego Serious Play an effective innovation tool. These factors include the use of hands-on building activities, the emphasis on storytelling and narrative, and the encouragement of active participation from all team members. By utilizing these factors, Lego Serious Play fosters a collaborative environment that encourages innovation and creative problem-solving.

Conclusion

The case study highlights the importance of innovative thinking and collaboration in the workplace and the role that Lego Serious Play can play in fostering these values. By providing a collaborative environment and using hands-on building activities, Lego Serious Play encourages team members to share their ideas and experiences, leading to innovative solutions to complex challenges.

INDUSTRY CONTEXT

The use of innovative and collaborative methods to tackle complex challenges in the field of computer operations and engineering.

CHALLENGES

- The increasing complexity of challenges faced by computer operators and engineers due to the prevalence of the Internet of Things, smart devices, and vast amounts of data.
- The need for innovative thinking and collaborative efforts to address these challenges.
- Overcoming barriers to participation and communication in team dynamics.

LESSONS LEARNED

- The Lego Serious Play methodology offers an alternative to traditional team-building methods and allows for a broader range of views and perspectives to be considered.
- Teams can achieve shared objectives by performing tasks reciprocally and leveraging the interconnectedness between participants.

QUESTIONS

1. How does the Lego Serious Play methodology promote collaborative efforts and overcome communication barriers within teams?
2. What are the key elements of the "think with hands" approach in Lego Serious Play, and how do they contribute to innovative thinking?
3. What are some potential applications of the Lego Serious Play methodology beyond the computer operations and engineering industries, and how might they differ from current uses?

UN SDGS: Quality Education (4); Decent Work and Economic Growth (8)

RESOURCES

Source: InnovationTraining

REFERENCES

1. Jensen, C. N., Seager, T. P., & Cook-Davis, A. (2018). LEGO® SERIOUS PLAY® In Multidisciplinary Student Teams. *International Journal of Management and Applied Research, 5*(4), 264-280.

2. Khan, A. H., & Matthews, B. (2019, March). Democratizing Soap: The Methodological Value of Using Constructive Assemblies as a Participatory Design Tool. *In Proceedings of the Thirteenth International Conference on Tangible*, Embedded, and Embodied Interaction (pp. 155-164).

3. Kurkovsky, S., Ludi, S., & Clark, L. (2019, February). Active Learning with LEGO for Software Requirements. *In Proceedings of the 50th ACM Technical Symposium on Computer Science Education* (pp. 218-224).

Navigating the AI Revolution: Implications and Opportunities

Themes: IoT, AI, Technology, Human intelligence, Management

TEACHING OBJECTIVES

The case study is intended to qualify students to:

- Understanding the potential benefits of artificial intelligence in enhancing organizational productivity and decision-making processes.
- Analyzing the challenges faced by Organizations in the adoption and integration of artificial intelligence into their business models.
- Exploring various strategies employed by Organizations to overcome the challenges of implementing artificial intelligence.

SYNOPSIS

As the world moves towards the era of Artificial Intelligence, employers are looking to increase productivity with these tools, while employees are worried about the future of their jobs. Experts predict that up to 60% of human tasks could be automated with AI and machine learning in the coming years. The adoption of AI and machine learning by organizations is essential in improving productivity and remaining competitive in the industry. However, the adoption of AI comes with its set of challenges, and companies need to develop strategies to handle these challenges effectively. The rapid progress of technology is a controversial issue for employees as they tend to work in comfortable environments, using specific techniques over an extended period. However, with the advent of AI, employees need to become more adaptable to change and develop new skills to remain relevant in the job market. Additionally, there is a shortage of qualified professionals with both fine arts or humanities qualifications and computer science experience. Hence, companies need to invest in employee training to ensure that their employees can effectively work with AI systems. Alternatively, organizations can hire AI interface developers who possess the necessary skills and expertise in the field, albeit at a higher cost.

Potential Benefits of AI Adoption

AI and machine learning can handle several tasks, including data analysis, prediction, and problem-solving. By leveraging AI, organizations can improve efficiency, reduce errors, and increase speed in decision-making processes. The use of AI and machine learning in business operations is crucial for remaining competitive in the industry.

Strategies for Successful AI Adoption

To overcome the challenges of AI adoption, companies can invest in employee training programs or hire AI interface developers with the necessary skills and expertise. Additionally, organizations can adopt a holistic approach to AI implementation, involving all stakeholders, and considering ethical and legal implications.

Human Intelligence and AI Collaboration

While AI can handle several tasks, human intelligence remains crucial in most situations, particularly in support and maintenance. Companies can leverage the strengths of AI and human intelligence by creating a symbiotic relationship between the two, where AI handles repetitive tasks, while humans focus on creativity, innovation, and problem-solving.

Conclusion

The case study highlights the importance of strategic planning and preparation for AI adoption in organizations. Companies must consider the potential benefits, challenges, and strategies for successful implementation. By adopting a holistic approach and leveraging the strengths of human intelligence and AI collaboration, companies can navigate the AI revolution and remain competitive in the industry.

INDUSTRY CONTEXT

With the increasing advancements in technology, Organizations are looking to adopt artificial intelligence (AI) to enhance their productivity and gain a competitive advantage.

CHALLENGES:

- Fear of job displacement among employees due to AI implementation
- Lack of technical knowledge and skills among employees to work with AI systems
- Algorithms may only be effective in specific problem-solving scenarios

LESSONS LEARNED

- Companies need to invest in employee training or hire AI interface developers to implement AI systems effectively
- The human presence is still necessary for most situations where AI systems are implemented

QUESTIONS

1. What are the potential benefits and challenges of adopting artificial intelligence in an organization?

2. How can organizations ensure that their employees have the necessary skills and training to effectively work with AI systems?

3. What are some strategies that organizations can use to balance the use of AI with the need for human involvement?

UN SDGS: Decent work and Economic Growth (8); Industry, innovation, and infrastructure (9)

RESOURCES

ARTIFICIAL INTELLIGENCE VS HUMAN INTELLIGENCE

Enter your sub headline here

Artificial Intelligence		Human Intelligence
Created by human intelligence	1	Created by Divine intelligence
Process information faster	2	Process information slower
Highly objective	3	May be subjective
More accurate	4	May be less accurate
Uses 2 watts	5	Uses 25 watts
Cannot adapt to changes well	6	Can easily adapt to changes
Cannot multitask that well	7	Can easily multitask
Below average social skills	8	Excellent social skills
Still working towards self-awareness	9	Has self-awareness
Optimization	10	Innovation

Source: Author

REFERENCES

1. Alsheibani, S., Cheung, Y., & Messom, C. (2018). *Artificial Intelligence Adoption: AI-readiness at Firm-Level*. In PACIS (p. 37).

2. Blanco, J. L., Fuchs, S., Parsons, M., & Ribeirinho, M. J. (2018). Artificial Intelligence: Construction technology's next frontier. *Building Economist*, The, (Sep 2018), 7-13.

3. Donahoe, E., & Metzger, M. M. (2019). Artificial Intelligence and human rights. *Journal of Democracy, 30*(2), 115-126.

Tackling Student Enrolment Challenges in Abu Dhabi: A Design Thinking Approach

Themes: Marketing, Economic, Economic sector, Leadership, Higher education

TEACHING OBJECTIVES

The case study is intended to qualify students to:

- Critically analyze Abu Dhabi's standing as an educational hub for international students.
- Assess the demographic and economic factors that contribute to Abu Dhabi's appeal as a destination for global citizens.
- Utilize design thinking methodology to develop an innovative solution to address the challenges highlighted in the case study.

SYNOPSIS

The city of Abu Dhabi in the United Arab Emirates has emerged as a popular destination for people seeking a high quality of life, security, and a variety of economic opportunities. Abu Dhabi has become a hub for various industries, with investors from diverse backgrounds investing in different sectors. Education has become a priority for the government of Abu Dhabi, and the city has grown as a leader in the educational sector. The government of Abu Dhabi has incorporated education as an important element in the Sustainability and Development Goals of the city. Despite the efforts of the government, there has been a decline in student enrollment numbers in federal institutions compared to non-federal institutions. This decline raises concerns about the quality of education and student satisfaction in federal institutions. The case study focuses on Abu Dhabi as a significant center in the higher education sector and examines enrollment trends of students in federal and non-federal higher educational institutions. Additionally, the case study analyzes how the design thinking process can be applied to develop a solution to address the issue of declining enrollment in federal institutions.

Abu Dhabi as an Educational Hub

Abu Dhabi has emerged as a popular destination for people seeking a high quality of life, security, and a variety of economic opportunities. It has become a hub for various industries, with investors from diverse backgrounds investing in different sectors. Education has become a priority for the government of Abu Dhabi, and the city has grown as a leader in the educational sector. The government has incorporated education as an important element in the Sustainability and Development Goals of the city.

Enrollment Trends in Abu Dhabi's Higher Educational Institutions

Despite the efforts of the government, there has been a decline in student enrollment numbers in federal institutions compared to non-federal institutions. This decline raises concerns about the quality of education and student satisfaction in federal institutions. The decline can be attributed to several factors, including the perception of a lack of innovation in federal institutions, difficulty in obtaining visas, language barriers, and high tuition fees.

Design Thinking Approach

The case study explores how the design thinking process can be applied to develop an innovative solution to address the issue of declining enrollment in federal institutions. The design thinking approach involves understanding the problem, empathizing with the stakeholders, defining the problem, ideating and prototyping possible solutions, and testing and implementing the solution. By utilizing the design thinking approach, Abu Dhabi's government and educational institutions can develop innovative strategies to attract more international students to its federal institutions of higher education.

Conclusion

The case study highlights the importance of innovation and design thinking in addressing challenges faced by the educational sector. The decline in student enrollment numbers in Abu Dhabi's federal institutions can be addressed through the design thinking approach. By understanding the challenges faced by international students and utilizing design thinking to develop innovative solutions, Abu Dhabi can continue to grow as a leader in the educational sector and attract more international students to its federal institutions.

CHALLENGES

- A decline in student enrollment in federal institutions
- Risk of losing the perception of federal institutions as being strong in ensuring learner satisfaction
- Perception of federal institutions being weaker than non-federal institutions

LESSONS LEARNED

- Prioritizing education can lead to significant growth and development in the educational sector
- The decline in student enrollment can be detrimental to the perception of educational institutions

QUESTIONS

1. What are the reasons for the decline in student enrollment in federal institutions compared to non-federal institutions in Abu Dhabi?

2. How can the design thinking process be applied to address the issue of declining enrollment in federal institutions?
3. What steps can the government of Abu Dhabi take to ensure that federal institutions are perceived as strong in ensuring learner satisfaction?

UN SDGS: Quality Education (4); Industry, innovation, and Infrastructure (9)

RESOURCES

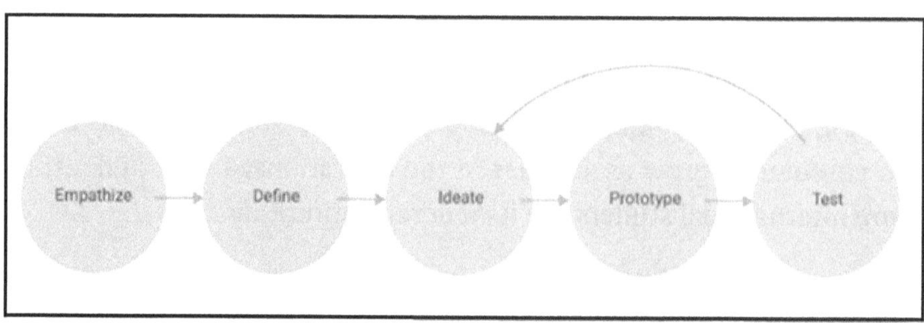

Source: Higher Education

REFERENCES

1. Design Thinking Comes of Age. (2015, September). *Harvard Business Review*, 66–71. https://hbr.org/2015/09/design-thinking-comes-of-age
2. Design Thinking. (2008). *Harvard Business Review*, 15–20. https://hbr.org/2008/06/design-thinking
3. Using Design Thinking in Higher Education. (2015, January 12). Using Design Thinking in Higher Education. https://er.educause.edu/articles/2015/1/using-design-thinking-in-higher-education

Case Study **13**

Amazon's AI Vanguard: Pioneering the Digital Frontier for SMEs

Themes: SMEs, Operations, Economic, Private, Sustainability

TEACHING OBJECTIVES

The case study is intended to qualify students to:

- To comprehend the significance of efficient operations management in Small and Medium Enterprises (SMEs) in the UAE.
- To evaluate the potential operational challenges that SMEs may face while conducting business in the UAE market.
- To explore effective strategies that SMEs can adopt to overcome operational challenges and enhance their business performance.

SYNOPSIS

Small and Medium Enterprises (SMEs) play a significant role in the UAE's economic growth, comprising about 85% of operational units and 55% of employed staff. These businesses are known to be job creators, catalysts for economic development, and essential components of the national economy. However, SMEs in the UAE face challenges due to intense competition, rapidly changing market demands, and limited resources, including knowledge, creativity, and innovation. One of the significant challenges faced by SMEs in the UAE is hiring qualified staff to manage their operations, resulting in limited financial information compared to larger companies. Consequently, SMEs may not be able to provide an audit of financial statements, which is essential for obtaining loans from financiers. Additionally, private firms may provide lower-quality information compared to government firms, leading to an information asymmetry issue between consumers and suppliers of loans.

Addressing Information Asymmetry

The UAE economy heavily relies on managing information, and addressing the information asymmetry issue is crucial for SMEs. While large firms can disseminate information through stock markets and securities, SMEs may face difficulties due to a lack of data. The Loan Risk database can be used to assess SMEs as it maintains both financial and non-financial data, providing a vast amount of information that is critical for evaluating SMEs. This database can help financiers evaluate SMEs and determine their creditworthiness, which can help SMEs obtain loans.

Effective Strategies for SMEs

To support SMEs, the UAE government can provide training on adopting the latest technology in business procedures through chambers of commerce. This will help SMEs overcome their limitations and provide quality information to financiers. Additionally, the government can provide SMEs with tax exemptions, subsidies, and access to low-interest loans to improve their financial status. SMEs can also adopt innovative strategies such as leveraging artificial intelligence, digital marketing, and e-commerce platforms to enhance their business operations and remain competitive.

Conclusion

The case study highlights the significance of efficient operations management for SMEs in the UAE and the challenges faced by SMEs in obtaining loans due to limited financial information. Addressing information asymmetry is critical for SMEs to obtain loans, and the

Loan Risk database can provide financiers with valuable information to assess the creditworthiness of SMEs. Additionally, effective strategies such as training on the latest technology and innovative approaches can help SMEs overcome challenges and enhance their business performance. The UAE government can provide SMEs with tax exemptions, subsidies, and access to low-interest loans to support their growth and promote economic development.

INDUSTRY CONTEXT

Small and Medium Enterprises (SMEs) are an integral part of the UAE's economy, providing employment to 55% of the UAE's workforce and constituting about 85% of the total operational units in the UAE.

CHALLENGES

- SMEs struggle to hire qualified staff to oversee their tasks, resulting in insufficient financial information compared to larger companies.
- SMEs face challenges in sustaining the frequently altering market demand, technological advancement, and competence constraints regarding knowledge, inventiveness, and creativity.
- Information asymmetry issue between consumers and suppliers of loans in general.

LESSONS LEARNED

- Providing training on adopting the latest technology in business procedures can help SMEs overcome their limitations and provide quality information to financiers.
- Evaluating financial and non-financial accounts is challenging for SMEs, and the Loan Risk database can be used to assess SMEs.

QUESTIONS

1. What are the most significant challenges faced by SMEs in the UAE?
2. How can SMEs in the UAE overcome the challenges of hiring qualified staff and obtaining loans from financiers?
3. What initiatives can the UAE government undertake to support the growth of SMEs in the country?

UN SDGS: Decent work and Economic Growth (8); Industry, innovation, and infrastructure (9)

RESOURCES

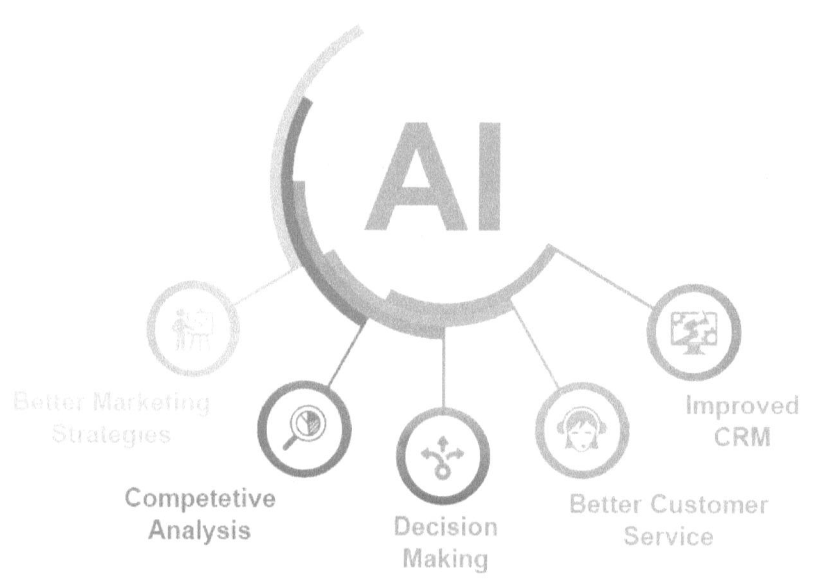

Source: Author

REFERENCES

1. Alefari, M., Almanei, M., & Salonitis, K. (2020). Lean manufacturing, leadership, and employees: the case of UAE SME manufacturing companies. *Production & Manufacturing Research*, 8(1), 222-243.

2. Alsharji, A., Jabeen, F., & Ahmad, S. Z. (2019). Factors affecting social media adoption in small and medium enterprises: evidence from the UAE. *International Journal of Business Innovation and Research*, 19(2), 162-182.

3. Aziz, W. A. (2019). Business process reengineering impact on SMEs operations: evidence from GCC region. *International Journal of Services and Operations Management*, 33(4), 545-562.

DEWA's Visionary Strategy for a Sustainable Future

Themes: Future foresight, Sustainability, DEWA, Electricity, Strategy

TEACHING OBJECTIVES

The case study is intended to qualify students to:

- Comprehend the significance of sustainable strategic future foresight in the context of IT governance.
- Assess the speed and magnitude of challenges faced by DEWA in its IT governance.
- Critically evaluate strategic foresight techniques that can aid in supporting sustainable strategic initiatives of DEWA.

SYNOPSIS

In 2015, DEWA experienced significant success and progress, with the Chief of Efficienology Officer, Arwa Alhassan, leading initiatives related to technology and efficiency. Alhassan's team, which includes female engineers who share her passion, is responsible for adopting the "Energy Efficiency and Retrofit" program, reflecting DEWA's commitment to conservation and sustainability. However, the rapid pace of challenges in IT governance poses a significant threat to DEWA's ability to keep up with everyday situations and plan for the future. To address this, Alhassan believes that a dynamic leader who can motivate team members to achieve strategic objectives is necessary. DEWA needs to create a strategic foresight system in IT governance that enables the sustainable and up-to-date practice of strategic foresight, with extensive application to policymaking.

DEWA's Strategic Foresight System

DEWA has developed a strategic foresight system in IT governance that enables sustainable and up-to-date practices of strategic foresight. The company has hired employees with relevant skills and experience and provided specialized coaching courses to engage employees in foresight procedures at their workplaces. DEWA's commitment to staying ahead of the curve and addressing future challenges and opportunities is reflected in its proactive approach to strategic foresight in IT governance. Creating foresight capacity is not the responsibility of a small team of experts or projects with limited influence. DEWA has implemented several strategies to build these capacities, such as hiring employees with relevant skills and experience and providing specialized coaching courses to engage employees in foresight procedures at their workplaces. DEWA's commitment to staying ahead of the curve and addressing future challenges and opportunities is reflected in its proactive approach to strategic foresight in IT governance. By prioritizing sustainability and efficiency, DEWA aims to ensure that it remains well-positioned to address the needs of its stakeholders and the broader community.

Sustainability and Efficiency

DEWA's commitment to sustainability and efficiency is reflected in its adoption of the "Energy Efficiency and Retrofit" program, which aims to reduce energy and water consumption and lower carbon emissions. The program is an example of DEWA's dedication to the Sustainable Development Goals, which aim to promote sustainable development globally.

Leadership

The case study emphasizes the importance of leadership in fostering sustainable strategic future foresight in IT governance. Arwa Alhassan, the Chief of Efficienology Officer, has played a significant role in leading DEWA's initiatives related to technology and efficiency. She believes that a dynamic leader who can motivate team members to achieve strategic objectives is necessary for DEWA to address future challenges effectively.

Conclusion

DEWA's commitment to sustainability and efficiency is reflected in its proactive approach to strategic foresight in IT governance. The company's adoption of sustainable initiatives such as the "Energy Efficiency and Retrofit" program is a testament to its commitment to promoting sustainable development globally. The case study highlights the importance of sustainable strategic future foresight in IT governance and the critical role of leadership in fostering innovation and efficiency in organizations.

INDUSTRY CONTEXT

DEWA operates in the energy and utilities industry, which is essential for economic growth and development. The industry is characterized by a high level of government regulation, increased competition, and the adoption of innovative technologies to enhance sustainability and efficiency.

CHALLENGES

- The rapid pace of technological change requires companies to remain agile and adapt quickly to stay competitive.

- The industry is subject to increasing government regulations and policies, which can impact business operations and profitability.
- Environmental concerns and the need for sustainable practices are becoming more important, necessitating investment in renewable energy and energy efficiency initiatives.

LESSONS LEARNED

- Developing a strategic foresight system can help Organizations anticipate and prepare for future challenges.
- Investing in employee training and development can build internal capabilities to support sustainable and innovative practices.

QUESTIONS

1. How can companies balance the need for sustainability and efficiency with the need for profitability in the energy and utilities industry?
2. What role do government regulations play in shaping the strategies and operations of companies in the energy and utilities industry?
3. How can Organizations use strategic foresight to address challenges related to innovation and technological change in the energy and utilities industry?

UN SDGS: Decent work and Economic Growth (8); Industry, innovation, and infrastructure (9)

RESOURCES

Source: Dewa

REFERENCES

1. Abdennadher, S., Grassa, R., Abdulla, H., & Alfalasi, A. (2021). The effects of blockchain technology on the accounting and assurance profession in the UAE: an exploratory study. *Journal of Financial Reporting and Accounting.*

2. Al Darwish, M. A. The Effect Of Artificial Intelligence In Smart Decision-Making In The UAE Government.

3. Al-Sarihi, A., & Mason, M. (2020). Challenges and opportunities for climate policy integration in oil-producing countries: the case of the UAE and Oman. *Climate Policy, 20*(10), 1226-1241.

Overcoming Supply Chain Disruptions in the UAE During COVID-19

Themes: Supply chain management, Barriers, IMF, Supply disruption, Supply chain challenges

TEACHING OBJECTIVES

The case study is intended to qualify students to:

- Understand the impact of the COVID-19 pandemic on supply chain management.
- Analyze the challenges faced by Organizations regarding supply chain management during the pandemic.
- Develop recommendations to enhance supply chain procedures to prepare for future disruptions.

SYNOPSIS

This case study highlights the impact of the COVID-19 pandemic on the United Arab Emirates (UAE) and its efforts to maintain its goals for technology, investment, and labor in the context of globalization. Despite the UAE's progress, the pandemic has significantly affected its supply chain procedures, highlighting the need for comprehensive supply chain management. The disruptions caused by the pandemic have led to challenges in transportation, border closures, and supply shortages, emphasizing the need for companies in the UAE to understand the flow of materials during supply chain procedures. This understanding will allow them to address problems at the beginning of the process and avoid supply chain setbacks.

To achieve this, the UAE must implement sustainable policies that incorporate real-time data collection, supply chain reconfiguration, and prompt responses using modern communication technologies such as smartphones. By doing so, firms can adapt to the new realities brought by the pandemic and ensure long-term flexibility in a changing global landscape. Overall, this case study aims to highlight the importance of supply chain management during times of crisis and the role of technology in addressing the challenges posed by the COVID-19 pandemic. By understanding the impact of the pandemic on the global economy and the UAE's goals for technology, investment, and labor, students can develop a deeper understanding of the complexities involved in managing supply chains and identifying opportunities for improvement.

Recommendations for Future Preparedness

To prepare for future supply chain disruptions, the UAE should implement sustainable policies that incorporate real-time data collection, supply chain reconfiguration, and prompt responses using modern communication technologies such as smartphones. By doing so, firms can adapt to the new realities brought by the pandemic and ensure long-term flexibility in a changing global landscape.

Importance of Technology

The case study highlights the role of technology in addressing the challenges posed by the COVID-19 pandemic. Companies that adopt digital technologies to optimize their supply chain management procedures will be better equipped to handle future disruptions. The UAE's reliance on technology is significant, and digital transformation has become a crucial aspect of the country's development plans.

Importance of Supply Chain Management

The case study emphasizes the importance of supply chain management during times of crisis. Companies that understand the impact of disruptions on the global economy and the UAE's goals for technology, investment, and labor can develop a deeper understanding of the complexities involved in managing supply chains and identifying opportunities for improvement.

Conclusion

The case study highlights the importance of supply chain management in the context of the COVID-19 pandemic and the role of technology in addressing the challenges faced by companies in the UAE. The recommendations provided in the case study emphasize the need for comprehensive supply chain management and the importance of digital transformation in ensuring long-term flexibility in a changing global landscape.

INDUSTRY CONTEXT

The case study is situated in the United Arab Emirates (UAE), which has set ambitious goals for technology, investment, and labor in the context of globalization. The COVID-19 pandemic has significantly impacted the country's economy, highlighting the importance of supply chain management and technological innovation.

CHALLENGES

- Disruptions in transportation, border closures, and supply shortages caused by the COVID-19 pandemic have created significant challenges for supply chain management in the UAE.
- The interdependence and connectivity of global supply chains have increased the risk of supply chain disruptions during times of crisis.

- Balancing the need for supply chain flexibility with the need for cost-effectiveness and efficiency remains a significant challenge for Organizations.

LESSONS LEARNED

- Developing comprehensive supply chain management procedures is critical to identifying and addressing problems before they escalate.
- Investing in technology, such as real-time data collection and communication, can improve supply chain resilience and responsiveness during times of crisis.

QUESTIONS

1. How can organizations balance the need for supply chain flexibility with cost-effectiveness and efficiency?
2. What role do interdependence and connectivity play in supply chain disruptions, and how can organizations mitigate these risks?
3. How can organizations leverage technology, such as real-time data collection and communication, to enhance their supply chain resilience and responsiveness?

UN SDGS: Decent work and Economic Growth (8); Industry, innovation, and infrastructure (9)

RESOURCES

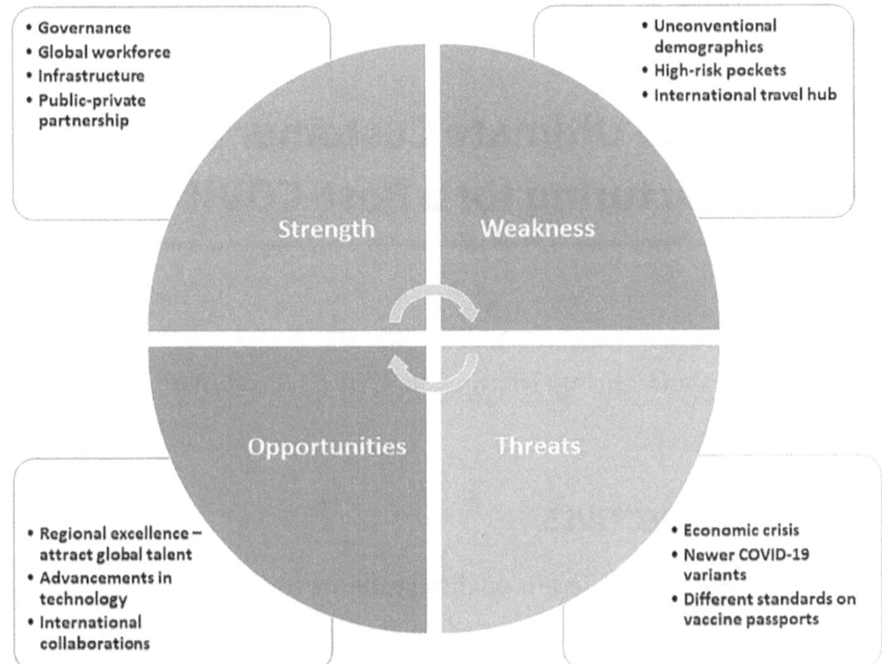

Source: Author

REFERENCES

1. Butt, A. S. (2021). Strategies to mitigate the impact of COVID-19 on supply chain disruptions: a multiple case analysis of buyers and distributors. *The International Journal of Logistics Management*.

2. D'Adamo, I., Gastaldi, M., & Morone, P. (2020). The post-COVID-19 green recovery in practice: Assessing the profitability of a policy proposal on residential photovoltaic plants. *Energy policy, 147,* 111910.

Crafting the Ultimate Customer Experience in Manufacturing for a Post-COVID World

Themes: Manufacturing, Disruption, COVID, Leadership, Business Impact

TEACHING OBJECTIVES

The case study is intended to qualify students to:

- Understand the significance of customer experience in the manufacturing industry, particularly in the post-pandemic world.
- Examine strategies implemented by manufacturing firms to enhance customer experience in the post-pandemic world.
- Evaluate the role of digital transformation in the manufacturing industry and its impact on customer experience.

SYNOPSIS

The impact of the COVID-19 pandemic on manufacturing firms is evident, with disruptions to global supply chains and employee availability posing significant challenges. Manufacturing firms must now navigate through the crisis by considering the situation beyond the haze of uncertainty toward possible future alterations to the manufacturing sector. To respond to the crisis, manufacturing companies are increasingly adopting new technologies, recognizing the need for precise tools to predict changes in consumer demand and alleviate supply sources. Adopting flexible operating frameworks is crucial to remain relevant and adapt to changing customer behaviors. Digital transformation is becoming an essential part of the customer buying journey, and managing customer relationships efficiently is critical in the current environment.

Strategies to Enhance Customer Experience

Manufacturing firms are increasingly adopting new technologies and flexible operating frameworks to remain competitive and navigate the challenges of the pandemic. The focus on customer experience has become essential, and managing customer relationships efficiently is critical in the current environment. Adopting flexible operating frameworks is crucial to remain relevant and adapt to changing customer behaviors.

Digital Transformation

Digital transformation is becoming an essential part of the customer buying journey, and manufacturing firms are recognizing the need for precise tools to predict changes in consumer demand and alleviate supply sources. Students need to examine the role of digital transformation in the manufacturing industry and its impact on customer experience. By understanding how digital transformation can enhance customer experience and improve operational efficiency, students can provide practical insights into the potential benefits and challenges of adopting new technologies.

Leadership

The case study emphasizes the importance of leadership in fostering innovation and efficiency in the manufacturing industry. Effective leadership is necessary to ensure that manufacturing firms can adapt to changing market conditions, navigate through the challenges of the pandemic, and remain competitive in the future.

Conclusion

The COVID-19 pandemic has significantly impacted the manufacturing industry, leading to disruptions in global supply chains and employee availability. Manufacturing firms need to focus on enhancing customer experience and adopting new technologies and flexible operating frameworks to remain competitive and navigate through the crisis. The case study highlights the importance of leadership in fostering innovation and efficiency in the manufacturing industry and the critical role of digital transformation in enhancing customer experience. Students need to examine real-world examples and develop practical recommendations to navigate the complexities of the current crisis and remain competitive in the future.

INDUSTRY CONTEXT

The case study is situated in the manufacturing industry, which has been significantly impacted by the COVID-19 pandemic. The disruptions to global supply chains and employee availability have posed significant challenges for manufacturing firms.

CHALLENGES

- Global supply chain disruptions have created challenges for manufacturing firms in sourcing materials and components.
- The pandemic has accelerated the need for digital transformation in the manufacturing industry, but many firms lack the necessary resources and expertise to implement new technologies.
- Customer expectations have shifted in the post-COVID world, with a greater emphasis on personalized experiences and seamless customer service.

LESSONS LEARNED

- Customer experience is critical to the success of manufacturing firms, particularly in the post-COVID world.
- Digital transformation can help manufacturing firms enhance customer experience and improve business outcomes.

QUESTIONS

1. How can manufacturing firms effectively manage global supply chain disruptions?
2. What are the key challenges associated with implementing digital transformation in the manufacturing industry, and how can firms overcome them?
3. How can manufacturing firms enhance customer experience in the post-COVID world, and what role does technology play in this process?

UN SDGs: Sustainable cities and communities (11); Industry, innovation, and infrastructure (9)

RESOURCES

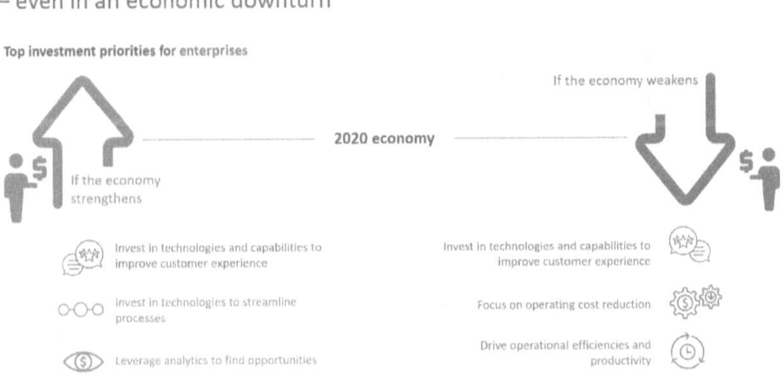

Source: Everest Group

REFERENCES

1. Altig, D., Baker, S., Barrero, J. M., Bloom, N., Bunn, P., Chen, S., ... & Thwaites,
2. G. (2020). Economic uncertainty before and during the COVID-19 pandemic. *Journal of Public Economics*, 191, 104274.
3. Ilinova, A., Dmitrieva, D., & Kraslawski, A. (2021). Influence of COVID-19 pandemic on fertilizer companies: The role of competitive advantages. Resources Policy, 71, 102019.

DEWA's Tech Governance Transformation: A Blueprint for Excellence

Themes: Transformation, Excellence, DEWA, Technology, Governance, Performance, Digital

TEACHING OBJECTIVES

The case study is intended to qualify students to:

- Understand the importance of technology governance and its impact on business outcomes.
- Analyze the factors that contribute to achieving excellence in technology governance, including leadership, culture, and talent.
- Evaluate strategies for managing operational key performance indicators (KPIs) and improving organizational performance.

SYNOPSIS

The Dubai Electricity and Water Authority (DEWA) has established itself as the UAE's leading energy provider, raising significant funds in 2018 and 2020. However, the company's CEO, Dr. Rashid, is now concerned about the impact of IT governance key performance indicators (KPIs) on DEWA's operational excellence. Dr. Rashid believes that the monitoring of operational performance is a significant gap in DEWA, leading to erroneous measurements and logic that hinder decision-making. One of the key challenges DEWA faces is the complicated distribution network with numerous stakeholders, such as customers, that are integrated into distribution transformer centers (DTCs), substations, feeders, and the network as a whole. This complexity poses significant limitations in the management of the distribution system. While DEWA has a set of operational KPIs, they are not sufficient for development, and follow-up interventions are necessary. The company is committed to achieving excellence in technology governance and has implemented several initiatives to achieve this objective.

Strategies for Excellence in Technology Governance

To address these challenges, DEWA's management team should focus on taking customer engagement and digital innovation to the next level by consolidating smart services in all functions to improve water and energy efficiency, refurbish government work to high standards, improve customer experience and attain happiness for everybody. This will require DEWA to make full use of the management information system created to manage the distribution system efficiently. Additionally, DEWA's management team needs to develop a compelling set of operational KPIs that provides efficient causative analysis of any network issues. These KPIs should enable DEWA to monitor operational performance more effectively and make informed decisions to ensure the company's continued success in the energy sector.

Factors Contributing to Excellence in Technology Governance

Several factors contribute to achieving excellence in technology governance, including leadership, culture, and talent. DEWA's leadership plays a critical role in driving the company's technology governance transformation, while its organizational culture fosters a sense of innovation and collaboration. DEWA also focuses on attracting and retaining top talent in the industry, recognizing the critical role that skilled employees play in achieving excellence in technology governance.

Improving Organizational Performance

DEWA's commitment to technology governance transformation has resulted in several improvements in organizational performance, including increased efficiency, reduced costs, and enhanced customer experience. By implementing a compelling set of operational KPIs and adopting digital innovations, DEWA has been able to streamline its operations and provide better services to its stakeholders.

Conclusion

DEWA's commitment to achieving excellence in technology governance provides a blueprint for other organizations seeking to transform their operations and enhance their performance. The case study highlights the importance of leadership, culture, and talent in driving technology governance transformation and improving organizational performance. By examining real-world examples and developing practical recommendations, students will be better equipped to navigate the complexities of technology governance and achieve excellence in their organizations.

INDUSTRY CONTEXT

DEWA is a leading energy provider in the UAE, which has experienced significant growth in the past decade. However, the company faces challenges in monitoring operational performance and making informed decisions due to the complicated distribution network with numerous stakeholders.

CHALLENGES

- Monitoring operational performance in a complicated distribution network with numerous stakeholders
- Developing a compelling set of operational KPIs that provides efficient causative analysis of any network issues

- Making full use of the management information system created to manage the distribution system efficiently

LESSONS LEARNED

- Effective leadership and a culture of continuous improvement are critical to successfully implementing customer-centric strategies and driving business impact in the energy sector.
- Adopting innovative digital technologies such as artificial intelligence, machine learning, and the Internet of Things can improve customer interactions and streamline operations.

QUESTIONS

1. How can DEWA effectively manage the complicated distribution network with numerous stakeholders?
2. What steps can DEWA take to develop a compelling set of operational KPIs that provide efficient causative analysis of any network issues?
3. How can DEWA ensure effective leadership and a culture of continuous improvement to drive business impact in the energy sector?

UN SDGS: Decent work and Economic Growth (8); Industry, innovation, and infrastructure (9)

RESOURCES

Source: Dewa.gov.ae

REFERENCES

1. HAMDAN, D. (2018). *Government Data Governance and Management Frameworks Positive Collaborations, to Enhance Data Sharing and Efficiency of Government Services in Smart Cities* (Doctoral dissertation, The British University in Dubai (BUiD)).

2. Ilmudeen, A. (2021). IT Governance and Business-IT Alignment Frameworks, Models, and the Best Practices. In *Corporate Governance and Its Implications on Accounting and Finance* (pp. 85-103). IGI Global.

3. Kustin, B., Johnstone-Louis, M., & Chan, J. (2019). The future of corporate ownership and governance.

Embracing AI in Supply Chain Management: A Paradigm Shift

Themes: SCM, AI, Technology, Operations, Process, Improvement

TEACHING OBJECTIVES

The case study is intended to qualify students to:

- Understand how advanced technologies, particularly artificial intelligence, are used in supply chain management.
- Explore the benefits that artificial intelligence can bring to supply chain management, such as improving efficiency, reducing costs, and shortening lead times.
- Evaluate the impact of the COVID-19 pandemic on supply chain management and consider the changes that need to be made to create a more resilient and adaptable supply chain in the post-pandemic world.

SYNOPSIS

The COVID-19 pandemic has brought significant challenges to businesses worldwide, particularly in the supply chain management sector. The pandemic has shown that responsive and adaptable supply chains are vital to the survival of businesses during times of crisis. To remain competitive, firms must think creatively and develop new strategies to manage supply chain disruptions caused by the pandemic and other risks. The impact of the pandemic is far-reaching and will continue to shape how businesses operate in the post-COVID world. To prepare for future challenges, firms must create enduring flexibility in their supply chains. They should focus on developing a robust framework that includes a flexible and responsive risk management capability, driven by advanced technologies such as artificial intelligence, applied analytics, and machine learning. These technologies can help firms to better manage risk and make more informed decisions in real time.

Benefits of AI in SCM

AI offers numerous benefits in SCM, such as improving efficiency, reducing costs, and shortening lead times. AI-driven supply chains can predict demand patterns and make informed decisions in real time. This results in lower inventory costs and fewer stockouts, improving customer satisfaction.

Impact of COVID-19

The pandemic has caused significant disruptions in supply chains, highlighting the need for firms to create enduring flexibility in their SCM. Firms must consider various risks that may challenge supply chain networks, such as political, economic, health, and environmental crises. To prepare for future challenges, firms must have a well-planned and integrated SCM system that can adapt to new circumstances quickly.

Advanced Technologies

To manage risk and prepare for future challenges, firms must adopt advanced technologies such as AI, applied analytics, and machine learning. These technologies can help firms to better manage risk and make more informed decisions in real time.

Flexibility in SCM

Firms must also create sufficient suppleness in their supply chains to protect themselves against future disruptions. This requires a general approach that considers various risks that may challenge supply chain networks.

Conclusion

The pandemic has highlighted the importance of advanced technologies in SCM, and firms must adopt these technologies to remain competitive. By creating enduring flexibility and developing a robust framework that includes advanced technologies and a flexible and responsive risk management capability, firms can manage risk and prepare for future challenges. Overall, firms must embrace a paradigm shift in SCM and adopt new strategies to remain competitive in the post-pandemic world.

In addition to advanced technologies, firms should also create sufficient suppleness in their supply chains to protect themselves against future disruptions. This requires a general approach that considers various risks that may challenge supply chain networks, such as political, economic, health, and environmental crises. To achieve this, firms must have a well-planned and integrated supply chain management system that can adapt to new circumstances quickly.

Overall, the pandemic has highlighted the importance of advanced technologies in supply chain management, and firms must adopt these technologies to remain competitive. By creating enduring flexibility and developing a robust framework that includes advanced technologies and a flexible and responsive risk management capability, firms can manage risk and prepare for future challenges.

INDUSTRY CONTEXT

The COVID-19 pandemic has had a significant impact on global supply chains, causing widespread disruption and forcing businesses to reassess their supply chain strategies. As a result, many companies are turning to advanced technologies like artificial intelligence (AI) to improve the efficiency and agility of their supply chains.

CHALLENGES

- Managing supply chain disruptions caused by the pandemic and other crises
- Balancing cost efficiency with supply chain resilience
- Overcoming the challenges of integrating AI and other advanced technologies into existing supply chain systems

LESSONS LEARNED

- The importance of building flexible and agile supply chains that can adapt to changing circumstances
- The potential of AI and advanced technologies to improve supply chain efficiency and resilience

QUESTIONS

1. How can companies strike a balance between cost efficiency and supply chain resilience in the post-COVID world?
2. What are some potential challenges of integrating AI and other advanced technologies into existing supply chain systems?
3. How can companies ensure that their supply chains are flexible and agile enough to adapt to future disruptions and crises?

UN SDGS: Industry, innovation, and infrastructure (9); Sustainable cities and communities (11)

RESOURCES

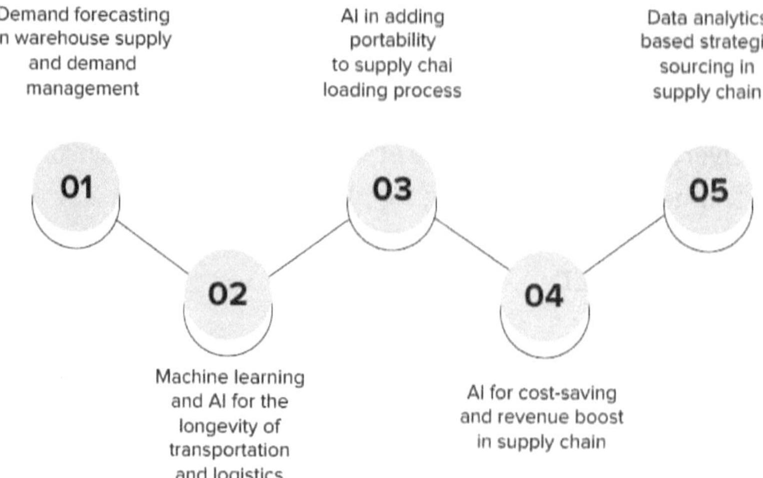

Source: Appinventiv

REFERENCES

1. Acemoglu, D., & Restrepo, P. (2018). *Artificial intelligence, automation, and work* (No. w24196). National Bureau of Economic Research.

2. Brynjolfsson, E., & Mcafee, A. N. D. R. E. W. (2017). The business of artificial intelligence. *Harvard Business Review*, 1-20.

3. Calatayud, A., Mangan, J., & Christopher, M. (2019). The self-thinking supply chain. *Supply Chain Management: An International Journal. UCDL Rev., 51*, 399.

Navigating the Ethical Landscape of AI-Driven Organizations

Themes: Artificial Intelligence, Corporate, Ethics, Ethical AI, Ethics significance

TEACHING OBJECTIVES

The case study is intended to qualify students to:

- Understand the significance of artificial intelligence and advanced technologies in corporate organizations.
- Examine the advantages of artificial intelligence and technologies in corporate organizations.
- Evaluate the ethical implications of artificial intelligence in corporate organizations.

SYNOPSIS

Artificial intelligence (AI) is revolutionizing numerous industries in the UAE with its transformative potential. It allows firms to leverage vast amounts of big data, utilize cloud computing platforms, and implement sophisticated machine learning algorithms. Despite its numerous advantages, AI also brings various challenges and ethical concerns. One significant challenge is the potential for errors and malicious content that could lead to destructive impacts. As technology advances, AI systems are becoming more proficient at creating fake pictures, conversations, and videos, leading to ethical concerns about its use. Furthermore, there is a risk of powerful AI methods being used inappropriately, causing significant harm. Therefore, firms, corporate organizations, and individuals must question and address the ethical considerations of AI while fighting against bots and harmful attacks. The development of ethical AI is essential to ensure that it is used appropriately and beneficially.

Advantages of AI in Corporate Organizations

AI has numerous advantages in corporate organizations, including increased efficiency, improved decision-making, and reduced costs. By analyzing vast amounts of data, AI can generate valuable insights that help firms to make informed decisions, boost productivity, and gain a competitive edge in the market.

Ethical Implications of AI in Corporate Organizations: Despite its advantages, AI also brings ethical concerns, such as the potential for errors and malicious content that could lead to destructive impacts. Moreover, the risk of powerful AI methods being used inappropriately causes significant harm. Therefore, firms and corporate organizations must address the ethical considerations of AI while ensuring that it is used appropriately and beneficially.

The Importance of Ethical AI

The development of ethical AI is critical to ensure that AI is used appropriately and beneficially. Ethical AI considers the potential impact of AI on individuals, communities, and society as a whole. It promotes transparency, accountability, and fairness in the development and use of AI.

Navigating the Ethical Landscape of AI-Driven Organizations

The case study aims to equip students with the necessary skills to analyze and evaluate the potential benefits and risks of AI while fostering an ethical framework for its implementation in corporate organizations. By examining real-life examples of firms that have successfully implemented ethical AI frameworks, students will be better equipped to navigate the ethical landscape of AI-driven organizations. The case study will also encourage students to consider the impact of AI on individuals, communities, and society as a whole.

Conclusion

The case study highlights the importance of ethical AI in corporate organizations, emphasizing the potential benefits and risks of AI while fostering an ethical framework for its implementation. The case study aims to equip students with the necessary skills to analyze and evaluate the potential benefits and risks of AI while promoting transparency, accountability, and fairness in its development and use.

INDUSTRY CONTEXT

The widespread adoption of artificial intelligence (AI) in various industries has led to significant advancements in technology.

CHALLENGES

- Ensuring the ethical use of AI in corporate organizations
- The potential misuse of AI and its impact on individuals and society
- The need to continually address and mitigate the risks and consequences of AI malfunction

LESSONS LEARNED

- AI can greatly benefit industries, but it is essential to ensure its responsible and ethical use.
- The development of effective AI governance and regulations is crucial to ensure accountability and prevent misuse.

QUESTIONS

1. What are the potential ethical concerns of using AI in corporate organizations?
2. How can organizations balance the benefits of AI with its potential risks and consequences?
3. What measures should be taken to ensure the responsible and ethical use of AI in industries?

UN SDGS: Industry, innovation, and infrastructure (9); Sustainable cities and communities (11)

RESOURCES

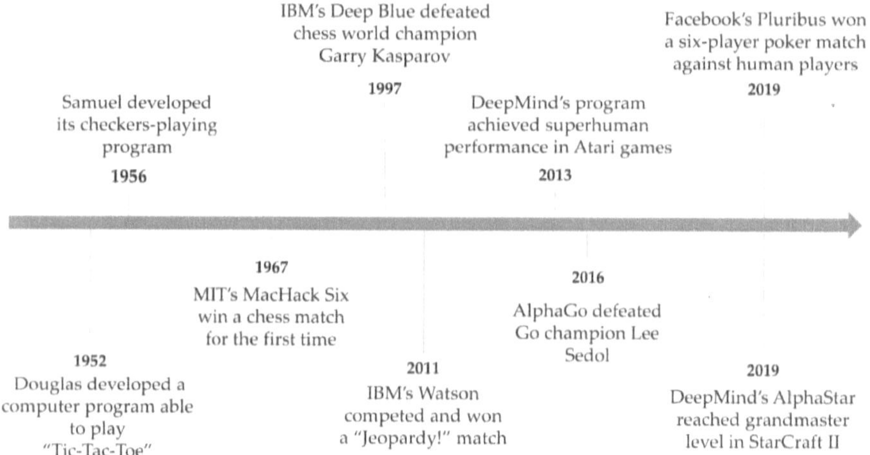

Source: Enrico et al., 2022

REFERENCES

1. Carrillo, M. R. (2020). Artificial intelligence: From ethics to law. *Telecommunications Policy, 44*(6), 101937.
2. Nath, R., & Sahu, V. (2020). The problem of machine ethics in artificial intelligence. *AI & SOCIETY, 35*(1), 103-111.
3. Rajakishore, N., & Vineet, S. (2020). The problem of machine ethics in artificial intelligence. *AI & Society, 35*(1), 103-111.

Empowering Marketing Leaders to Revolutionize Customer Experience

Themes: Competitive advantage, Customer experience, Leadership, Strategy

TEACHING OBJECTIVES

The case study is intended to qualify students to:

- Understand the importance of customer experience in achieving a competitive advantage.
- Explore the role of market leaders in enhancing customer experience.
- Develop recommendations to improve the overall customer experience.

SYNOPSIS

Marketing budgets for customer experience initiatives are increasing daily to achieve a competitive advantage in today's market. Firms are recognizing the significance of customer experience as a key differentiator and are investing heavily in marketing initiatives that prioritize customer satisfaction. In addition to collecting accurate data, marketing leaders need to establish a shared vision of customer experience and ensure that a common set of customer experience KPIs are easily accessible throughout the company. This requires creating a culture of cross-functional team collaboration and aligning all departments toward achieving customer-centric goals. Marketing not only manages data but also coordinates the company's customer experience strategy by sharing results and best practices with other departments.

However, achieving a high level of customer experience poses significant challenges for firms. In addition to data uncertainty, firms need to ask for feedback from previous, current, and future customers. Customer voice programs can be integrated into the firm's marketing agenda to gather feedback from customers and use it to improve customer experience. This requires firms to have a deep understanding of customer preferences and expectations and to be able to act on the insights they gain. Additionally, there is a need to attract and develop talent experienced in customer experience to execute customer-centric strategies effectively.

The COVID-19 pandemic has created a unique set of challenges for firms aiming to enhance their customer experience. With employees widely isolated, the importance of investing in the customer service revolution needs to be proven, while also providing competency objectives for remote workers. This has created a challenging to-do list for marketing and their firms.

The Role of Marketing Leaders

Marketing leaders not only manage data but also coordinate the company's customer experience strategy by sharing results and best practices with other departments. They need to establish a culture of cross-functional team collaboration and align all departments toward achieving customer-centric goals. Marketing leaders must also ensure that a common set of customer experience KPIs are easily accessible throughout the company.

COVID-19 Pandemic

The COVID-19 pandemic has created a unique set of challenges for firms aiming to enhance their customer experience. With employees widely isolated, the importance of investing in the customer service revolution needs to be proven, while also providing competency objectives for remote workers. This has created a challenging to-do list for marketing and their firms.

Conclusion

In conclusion, firms must invest in marketing initiatives that prioritize customer satisfaction to achieve a competitive advantage in the market. Marketing leaders play a vital role in enhancing customer experience by collecting accurate data and establishing a shared vision of customer experience. However, achieving a high level of customer experience poses significant challenges for firms, and marketing leaders need to establish a culture of cross-functional team collaboration and align all departments toward achieving customer-centric goals. Additionally, firms must attract and develop talent experienced in customer experience to execute customer-centric strategies effectively. The COVID-19 pandemic has created a unique set of challenges for firms aiming to enhance their customer experience, and they need to invest in the customer service revolution while also providing competency objectives for remote workers.

INDUSTRY CONTEXT

The marketing industry is rapidly evolving with a focus on customer experience and its impact on the overall success of a business.

CHALLENGES

- Gathering accurate and reliable customer data to inform customer experience strategies.
- Creating a shared vision of customer experience across the organization and establishing a culture of cross-functional team collaboration.
- Attracting and developing talent experienced in customer experience and navigating the challenges posed by COVID-19.

LESSONS LEARNED

- Effective customer experience strategies require collaboration across all functional areas of the organization.
- Gathering and integrating customer feedback into the marketing agenda is crucial for success.

QUESTIONS

1. How can companies improve their customer data collection and analysis methods to better inform customer experience strategies?
2. What are some effective strategies for creating a shared vision of customer experience and establishing a culture of cross-functional team collaboration?
3. How can companies attract and develop talent experienced in customer experience and navigate the challenges posed by COVID-19?

UN SDGS: Reduced Inequalities (10); Industry, innovation, and Infrastructure (9)

RESOURCES

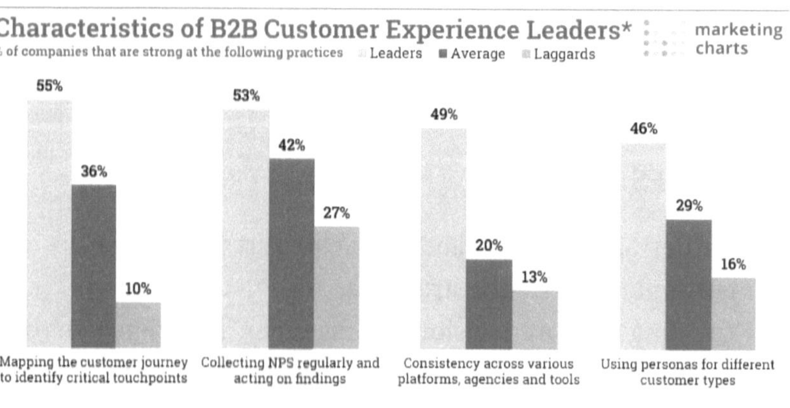

Source: MarketingCharts

REFERENCES

1. Aghina, W., Handscomb, C., Ludolph, J., Rona, D., & West, D. (2020). Enterprise agility: buzz or business impact. *McKinsey & Company*.
2. D'Antonio, M. (2019). Ovum Market Radar: Customer Data Platforms.
3. Hajdas, M., & Kłeczek, R. (2021). The real purpose of purpose-driven branding: consumer empowerment and social transformations. *Journal of Brand Management*, 1-15.

Embracing the Metaverse: The Future of Virtual Reality and Business Opportunities

Themes: Operational challenges, Customer excellence, Facilities, Prediction, Management

TEACHING OBJECTIVES

The case study is intended to qualify students to:

- Analyze the concept of the metaverse and its potential impact on business opportunities.
- Explore the role of virtual reality in creating immersive experiences for customers.
- Evaluate the challenges and opportunities that businesses face when embracing the metaverse.

SYNOPSIS

The concept of the metaverse has been around for decades, but it is now gaining more attention and momentum as technology advances. The metaverse is a virtual world where people can interact with each other and digital objects in a seamless and immersive way. It is a three-dimensional virtual space that can be accessed through virtual reality or augmented reality devices. The metaverse is not just a video game; it offers limitless possibilities for socializing, gaming, education, and commerce. As virtual reality technology continues to advance, the potential of the metaverse becomes more significant. The metaverse has the potential to be the next big thing for businesses, providing new opportunities for engaging with customers and creating innovative products and services. The rise of the metaverse presents significant challenges for businesses. One of the primary challenges is technological limitations. The current virtual reality and augmented reality technologies are still in the early stages of development, and many technical issues need to be resolved before the metaverse can become a mainstream technology. Another challenge is ethical concerns related to privacy, data protection, and cybersecurity. As businesses collect more data in the metaverse, there is a need for standardization to ensure data security and privacy. Additionally, businesses need to consider how they will address the potential impact of the metaverse on society.

To be successful in the metaverse, businesses need to have a clear strategy and understanding of the technology. They need to be creative in their approach and prioritize user experience. The user experience is essential in the metaverse, and businesses need to focus on creating a seamless and immersive experience that meets users' needs. Additionally, businesses need to consider how they can use the metaverse to engage with their customers and create innovative products and services.

Virtual Reality and the Metaverse

Virtual reality is transforming the way people interact with technology, and the concept of the metaverse takes this interaction to the next level. It is a three-dimensional virtual space where people can interact with each other and digital objects seamlessly. Businesses can use the metaverse to create immersive experiences for their customers, providing new opportunities for commerce, education, and socializing.

Opportunities

While the potential benefits of the metaverse are significant, businesses also face several challenges when embracing this new technology.

Technological limitations are one of the primary challenges, as the current virtual reality and augmented reality technologies are still in the early stages of development. Additionally, ethical concerns related to privacy, data protection, and cybersecurity must be addressed. The impact of the metaverse on society must also be considered.

Strategy and User Experience

To succeed in the metaverse, businesses need to have a clear strategy and understanding of the technology. A focus on user experience is essential, and businesses need to prioritize creating immersive experiences that meet users' needs. Additionally, businesses should consider how they can use the metaverse to engage with customers and create innovative products and services.

Conclusion

The metaverse has the potential to be the next big thing for businesses, offering new opportunities for customer engagement and innovative products and services. However, businesses must address the challenges and ethical concerns associated with this new technology. By developing a clear strategy and prioritizing user experience, businesses can embrace the metaverse and succeed in this new virtual world.

INDUSTRY CONTEXT

The metaverse has its roots in gaming and virtual reality technology, but it has since expanded into a broader concept that encompasses a range of virtual experiences, including social media platforms and e-commerce. Companies such as Facebook, Google, and Microsoft have made significant investments in virtual reality and are positioning themselves to take advantage of the potential opportunities in the metaverse.

CHALLENGES

- Technological limitations and the need for high-speed internet connectivity
- Ethical concerns around privacy, data collection, and addiction
- Adapting to a new form of digital communication and customer interaction

LESSONS LEARNED

- Businesses need to stay on top of technological advancements to remain competitive in the metaverse.
- Building ethical and transparent practices around data collection and privacy is essential.
- Adopting a customer-centric approach is critical to success in the metaverse.

QUESTIONS

1. How can businesses effectively balance immersive experiences with ethical considerations in the metaverse?
2. What are the potential drawbacks of the metaverse for individuals and society as a whole?
3. How might the metaverse change the way businesses operate and interact with customers in the future?

UN SDGS: Decent work and Economic Growth (8); Industry, innovation, and infrastructure (9)

RESOURCES

Opportunities in a Metaverse (Now and in the Future)

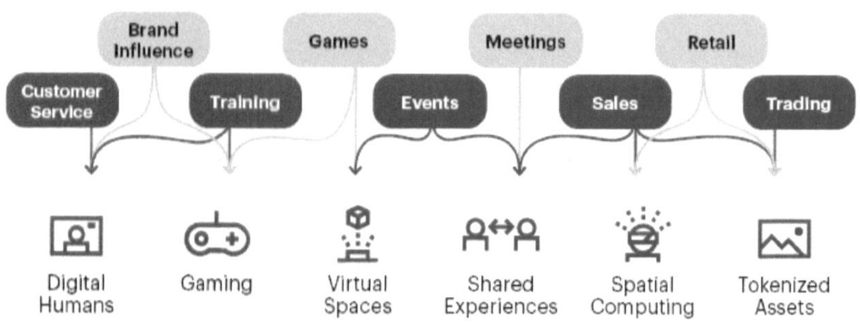

Source: Gartner

REFERENCES

1. Bento, F., & Garotti, L. (2019). Resilience beyond formal structures: A network perspective towards the challenges of an aging workforce in the oil and gas industry. *Journal of Open Innovation: Technology, Market, and Complexity, 5*(1), 15.

2. Gooneratne, C. P., Magana-Mora, A., Otalvora, W. C., Affleck, M., Singh, P., Zhan, G. D., & Moellendick, T. E. (2020). Drilling in the fourth industrial revolution—Vision and challenges. *IEEE Engineering Management Review, 48*(4), 144-159.

3. Koroteev, D., & Tekic, Z. (2021). Artificial intelligence in oil and gas upstream: Trends, challenges, and scenarios for the future. *Energy and AI, 3*, 100041.

Reshaping Corporate Competitive Advantage with Cutting-Edge Technologies

Themes: Strategy, Management, Technologies, Competitive advantage, Strategy, Future

TEACHING OBJECTIVES

The case study is intended to qualify students to:

- Understand the importance of information technology in staying competitive.
- Examine the process of implementing new technology in a step-by-step manner.
- Explore the critical factors that help firms stay competitive in the marketplace.

SYNOPSIS

In today's digital age, managers need to assess the role of Information Systems (IS) to determine their firm's competitive position. IS can add value to the firm's products and services, and can also be essential for the firm's competitive survival. For example, a distributor can launch a novel electronic channel for its customers, providing an advanced service to attract and retain customers. However, investing in electronic systems can create significant cost inflexibility and exit barriers, making it challenging to exit the industry during tough economic times. The implementation of new technology requires a step-by-step approach, starting with a clear understanding of the firm's goals, followed by selecting the appropriate technology and vendor, developing a detailed implementation plan, and testing the system before the final launch. By following these steps, the firm can ensure a successful implementation and reap the benefits of the new technology. To stay competitive, firms need to consider significant factors such as market trends, customer needs, and technological advancements. By continually evaluating these factors, firms can adapt to changes in the market and maintain a competitive edge. Additionally, firms need to prioritize user experience to ensure that the technology they implement meets the needs of their customers and enhances their overall experience.

Systematic Approach

The implementation of new technology requires a systematic approach, starting with a clear understanding of the firm's goals, followed by selecting the appropriate technology and vendor, developing a detailed implementation plan, and testing the system before the final launch. Managers need to develop a detailed implementation plan that considers various factors, such as the cost of the new technology, the impact on the firm's operations, the timeline for implementation, and the training required for employees to use the new system. The success of the new technology depends on the effectiveness of the implementation plan and how well it aligns with the firm's strategic goals.

Gaining Competitive Advantage

To stay competitive, firms need to evaluate significant factors such as market trends, customer needs, and technological advancements continually. Market trends and customer needs can change rapidly, and firms need to be agile and adaptable to stay competitive. Additionally, firms need to prioritize user experience to ensure that the technology they implement meets the needs of their customers and enhances their overall experience. This requires a deep understanding of customer preferences, behaviors, and expectations, and the ability to act on the insights gained from customer feedback.

Conclusion

In conclusion, firms need to evaluate the role of IS in their competitive position, follow a systematic approach to implementing new technology, and continually evaluate significant factors such as market trends, customer needs, and technological advancements to stay competitive. By doing so, firms can leverage technology to gain a competitive advantage and stay ahead in the marketplace.

INDUSTRY CONTEXT

The case study examines the role of information technology in firms and their competitive position. Information technology has become an integral part of most industries, and companies need to assess its significance to stay competitive.

CHALLENGES

- Distinguishing the supporting role of information technology in the firm from its essential role
- Balancing the potential benefits of investing in electronic systems with the cost inflexibility and exit barriers
- Managing a range of innovations to create a beneficial image and maintain a competitive edge

LESSONS LEARNED

- Managers need to assess the role of information systems in their firms to determine their competitive position, considering the potential benefits and risks of investing in electronic systems.
- A range of innovations can help a firm maintain a competitive edge even if it struggles to sustain a single advantage.

QUESTIONS

1. What are the benefits and risks of investing in electronic systems for firms?
2. How can firms assess the role of information systems in their competitive position?
3. What strategies can firms use to manage a range of innovations to create a beneficial image and maintain a competitive edge?

UN SDGS: Quality Education (4); Industry, innovation, and Infrastructure (9)

RESOURCES

Source: Letycja and Adam, 2020

REFERENCES

1. Chan, D. W., Olawumi, T. O., & Ho, A. M. (2019). Perceived benefits of and barriers to Building Information Modelling (BIM) implementation in construction: The case of Hong Kong. *Journal of Building Engineering, 25*, 100764.

2. Darko, A., Chan, A. P., Owusu-Manu, D. G., & Ameyaw, E. E. (2017). Drivers for implementing green building technologies: An international survey of experts. *Journal of cleaner production, 145*, 386-394.

3. Demirkesen, S., & Ozorhon, B. (2017). Impact of integration management on construction project management performance. *International Journal of Project Management, 35*(8), 1639-1654.

Cybersecurity Challenges in the Era of Advanced Information Technologies

Themes: Cybersecurity, Information, Technology, Vulnerabilities

TEACHING OBJECTIVES

The case study is intended to qualify students to:

- Understand the importance of cybersecurity in modern organizations.
- Analyze the potential risks and threats that organizations face in terms of cybersecurity.
- Evaluate the strategies and techniques used to mitigate cybersecurity threats and vulnerabilities.

SYNOPSIS

In today's hyper-connected world, digital firms face an ever-increasing risk of cybersecurity threats, which can leave important data vulnerable and critical functions at risk. While firms prioritize new product development, security standards and government regulations often lag, leaving a gap in cybersecurity. The COVID-19 pandemic has exacerbated the risk, as employees work remotely, making it necessary to share sensitive information outside the firm's walls. Cybercriminals have exploited this opportunity through phishing schemes that lure email users to click on malicious links. Therefore, digital firms need to transform IP addresses, usernames, and passwords into practical aspects that assist in underpinning cybersecurity. The evolving digital ecosystem requires a rethinking of conventional aspects of computing, such as networking, mainframes, applications, and operating systems. Digital firms must prioritize cybersecurity to protect important data and critical functions from cyber criminals.

Implementing cyber security measures

One of the primary challenges in implementing effective cybersecurity measures is the lag in security standards and government regulations compared to new product development. The COVID-19 pandemic has made the situation more complex, as employees are working remotely and sharing sensitive information outside the firm's walls, providing cybercriminals with an opportunity to exploit weaknesses in the security system. Cybercriminals use phishing schemes that lure email users to click on malicious links or attachments, leading to unauthorized access to the Organization's network and critical data.

Mitigating cybersecurity threats

To mitigate cybersecurity threats and vulnerabilities, Organizations must transform IP addresses, usernames, and passwords into practical aspects that help underpin cybersecurity. The evolving digital ecosystem requires a rethinking of conventional aspects of computing, such as networking, mainframes, applications, and operating systems. Organizations must prioritize cybersecurity to protect their data and critical functions from cyber criminals. They can implement various cybersecurity measures, such as using multi-factor authentication, deploying firewalls and intrusion detection and prevention systems, conducting regular security audits, and establishing incident response and disaster recovery plans.

Conclusion

Cybersecurity is a crucial issue for modern Organizations that must prioritize the protection of sensitive data and critical functions. With the increasing number of cyberattacks and the COVID-19 pandemic's impact on remote work, Organizations must be proactive in implementing robust cybersecurity strategies and techniques to mitigate the risks and vulnerabilities. By developing effective cybersecurity measures, Organizations can safeguard their assets against cyber threats and maintain their competitive edge in the market.

INDUSTRY CONTEXT

Digital firms operate in a hyperconnected world, where technology advances and a growing reliance on digital infrastructure pose significant cybersecurity risks.

CHALLENGES

- The risk of cybersecurity breaches is ever-increasing in the evolving digital ecosystem.
- Prioritizing cybersecurity is challenging when firms focus on new product development and lag in security standards.
- The COVID-19 pandemic has increased the risk of cyber threats as employees work remotely.

LESSONS LEARNED

- Digital firms must prioritize cybersecurity to protect important data and critical functions from cyber criminals.
- The evolving digital ecosystem requires a rethinking of conventional aspects of computing to create practical aspects that underpin cybersecurity.

QUESTIONS

1. What steps can digital firms take to prioritize cybersecurity in their organizations?
2. How can firms balance the need for new product development with maintaining robust cybersecurity measures?

3. What role should government regulations play in ensuring cybersecurity in the evolving digital ecosystem?

UN SDGS: Decent work and Economic Growth (8); Industry, innovation, and infrastructure (9)

RESOURCES

The elements of strategic vision for cybersecurity as a business decision

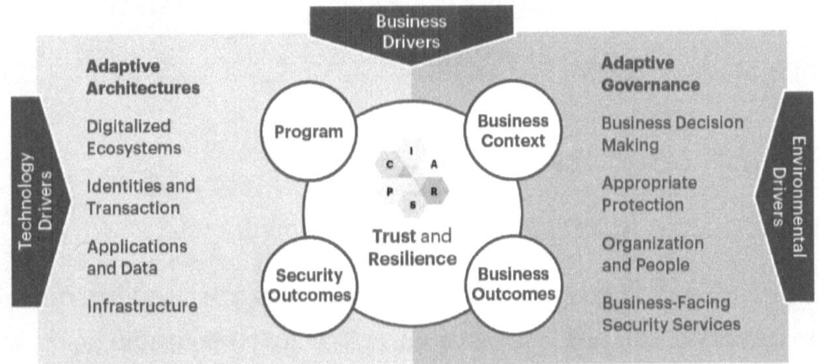

Source: Gartner

REFERENCES

1. Abeshu, A., & Chilamkurti, N. (2018). Deep learning: The frontier for distributed attack detection in fog-to-things computing. *IEEE Communications Magazine, 56*(2), 169-175.

2. Kim, K., Kim, J. S., Jeong, S., Park, J. H., & Kim, H. K. (2021). Cybersecurity for autonomous vehicles: Review of attacks and defense. *Computers & Security*, 102150.

3. Kimani, K., Oduol, V., & Langat, K. (2019). Cyber security challenges for IoT-based smart grid networks. *International Journal of Critical Infrastructure Protection, 25*, 36-49.

Case Study **24**

Harnessing Advanced Technologies in UAE Firms

Themes: Technology, Firms, R&D, Capability, Management

TEACHING OBJECTIVES

The case study is intended to qualify students to:

- Understand how advanced technology can be used in a business.
- Analyze the process of adopting advanced technology.
- Evaluate key factors that contribute to the successful adoption of advanced technology.

SYNOPSIS

Advanced technologies such as virtual reality, artificial intelligence, and big data are revolutionizing businesses, presenting new opportunities and challenges. UAE firms are embracing these technologies to improve their operations and gain a competitive advantage in the market. However, with the adoption of new technologies, businesses must also address the potential risks and ethical implications.

Advantages of Advanced Technologies in UAE Firms

Advanced technologies offer numerous advantages to UAE firms, including increased efficiency, improved decision-making, and enhanced customer experience. Virtual reality can create immersive experiences for customers, while big data can provide valuable insights to inform business strategies. Artificial intelligence can automate processes, reduce costs, and improve productivity, among other benefits.

Adopting Advanced Technologies

The adoption of advanced technologies requires a step-by-step approach, starting with a clear understanding of the firm's goals, selecting the appropriate technology and vendor, developing a detailed implementation plan, and testing the system before the final launch. The adoption process also requires investment in resources and talent to ensure successful implementation and adoption.

Risks of Advanced Technologies

The adoption of advanced technologies also presents challenges and potential risks, such as cybersecurity threats, data privacy concerns, and the need to reskill or upskill employees to adapt to new technologies. Businesses must address these challenges and mitigate potential risks to ensure successful adoption and implementation.

Factors Contributing to Successful Adoption

Several factors contribute to the successful adoption of advanced technologies, including a clear strategy, effective leadership, stakeholder involvement, and prioritizing user experience. By considering these factors, businesses can ensure the successful adoption and implementation of advanced technologies, ultimately gaining a competitive advantage in the market.

Conclusion

The case study highlights the importance of adopting advanced technologies for UAE firms to remain competitive in the market, emphasizing the potential benefits and risks. It also emphasizes the need to address potential risks and ethical implications, prioritize user experience, and invest in resources and talent to ensure successful implementation and adoption.

INDUSTRY CONTEXT

With the rise of technology, companies across various industries are embracing advanced information technology to improve their operations and stay competitive.

CHALLENGES

- Resistance to change and adoption of new technology
- Identifying the right technology to invest in
- Integration of new technology with existing systems

LESSONS LEARNED

- Involving users in the design stage can increase user satisfaction and adoption
- Heavy investment by developers early in the project is necessary for successful implementation

QUESTIONS

1. How to involving users in the design stage to increase user satisfaction?
2. Will heavy investment in technology improve user experience?
3. What are the types of critical resources required by organizations for successful implementation?

UN SDGS: Decent work and Economic Growth (8); Industry, innovation, and infrastructure (9)

RESOURCES

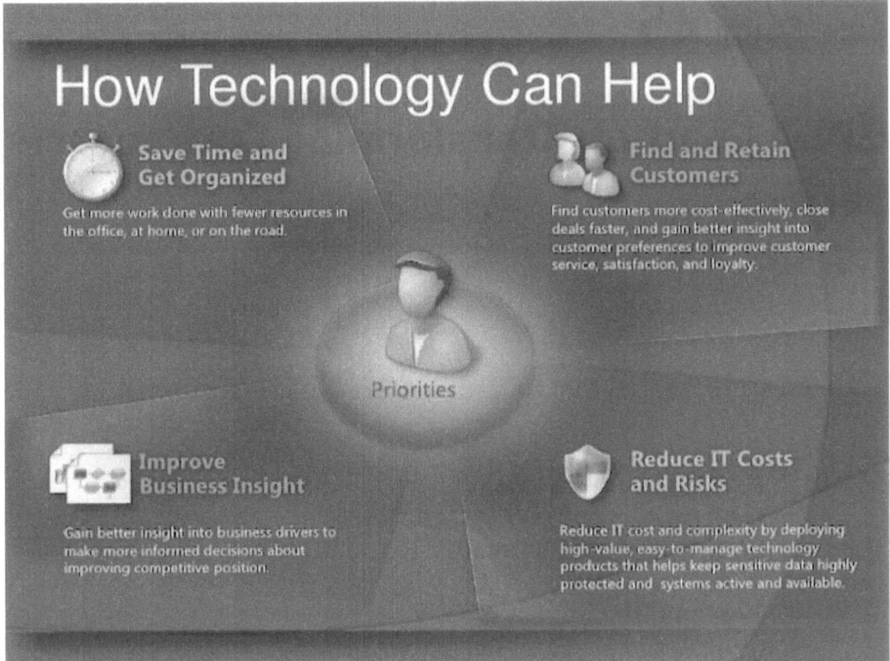

Source: Clutch

REFERENCES

1. Batista, A. A. D. S., & Francisco, A. C. D. (2018). Organisational sustainability practices: A study of the firms listed by the corporate sustainability index. *Sustainability, 10*(1), 226.

2. Franco, M., & Garcia, M. (2018). Drivers of ICT acceptance and implementation in micro-firms in the estate agent sector: influence on Organisational performance. *Information Technology for Development, 24*(4), 658-680.

3. Frank, A. G., Dalenogare, L. S., & Ayala, N. F. (2019). Industry 4.0 technologies: Implementation patterns in manufacturing companies. *International Journal of Production Economics, 210,* 15-26.

GPT-4 Chatbots Transforming Customer Service

Themes: GPT-4, Chatbots, Customer Services, Transformation

TEACHING OBJECTIVES

The case study is intended to qualify students to:

- Understand the impact of GPT-4 chatbots on customer service in various industries
- Analyze the benefits and challenges of implementing GPT-4 chatbots in customer service
- Evaluate strategies for successful integration of GPT-4 chatbots in customer service

SYNOPSIS

The increasing adoption of GPT-4 chatbots in customer service is a response to the need for more efficient and effective customer service operations in today's fast-paced business environment. Chatbots are designed to provide personalized responses to customers by understanding natural language and using machine learning algorithms to improve their performance over time. This technology has significantly impacted various industries, including healthcare, retail, finance, and telecommunications. While the benefits of GPT-4 chatbots are undeniable, there are significant challenges that businesses must address. One major challenge is technical issues, such as chatbot errors, system crashes, and data breaches, that may negatively impact customer satisfaction and trust. Another challenge is data privacy concerns, as chatbots collect and store large amounts of sensitive customer information. Proper training and maintenance are also essential to ensure that the chatbots function effectively and accurately.

Benefits of GPT-4 Chatbots: GPT-4 chatbots offer several benefits to businesses, such as increased efficiency, reduced costs, and improved customer satisfaction. The chatbots can handle repetitive and mundane tasks, allowing customer service representatives to focus on more complex issues. Additionally, chatbots can provide 24/7 customer service, leading to faster response times and improved customer satisfaction.

Impact on Human Jobs

The adoption of GPT-4 chatbots in customer service may also impact human jobs, especially in areas that involve repetitive tasks. The technology has the potential to automate tasks and reduce the need for human interaction in customer service, leading to job displacement and the need for reskilling and upskilling. Therefore, businesses must strike a balance between the use of technology and the preservation of human jobs.

Strategies for Successful Integration

To successfully integrate GPT-4 chatbots in customer service, businesses must prioritize customer privacy and address technical issues promptly. Chatbots must be thoroughly trained and tested to ensure they function accurately and effectively. Businesses must also provide adequate training for their employees to work alongside the chatbots and effectively manage customer interactions.

Conclusion

GPT-4 chatbots have transformed customer service operations in various industries, leading to improved efficiency, reduced costs, and increased customer satisfaction. However, businesses must address significant challenges, such as technical issues, data privacy concerns, and job displacement. To successfully integrate chatbots, businesses must prioritize customer privacy, address technical issues promptly, and provide adequate training for their employees.

INDUSTRY CONTEXT

The use of GPT-4 chatbots is prevalent in various industries, including retail, healthcare, and finance. Retail businesses use chatbots to provide personalized recommendations to customers, while healthcare organizations use them to provide quick medical advice and support. Financial institutions use GPT-4 chatbots to provide automated customer service and support.

CHALLENGES

- Technical issues and integration challenges in implementing GPT-4 chatbots in customer service operations
- Data privacy concerns related to the collection and use of customer data by chatbots
- Impact on human jobs in customer service operations

LESSONS LEARNED

- Proper training and maintenance of GPT-4 chatbots are crucial for successful implementation and optimal performance
- The use of GPT-4 chatbots requires clear communication and transparency with customers about their use and capabilities

QUESTIONS

1. How can businesses address the potential impact of GPT-4 chatbots on human jobs in customer service?
2. What are the ethical considerations related to the collection and use of customer data by GPT-4 chatbots?

3. What strategies can businesses employ to ensure the successful implementation and adoption of GPT-4 chatbots in customer service operations?

UN SDGS: Decent Work and Economic Growth (8); Sustainable Cities and Communities (11)

RESOURCES

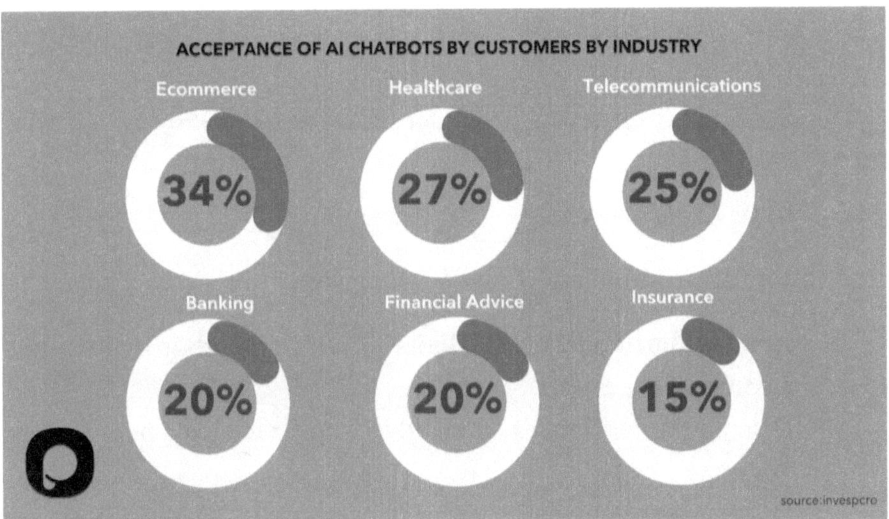

Source: PopupSmart

REFERENCES

1. George, A. S., George, A. H., Baskar, T., & Martin, A. G. (2023). Revolutionizing Business Communication: Exploring the Potential of GPT-4 in Corporate Settings. Partners *Universal International Research Journal, 2*(1), 149-157.

2. Roose, K. (2022). The brilliance and weirdness of ChatGPT. *The New York Times.*

3. https://openai.com/product/gpt-4

Digital Quality Revolution: Business Excellence in the Food Industry

Themes: Digital, Quality, Excellence, Food, Industry

TEACHING OBJECTIVES

The case study is intended to qualify students to:

- Analyze the importance of digital grading systems in maintaining a competitive edge.
- Discuss the challenges involved in implementing a new grading system.
- Propose strategies for effectively executing a business initiative using a grading system.

SYNOPSIS

Digital grading systems have become a necessity for businesses to remain competitive in today's fast-paced and constantly evolving business environment. These systems are designed to provide businesses with a comprehensive understanding of customer needs and preferences, allowing them to deliver exceptional customer service and experiences. By collecting customer feedback, tracking performance, and identifying areas for improvement, businesses can refine their operations and improve service quality.

Advantages of Digital Grading Systems in the Food Industry

The food industry is an example of a sector that has greatly benefited from digital grading systems. Digital grading systems enable food businesses to measure and maintain quality control throughout the food production and supply chain. By providing accurate and objective measures of quality, businesses can reduce waste and improve efficiency, leading to cost savings and increased customer satisfaction.

Implementing a New Grading System

Implementing a new grading system can be a complex process that requires careful planning and execution. One major challenge is the selection of appropriate grading criteria. The system's results depend on the accuracy of the grading criteria used. Businesses must carefully consider the key performance indicators (KPIs) that they wish to track and evaluate, as well as the data collection methods that will be used. Another challenge is designing a user-friendly interface that is intuitive and accessible to all users.

Strategies for Effective Execution of a Business Initiative using a Grading System

To effectively execute a business initiative using a grading system, businesses must consider several strategies. First, businesses should involve all stakeholders in the planning and implementation process to ensure that the system meets their needs and expectations. Second, businesses should prioritize data privacy and security by implementing robust data security protocols and complying with relevant regulations. Third, businesses should regularly review and update the grading criteria and KPIs to ensure that they remain relevant and accurate. Lastly, businesses should use the data collected by the grading system to identify areas for improvement and refine their operations accordingly.

Conclusion

Digital grading systems have become an essential tool for businesses to remain competitive in today's fast-paced business environment. The food industry is an example of a sector that has greatly benefited from digital grading systems. However, implementing a new grading system can be a complex process that requires careful planning and execution. To effectively execute a business initiative using a grading system, businesses must consider several strategies, including involving stakeholders, prioritizing data privacy and security, regularly reviewing and updating the grading criteria and KPIs, and using the data collected to refine operations.

INDUSTRY CONTEXT

Digital grading systems are used in various industries, including hospitality, healthcare, education, and e-commerce. In hospitality, grading systems are used to rate the quality of accommodation, restaurants, and transportation services.

CHALLENGES

- Selecting appropriate grading criteria
- Designing a user-friendly interface
- Ensuring data privacy and security

LESSONS LEARNED

- Careful planning and effective communication with stakeholders is crucial for successful implementation
- Continuous evaluation and adjustment of the grading system are necessary to ensure its effectiveness

QUESTIONS

1. How can businesses use digital grading systems to enhance customer experience and maintain a competitive edge?
2. What are the potential challenges and risks involved in implementing a new grading system?
3. How can businesses ensure data privacy and security when collecting and storing customer feedback through a grading system?

UN SDGS: Health and well-being (3); Industry, innovation, and infrastructure (9)

RESOURCES

Source: Ali et al., 2022

REFERENCES

1. Azam, T., Wang, S., Mohsin, M., Nazam, M., Hashim, M., Baig, S. A., & Zia-ur-Rehman, M. (2021). Does Stakeholder Pressure Matters in Adopting Sustainable Supply Chain Initiatives? Insights from Agro-Based Processing Industry. *Sustainability, 13*(13), 7278.
2. Coulson-Thomas, C. (2020). Visionary leadership for fostering creativity, innovation, and business excellence.
3. Dhamija, P., & Bag, S. (2020). Role of artificial intelligence in operations environment: a review and bibliometric analysis. *The TQM Journal.*

Driving Business Value in the New Normal: Transforming Associations

Themes: Digital, Transformation, Business value, COVID-19

TEACHING OBJECTIVES

The case study is intended to qualify students to:

- Understand the importance of transforming associations in the new normal.
- Analyze the impact of the pandemic on firms' alliances and partnerships.
- Evaluate the critical success factors required to enhance firms' alliances and partnerships.

SYNOPSIS

The COVID-19 pandemic has created unprecedented challenges for firms and their relationships with partners and alliances. Many once-solid associations have been disrupted by the pandemic and the resultant economic downturn, leading firms to reassess and transform their alliances to remain competitive in the new normal. To drive business value in the current environment, firms must adopt a step-by-step approach to enhancing their alliances and partnerships. This includes strategically collaborating with other firms and leveraging technology to improve communication, productivity, and overall performance.

Additionally, firms must focus on customer needs, prioritizing their satisfaction and loyalty in all alliance-related activities. Furthermore, firms must be agile and adaptable, continuously evaluating and modifying their alliances to respond to changing circumstances and business environments. Ultimately, success in the new normal requires a holistic approach to transforming associations that balances short-term considerations with long-term objectives.

Impact of the Pandemic on Firms' Alliances and Partnerships

The pandemic has disrupted many once-solid associations, forcing firms to reassess and transform their partnerships to adapt to the changing business environment. As the pandemic continues to impact global supply chains and create economic uncertainty, firms must be agile and adaptable, continuously evaluating and modifying their alliances to respond to changing circumstances.

Transforming Associations in the Digital Age

To drive business value in the new normal, firms must adopt a step-by-step approach to enhancing their alliances and partnerships. This includes strategically collaborating with other firms and leveraging technology to improve communication, productivity, and overall performance. For example, firms can use digital tools to improve data sharing, project management, and workflow automation, reducing costs and improving efficiency.

Critical Success Factors for Enhancing Firms' Alliances and Partnerships

Firms must prioritize customer needs, focusing on their satisfaction and loyalty in all alliance-related activities. Moreover, they must ensure that their alliances align with their long-term objectives and values, balancing short-term considerations with long-term goals. Effective communication, transparency, and mutual trust are also essential for building and maintaining successful alliances.

Conclusion

The case study highlights the critical success factors required to enhance firms' alliances and partnerships in the digital age, emphasizing the importance of agility, adaptability, and the adoption of digital technologies. By strategically collaborating with other firms, leveraging technology, and prioritizing customer needs, firms can drive business value in the new normal while remaining competitive in an ever-changing business environment.

INDUSTRY CONTEXT

The pandemic has affected various industries, including healthcare, education, and travel, among others. These industries have had to adjust their partnerships and alliances to remain competitive in the new normal.

CHALLENGES

- Disruption of existing alliances and partnerships due to the pandemic
- Increased competition and pressure to drive business value in the new normal
- The need to adapt to the changing business environment and emerging technologies

LESSONS LEARNED

- Strategic collaborations and partnerships with other firms can help firms enhance their alliances and partnerships
- Agility and adaptability are critical success factors for firms to navigate the new normal

QUESTIONS

1. How can firms adapt their alliances and partnerships to remain competitive in the new normal?
2. What strategies can firms employ to enhance their alliances and partnerships?
3. How can firms balance the need for agility and adaptability with the need for stability in their alliances and partnerships?

UN SDGS: Decent work and Economic Growth (8); Industry, innovation, and infrastructure (9)

RESOURCES

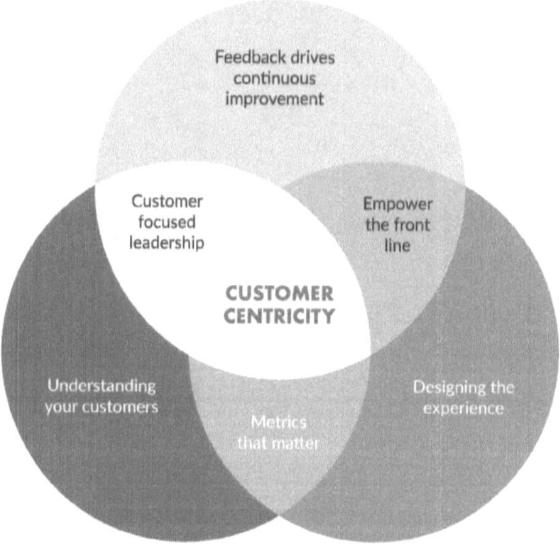

Source: SuperOffice

REFERENCES

1. Ahlstrom, D., Arregle, J. L., Hitt, M. A., Qian, G., Ma, X., & Faems, D. (2020). Managing technological, sociopolitical, and institutional change in the new normal. *Journal of Management Studies, 57*(3), 411-437.

2. Bhattacharyya, S. S., & Thakre, S. (2021). Coronavirus pandemic and economic lockdown; study of strategic initiatives and tactical responses of firms. *International Journal of Organisational Analysis.*

3. Cahapay, M. B. (2020). Rethinking education in the new normal post-COVID-19 era: A curriculum studies perspective. *Aquademia, 4*(2), ep20018.

Innovating Technical Talent Recruitment for a Competitive Edge

Themes: Diversification, Talent, Recruitment, Remote, Workplace

TEACHING OBJECTIVES

The case study is intended to qualify students to:

- Understand the importance of innovative recruitment practices for gaining a competitive edge in the job market.
- Analyze the significance of diversifying talent recruitment to achieve an inclusive and effective workforce.
- Evaluate the impact of remote work on recruitment strategies and workplace diversity.

SYNOPSIS

In today's competitive job market, innovative recruitment practices are essential for businesses to gain a competitive edge. Diversification of talent recruitment is crucial for creating a diverse and inclusive workforce that can provide fresh perspectives and innovative ideas. With the rise of remote work, companies must also adapt their recruitment procedures to ensure that they are inclusive and accessible to remote candidates. This case study explores the importance of innovative recruitment strategies in achieving a diverse and inclusive workforce and evaluates the impact of remote work on recruitment practices.

Advantages of Innovative Recruitment Practices

Innovative recruitment practices can provide several advantages, including a more diverse and inclusive workforce, better employee retention, and improved innovation and creativity. By implementing a variety of recruitment methods and diversifying the talent pool, companies can attract candidates with different backgrounds, perspectives, and skills. Offering flexible work arrangements can also improve employee satisfaction and work-life balance.

Impact of Remote Work on Recruitment Practices

With the rise of remote work, companies must adapt their recruitment procedures to ensure that they are inclusive and accessible to remote candidates. This can include utilizing video interviews, virtual job fairs, and online assessments. However, remote work may also present challenges, such as difficulty in building relationships with remote employees and maintaining a company culture.

Strategies for Successful Innovative Recruitment

To successfully diversify talent recruitment and attract a diverse and inclusive workforce, companies can implement strategies such as collaborating with educational institutions, offering internships and apprenticeships, and implementing blind hiring practices. Companies must also prioritize creating an inclusive culture and providing ongoing training and resources to support diversity and inclusion.

Conclusion

Innovative recruitment practices are critical for businesses to gain a competitive edge in today's job market. Diversifying talent recruitment is essential for creating a diverse and inclusive workforce that can provide fresh perspectives and innovative ideas. With the rise of remote work, companies must also adapt their recruitment procedures to ensure that they are inclusive and accessible to remote candidates. To successfully diversify talent recruitment, companies must implement a variety of strategies and prioritize creating an inclusive culture.

INDUSTRY CONTEXT

The job market is highly competitive, and companies are seeking ways to attract and retain top talent. The COVID-19 pandemic has further exacerbated this challenge, with remote work becoming the norm in many industries. As such, companies need to develop innovative recruitment practices that promote diversity and inclusivity.

CHALLENGES

- Developing effective recruitment strategies that promote diversity and inclusivity
- Ensuring that remote work does not hinder the recruitment process
- Overcoming unconscious bias and traditional hiring practices

LESSONS LEARNED

- Diversifying the talent pool can lead to improved creativity, productivity, and innovation.
- Innovative recruitment strategies can help companies gain a competitive edge in the job market.

QUESTIONS

1. What are the benefits of diversifying the talent pool, and how can companies achieve this?
2. How has remote work impacted recruitment strategies, and what are the challenges associated with this?
3. What are some innovative recruitment practices that companies can implement to gain a competitive edge in the job market?

UN SDGS: Decent work and Economic Growth (8); Industry, innovation, and infrastructure (9)

RESOURCES

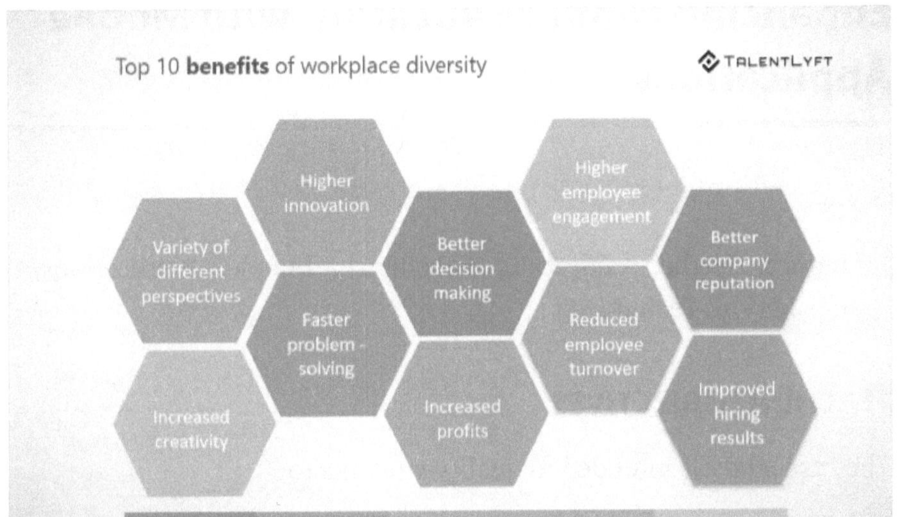

Source: talentlyft.com

REFERENCES

1. Burrell, D. N., & Nobles, C. (2018). Recommendations to develop and hire more highly qualified women and minorities cybersecurity professionals. In *International Conference on Cyber Warfare and Security* (pp. 75-81). Academic Conferences International Limited.

2. Carver-Thomas, D. (2017). Diversifying the Field: Barriers to Recruiting and Retaining Teachers of Color and How to Overcome Them. Literature Review. *Equity Assistance Center Region II, Intercultural Development Research Association.*

3. Carver-Thomas, D. (2018). Diversifying the Teaching Profession: How to Recruit and Retain Teachers of Color. *Learning Policy Institute.*

Enhancing Higher Education with Mobile Applications

Themes: Higher education, Excellence, Mobile, Applications, Information, Technology

TEACHING OBJECTIVES

The case study is intended to qualify students to:

- Analyze the impact of mobile applications in the field of higher education.
- Examine the process of implementing a mobile application in educational institutions.
- Evaluate the factors that contribute to achieving educational excellence with the help of mobile applications.

SYNOPSIS

The integration of mobile applications in higher education has revolutionized the way students learn and interact with their educational institutions. Mobile applications provide access to a wide range of educational resources, including course materials, academic calendars, and online classes, making it easier for students to stay informed and engaged. Moreover, mobile applications enable educators to personalize learning experiences, track student progress, and provide timely feedback. The implementation of a mobile application in the educational sector requires careful planning, including the selection of the appropriate technology, designing a user-friendly interface, and ensuring data privacy and security. Additionally, effective communication with stakeholders and training educators on the new application are crucial for successful implementation.

Impact of Mobile Applications

Mobile applications have transformed higher education by providing students with easy access to course materials, academic calendars, and online classes. These applications allow educators to track student progress and provide timely feedback, making it easier to personalize learning experiences. Moreover, mobile applications enhance communication between students and educators, enabling them to stay informed and engaged.

Implementing a Mobile Application

The implementation of a mobile application in educational institutions requires careful planning, including selecting the appropriate technology, designing a user-friendly interface, and ensuring data privacy and security. Effective communication with stakeholders and training educators on the new application are also crucial for successful implementation.

Achieving Educational Excellence

Mobile applications can contribute significantly to achieving educational excellence by improving accessibility, engagement, and learning outcomes. They also facilitate communication and collaboration between students and educators, leading to a more dynamic and effective learning environment. However, institutional support, financial resources, and the availability of technological infrastructure are essential factors that influence the success of mobile applications in higher education.

Conclusion

Mobile applications have transformed the way students learn and interact with their educational institutions. The case study highlights the impact of mobile applications in higher education, including their potential to provide personalized learning experiences and enhance communication between students and educators. Successful implementation of mobile applications in educational institutions requires careful planning, effective communication with stakeholders, and institutional support. By leveraging the potential of mobile applications, educational institutions can achieve educational excellence and better prepare students for success in their careers.

INDUSTRY CONTEXT

The education industry is rapidly evolving, and technological advancements are changing the way students learn and engage with educational institutions. With the widespread use of smartphones and mobile devices, mobile applications have become an integral part of the higher education landscape. Educational institutions are adopting mobile applications to provide students with easy access to course materials, online classes, and academic resources.

CHALLENGES

- Selection of appropriate technology for the mobile application
- Designing a user-friendly interface
- Ensuring data privacy and security

LESSONS LEARNED

- Mobile applications can significantly enhance the learning experience and contribute to achieving educational excellence.
- The implementation of a mobile application in the educational sector requires careful planning and effective communication with stakeholders.

QUESTIONS

1. How can mobile applications contribute to achieving educational excellence?
2. What are some of the challenges that educational institutions face when implementing a mobile application?
3. What are the potential benefits and drawbacks of relying heavily on mobile applications for learning and educational resources?

UN SDGS: Quality Education (4); Industry, innovation, and Infrastructure (9)

RESOURCES

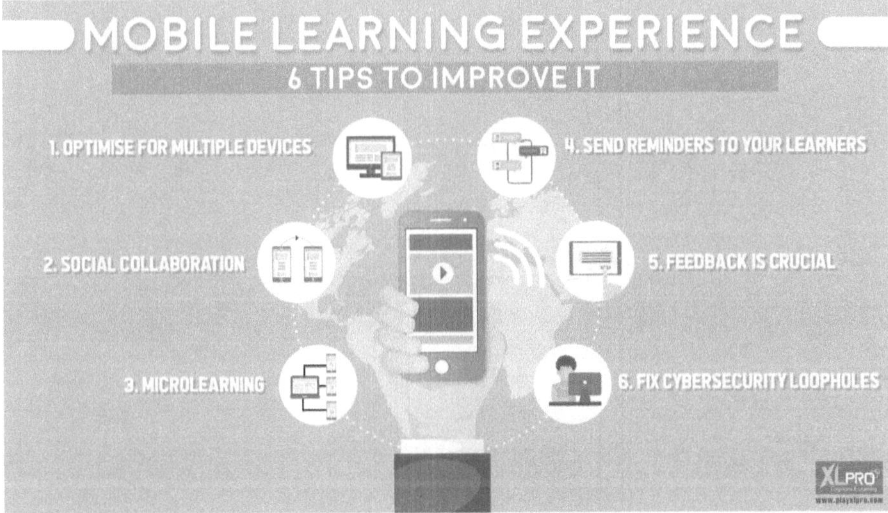

Source: XLPro

REFERENCES

1. Agus, R., & Samuri, S. M. (2018). Learning analytics contribution in education and child development: A review on learning analytics. *Asian Journal of Assessment in Teaching and Learning, 8*, 36-47.

2. Curran, V., Matthews, L., Fleet, L., Simmons, K., Gustafson, D. L., & Wetsch, L. (2017). A review of digital, social, and mobile technologies in health professional education. *Journal of Continuing Education in the Health Professions, 37*(3), 195-206.

3. De, S., & Nethi, V. (2020). Impact of Science Mobile Applications on Interest and Learning Among Undergraduate Science Students. *Quarterly Review of Distance Education, 21*(4), 37-75.

Customer Experience as a Pillar of Business Prosperity and Excellence

Themes: Customer, Experience, Prosperity, Business, Excellence

TEACHING OBJECTIVES

The case study is intended to qualify students to:

- Analyze the significance of customer experience to attain a competitive advantage
- Explore the role of market leaders to elevate the experience of customers
- Propose recommendations to upgrade the experience of customers

SYNOPSIS

In today's business landscape, customer experience is a critical pillar of success, as customers are increasingly demanding personalized and high-quality service. Enhancing the customer experience can help businesses differentiate themselves from competitors, increase customer loyalty, and drive revenue growth. To achieve this, businesses must understand their customers' needs and preferences, ensure that all customer touchpoints are optimized, and continuously evaluate and improve the customer experience. Market leaders can play a vital role in elevating the customer experience by setting industry standards and best practices. However, businesses also face challenges in enhancing the customer experience, such as managing data, ensuring privacy and security, and maintaining consistency across all channels. To overcome these challenges, businesses can adopt innovative technologies, invest in employee training, and develop a customer-centric culture.

Advantages of Enhancing Customer Experience

Enhancing the customer experience can provide numerous advantages to businesses, including differentiation from competitors, increased customer loyalty, and revenue growth. By understanding customers' needs and preferences, businesses can tailor their services to meet and exceed their expectations, leading to increased customer satisfaction and retention.

Role of Market Leaders

Market leaders can play a crucial role in elevating the customer experience by setting industry standards and best practices. By implementing innovative and customer-centric strategies, market leaders can inspire other businesses to adopt similar approaches and raise the bar for customer service excellence.

Recommendations for Upgrading Customer Experience

To overcome these challenges, businesses can adopt various strategies, including implementing innovative technologies such as AI and chatbots to provide personalized and efficient service, investing in employee training to improve customer service skills, and developing a customer-centric culture that prioritizes the customer experience. Additionally, businesses should continuously evaluate and improve their customer touchpoints, such as website design, mobile apps, and social media channels, to ensure that they are optimized for customer satisfaction.

Conclusion

This case study highlights the importance of customer experience in achieving business prosperity and excellence. It emphasizes the advantages of enhancing customer experience, the role of market leaders in setting industry standards, and the challenges businesses face in achieving this goal. By adopting innovative technologies, investing in employee training, and developing a customer-centric culture, businesses can upgrade their customer experience and gain a competitive advantage in the market.

INDUSTRY CONTEXT

The importance of customer experience in the business landscape is increasing, with customers demanding personalized and high-quality service. Businesses must prioritize enhancing the customer experience to differentiate themselves from competitors, increase customer loyalty, and drive revenue growth.

CHALLENGES

- Managing data and ensuring data privacy and security
- Maintaining consistency across all channels and touchpoints
- Investing in employee training and developing a customer-centric culture

LESSONS LEARNED

- Understanding customer needs and preferences is critical for enhancing the customer experience
- Market leaders play a vital role in setting industry standards and best practices for the customer experience

QUESTIONS

1. How can businesses use customer feedback to improve the customer experience?
2. What strategies can businesses use to maintain consistency across all channels and touchpoints?

3. How can businesses balance the need for data privacy and security with the desire for personalized service?

UN SDGs: No Poverty (1), Industry, innovation, and infrastructure (9); Sustainable cities and communities (11)

RESOURCES

The 5 Pillars of a
Good Customer Service Team

Source: UpWork

REFERENCES

1. Batat, W. (2019). *Experiential marketing: Consumer behavior, customer experience, and the 7Es.* Routledge.
2. Butner, K. (2019). Six strategies that define digital winners. *Strategy & Leadership.*
3. Gellweiler, C., & Krishnamurthi, L. (2020). How digital innovators achieve customer value.

Exploring the Rise of Data Storage as a Service

Themes: Data, Storage, Service, STaaS, Framework, Computing

TEACHING OBJECTIVES

The case study is intended to qualify students to:

- Understand the concept of data storage as a service and its potential benefits for organizations.
- Analyze the challenges faced by businesses in adopting data storage as a service, including technical limitations and security concerns.
- Evaluate the strategies used by organizations to effectively implement data storage as a service and maximize its potential.

SYNOPSIS

Data storage as a service (StaaS) has gained popularity as a means of enhancing organizational productivity and efficiency. StaaS provides businesses with a flexible and scalable data storage solution that can be accessed from anywhere, at any time, with a pay-per-use pricing model. However, the adoption of StaaS also presents challenges, including concerns about data security and privacy, technical limitations, and the need to integrate with existing IT infrastructure. Organizations must develop a framework for selecting a StaaS provider that addresses these challenges while providing an optimal solution. Implementation strategies such as data migration planning, performance testing, and ongoing monitoring can help organizations maximize the benefits of StaaS while minimizing disruption to existing operations. Overall, adopting StaaS can provide businesses with the agility and flexibility needed to meet the demands of a rapidly changing business environment.

Advantages of StaaS

StaaS offers several advantages to organizations, including flexibility and scalability, access from anywhere at any time, and pay-per-use pricing models. These benefits enable businesses to optimize their data storage and reduce costs while improving productivity and efficiency.

Strategies for Effective Implementation

To maximize the benefits of StaaS, organizations can adopt various strategies, including data migration planning, performance testing, and ongoing monitoring. These strategies can help organizations overcome technical limitations and ensure that the StaaS solution integrates seamlessly with existing IT infrastructure. Additionally, businesses must ensure that data security and privacy protocols are in place and that all StaaS providers comply with relevant regulations and standards.

Conclusion

This case study highlights the potential benefits of StaaS in enhancing organizational productivity and efficiency. It emphasizes the challenges faced by businesses in adopting StaaS, including data security and privacy concerns and technical limitations. By developing a framework for selecting the appropriate StaaS provider and implementing strategies such as data migration planning and ongoing monitoring, organizations can effectively adopt StaaS and maximize its potential.

INDUSTRY CONTEXT

The rise of cloud computing has led to increasing demand for data storage solutions that can keep pace with growing data volumes and provide greater flexibility and scalability. StaaS offers a solution to this challenge, allowing businesses to store and manage their data in the cloud, rather than relying on on-premises infrastructure.

CHALLENGES

- Security and privacy concerns: Storing sensitive data in the cloud raises concerns about data security and privacy.
- Technical limitations: Organizations must ensure that their existing IT infrastructure can integrate with StaaS solutions.
- Integration with existing systems: Integrating StaaS with existing IT systems and workflows can be a complex and time-consuming process.

LESSONS LEARNED

Developing a framework for selecting a StaaS provider that addresses security and privacy concerns, technical limitations, and integration with existing systems is essential. • Proper planning, testing, and monitoring can help Organizations overcome implementation challenges and maximize the benefits of StaaS.

QUESTIONS

1. How can organizations balance the benefits of StaaS with concerns about data security and privacy?
2. What are the key technical considerations that organizations must take into account when adopting StaaS?
3. How can organizations ensure a smooth integration of StaaS with their existing IT infrastructure and workflows?

UN SDGs: Quality Education (4); Decent Work and Economic Growth (8); Industry, innovation, and Infrastructure (9)

RESOURCES

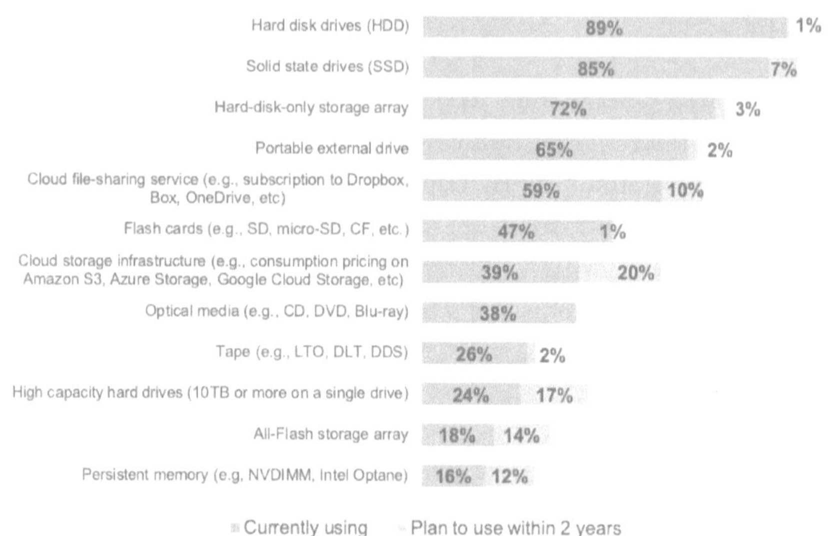

Source: Spiceworks

REFERENCES

1. Ferreira, A. M., Drummond, A. C., & de Araújo, A. P. F. (2017, June). Performance evaluation of a private cloud storage infrastructure service for document preservation. In *2017 12th Iberian Conference on Information Systems and Technologies (CISTI)* (pp. 1-7). IEEE.

2. Fu, Y., Qiu, X., & Wang, J. (2019, October). F2MC: Enhancing Data Storage Services with Fog-toMultiCloud Hybrid Computing. In *2019 IEEE 38th International Performance Computing and Communications Conference (IPCCC)* (pp. 1-6). IEEE.

3. Ghaffar, Z., Ahmed, S., Mahmood, K., Islam, S. H., Hassan, M. M., & Fortino, G. (2020). An improved authentication scheme for remote data access and sharing over cloud storage in cyber-physical-social-systems. *IEEE Access*, 8, 47144-47160.

Reinventing the Workplace with Emotion-sensing Technology

Themes: Workplace, Reformation, Emotion, Technology

TEACHING OBJECTIVES

The case study is intended to qualify students to:

- Analyze the potential benefits and risks of implementing emotion-sensing technology in the workplace.
- Evaluate the ethical considerations of using emotion-sensing technology in the workplace.
- Develop strategies for effectively implementing and managing emotion-sensing technology in the workplace.

SYNOPSIS

The use of emotion-sensing technology in the workplace is becoming increasingly popular as businesses seek to improve employee well-being and productivity. Emotion-sensing technology uses sensors and algorithms to analyze employee emotions, behaviors, and interactions, providing insights into employee engagement and overall workplace performance. While this technology can provide significant benefits, including identifying stress and burnout, improving team collaboration, and enhancing employee experiences, it also raises concerns about employee privacy, data security, and the potential for biased decision-making. Organizations must carefully consider the potential benefits and risks of implementing emotion-sensing technology and ensure that appropriate ethical standards and guidelines are in place to protect employee rights and privacy. Effective communication with employees about the purpose and use of the technology and providing training and support for its use are critical for successful implementation. Additionally, Organizations must continually evaluate the technology's performance, adjust its usage as necessary, and ensure compliance with relevant data privacy regulations.

Advantages

Emotion-sensing technology can provide numerous benefits to the workplace, including identifying stress and burnout, improving team collaboration, and enhancing employee experiences. However, it also raises concerns about employee privacy, data security, and the potential for biased decision-making.

Ethical Considerations

Organizations must consider ethical standards and guidelines for using emotion-sensing technology to protect employee rights and privacy. These guidelines should address issues such as data privacy, transparency, and informed consent.

Strategies

Organizations must effectively implement and manage emotion-sensing technology in the workplace by providing adequate training and support, continually evaluating the technology's performance, adjusting its usage as necessary, and ensuring compliance with relevant data privacy regulations. Effective communication with employees about the purpose and use of the technology is also critical for successful implementation.

Conclusion

This case study highlights the potential benefits and risks of implementing emotion-sensing technology in the workplace, the ethical considerations that must be taken into account, and strategies for effectively implementing and managing it. While emotion-sensing technology can provide significant benefits, organizations need to prioritize ethical considerations and ensure that employees' privacy rights are protected.

INDUSTRY CONTEXT

The use of emotion-sensing technology in the workplace is gaining traction in various industries, including healthcare, finance, and retail, as businesses seek to enhance employee well-being and productivity.

CHALLENGES

- Ensuring employee privacy and data security
- Addressing potential biases in decision-making
- Providing appropriate training and support for technology use

LESSONS LEARNED

- Ethical considerations are critical when implementing emotion-sensing technology in the workplace.
- Effective communication with employees is essential for successful implementation.

QUESTIONS

1. What are the potential benefits and risks of implementing emotion-sensing technology in the workplace, and how can Organizations balance these factors?
2. What ethical considerations must Organizations take into account when using emotion-sensing technology in the workplace, and how can they ensure that employee privacy and rights are protected?
3. How can Organizations effectively communicate the purpose and use of emotion-sensing technology to employees, and

what strategies can they use to provide appropriate training and support for its use?

UN SDGS: Decent Work and Economic Growth (8); Industry, innovation, and Infrastructure (9); Sustainable Cities and Communities (11)

RESOURCES

Implementation Barriers for Emotion-Sensing Technologies

Multiple measures are available to measure stress, attention, and decision-making. These measures present different cost-, complexity-, and privacy-related barriers.

ORGANIZATION OPPORTUNITY	RELEVANT MEASURES	COST-RELATED BARRIERS	COMPLEXITY-RELATED BARRIERS	PRIVACY-RELATED BARRIERS
Decision-making	Blood sugar	Low-medium	Low	Medium
	Electrodermal	Medium	Low	Medium
	EEG	High	Medium	High
Attention	Mouse/browser tracking	Low	Medium	Low-Medium
	Facial coding	Medium	Low	Medium
	Eye tracking	Medium-High	Low	Low-medium
Stress	Hormones	Low	Low	Low-Medium
	Heart rate	Low-medium	Medium	Medium
	Electrodermal	Medium	Low	Medium-high

Source: MIT Sloan

REFERENCES

1. Gu, Y., Wang, Y., Liu, T., Ji, Y., Liu, Z., Li, P., ... & Ren, F. (2019). EmoSense: computational intelligence-driven emotion sensing via wireless channel data. *IEEE Transactions on Emerging Topics in Computational Intelligence*, 4(3), 216-226.

2. Hasan, M., Rundensteiner, E., & Agu, E. (2019). Automatic emotion detection in text streams by analyzing Twitter

data. *International Journal of Data Science and Analytics, 7*(1), 35-51.

3. Kaur, S., & Sharma, R. (2021). Emotion AI: Integrating Emotional Intelligence with Artificial Intelligence in the Digital Workplace. In *Innovations in Information and Communication Technologies (IICT-2020)* (pp. 337-343). Springer, Cham.

Digital Customer Experience Strategies: Accelerating Digital Transformation 2023 and Beyond

Themes: Digital, Transformation, Strategies, Experience

TEACHING OBJECTIVES

The case study is intended to qualify students to:

- Analyze the role of digital customer experience in driving business growth and success.
- Evaluate the step-by-step implementation of digital customer experience strategies.
- Examine the challenges faced by Organizations in implementing digital customer experience and propose effective solutions.

SYNOPSIS

In today's digital landscape, implementing effective digital customer experience strategies has become a critical factor for Organizations to remain competitive and drive business growth. This case study will analyze the role of digital customer experience in driving success, evaluate the step-by-step implementation of digital customer experience strategies, and examine the challenges faced by Organizations in implementing digital customer experience.

Importance of Digital Customer Experience

The implementation of digital customer experience strategies can provide numerous benefits to Organizations, including improved customer engagement, increased customer loyalty, and revenue growth. By effectively integrating digital technology into the customer experience journey, Organizations can provide a seamless and convenient experience for their customers, ultimately leading to customer satisfaction and retention.

Steps for Implementation of Strategies

To effectively implement digital customer experience strategies, Organizations must first develop a clear understanding of the customer journey and identify key touchpoints. By using data analytics to gain insights into customer behavior and preferences, Organizations can tailor their digital customer experience strategy to meet their customers' needs. Additionally, Organizations must prioritize the integration of digital technology, such as mobile apps, chatbots, and social media, into their customer experience strategy to provide a seamless and convenient experience for their customers.

Effective Solutions

To overcome the challenges, Organizations can adopt various strategies, including creating cross-functional teams to ensure effective collaboration and communication, investing in employee training and development, and continuously evaluating and improving their digital customer experience strategy to keep up with changing customer expectations and technological advancements.

Conclusion

This case study highlights the importance of digital customer experience in driving business growth and success. It emphasizes the benefits of effective implementation of digital customer experience strategies, the step-by-step process of implementing such strategies, and the challenges Organizations face in doing so. By adopting innovative technologies, investing in employee training and development, and continuously evaluating and improving their digital customer experience strategy, Organizations can provide a seamless and convenient experience for their customers, leading to improved customer engagement, increased customer loyalty, and revenue growth.

INDUSTRY CONTEXT

In today's business landscape, customers expect seamless, personalized, and consistent experiences across all digital channels. This has led to the increasing adoption of digital customer experience strategies across various industries, including e-commerce, retail, finance, and healthcare.

CHALLENGES

- Data privacy and security concerns
- Limited employee expertise and training in digital customer experience
- Integrating digital customer experience strategies with existing systems

LESSONS LEARNED

- Understanding the customer journey is crucial for the effective implementation of digital customer experience strategies
- Continuous evaluation and improvement are necessary for the successful implementation
- Effective communication and collaboration with stakeholders are essential for a seamless implementation process.

QUESTIONS

1. What are the benefits of implementing digital customer experience strategies for organizations?
2. How can organizations overcome the challenges associated with implementing digital customer experience strategies?
3. What role does data analytics play in enhancing digital customer experience?

UN SDGS: Quality Education (4); Decent Work and Economic Growth (8); Industry, innovation, and Infrastructure (9)

RESOURCES

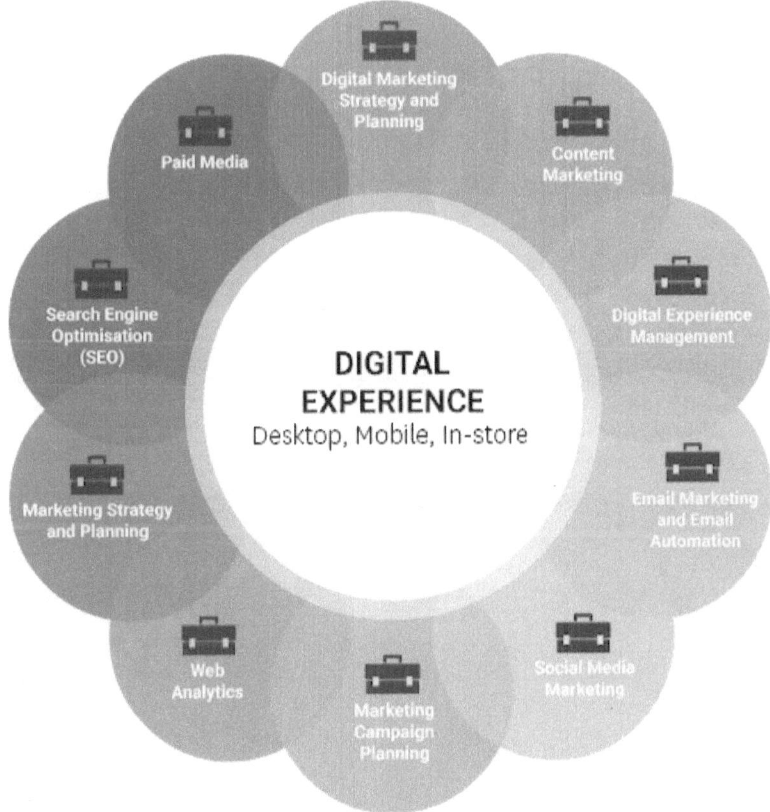

Source: Freshworks

REFERENCES

1. Gerster, V., Melonashi, P., & Nguyen, Q. C. (2021). Digital Customer Experience Matters.

2. Lattemann, C., & Robra-Bissantz, S. (2017). Digital customer experience.

3. Mbama, C. I., & Ezepue, P. O. (2018). Digital banking, customer experience, and bank financial performance: UK customers' perceptions. *International Journal of Bank Marketing.*

The Rise of Electric Vehicles: How Tesla Shaped the Auto Industry

Themes: Technology, Application, Tesla, Auto Industry

TEACHING OBJECTIVES

The case study is intended to qualify students to:

- Analyze the impact of electric vehicles on the auto industry.
- Evaluate the strategies used by Tesla to shape the electric vehicle market.
- Examine the challenges and opportunities presented by the electric vehicle market for traditional automakers.

SYNOPSIS

Tesla has emerged as a game-changer in the auto industry, revolutionizing the way people perceive and use electric vehicles. The company's innovative approach to electric vehicle design, battery technology, and manufacturing has propelled it to the top of the electric vehicle market. Tesla's success has also prompted traditional automakers to invest heavily in electric vehicle research and development to stay competitive. The electric vehicle market has significant potential for growth, with governments and consumers increasingly concerned about the environmental impact of gasoline-powered vehicles. However, there are significant challenges to the widespread adoption of electric vehicles, including battery cost and range limitations, charging infrastructure, and consumer perception.

Impact of Electric Vehicles

Electric vehicles have the potential to significantly reduce carbon emissions and improve air quality, leading to increased government and consumer interest in this technology. The electric vehicle market is expected to grow rapidly in the coming years, presenting significant opportunities for innovation and growth.

Tesla's Strategies

Tesla has disrupted the auto industry by developing innovative electric vehicle designs, improving battery technology, and creating a strong brand image. The company's direct-to-consumer sales model and focus on customer experience have also set it apart from traditional automakers. Tesla's success has prompted traditional automakers to invest heavily in electric vehicle research and development to remain competitive in the market.

Challenges and Opportunities

The widespread adoption of electric vehicles faces several challenges, including high battery costs, limited range, and a lack of charging infrastructure. However, these challenges also present opportunities for innovation and growth in the electric vehicle market. Traditional automakers must continue to invest in research and development to overcome these challenges and remain competitive in the market.

Conclusion

Tesla has demonstrated the potential of electric vehicles to transform the auto industry and drive innovation. The rapid growth of the electric vehicle market presents significant opportunities for traditional automakers to invest in research and development and meet the changing demands of consumers and governments. The success of electric vehicles will ultimately depend on the continued development of battery technology and charging infrastructure, along with the adoption of consumer-friendly business models that prioritize the customer experience.

INDUSTRY CONTEXT

The auto industry has traditionally been dominated by internal combustion engine vehicles. However, the rise of electric vehicles has disrupted this market, with new entrants like Tesla challenging established players. The push toward electric vehicles is driven by concerns over environmental sustainability, energy independence, and technological innovation.

CHALLENGES

- Developing cost-effective battery technology
- Expanding charging infrastructure
- Complying with government regulations and emission standards

LESSONS LEARNED

- Innovation and disruption can create new opportunities in established markets
- Customer demand can drive significant changes in industry trends

QUESTIONS

1. What are the long-term implications of the shift toward electric vehicles for the auto industry?
2. How can traditional automakers compete with new entrants like Tesla in the electric vehicle market?
3. What role will government regulations and policies play in shaping the future of the electric vehicle market?

UN SDGs: Decent work and Economic Growth (8); Industry, innovation, and infrastructure (9)

RESOURCES

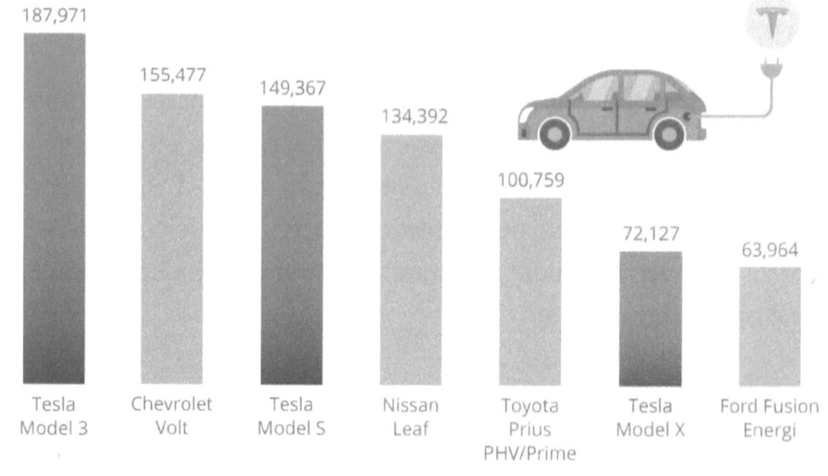

Source: Statista

REFERENCES

1. Hammi, B., Khatoun, R., Zeadally, S., Fayad, A., & Khoukhi, L. (2017). IoT technologies for smart cities. IET networks, 7(1), 1- 13.

2. Jameel, F., Chang, Z., Huang, J., & Ristaniemi, T. (2019). Internet of autonomous vehicles: architecture, features, and socio-technological challenges. IEEE Wireless Communications, 26(4), 21-29.

3. Malik, N., Nanda, P., He, X., & Liu, R. P. (2020). Vehicular networks with security and trust management solutions: proposed secured message exchange via blockchain technology. Wireless Networks, 26(6), 4207-4226.

Case Study **35**

Smart Solutions for Comprehensive Family Health Monitoring

Themes: SMART, Technology, Strategy, Solutions, Health, Tool

TEACHING OBJECTIVES

The case study is intended to qualify students to:

- Examine the role of advanced technology-based solutions in enhancing family health monitoring.
- Analyze the step-by-step implementation of a new health monitoring tool.
- Evaluate the benefits and challenges of using smart technology for family health monitoring.

SYNOPSIS

Smart solutions for comprehensive family health monitoring have become increasingly popular with the rise of digital health technologies. These solutions are designed to enable individuals and families to monitor and manage their health more effectively by providing access to health-related information and tools through smart devices. The implementation of these solutions requires careful planning and execution, including the selection of appropriate technology and tools, designing a user-friendly interface, and ensuring data privacy and security. Effective communication with stakeholders and training users on the new system are also crucial for successful implementation.

Additionally, continuous evaluation and improvement of the solution's performance are necessary to address any technical issues and improve the user experience.

The rise of digital health technologies has enabled the development of smart solutions for comprehensive family health monitoring. This case study examines the role of advanced technology-based solutions in enhancing family health monitoring, the step-by-step implementation of a new health monitoring tool, and the benefits and challenges of using smart technology for family health monitoring.

Benefits of Smart Health Monitoring

Smart health monitoring solutions provide several benefits, including early detection of health issues, improved disease management, and increased patient engagement. By providing users with real-time health-related information and tools, these solutions enable individuals and families to take an active role in managing their health, leading to improved health outcomes and quality of life.

Implementation of Smart Health Monitoring

The implementation of a smart health monitoring tool requires careful planning and execution. Organizations must first identify the appropriate technology and tools for their specific needs, design a user-friendly interface, and ensure data privacy and security. Effective communication with stakeholders and user training is also critical for successful implementation. Continuous evaluation and improvement of the system's performance are necessary to ensure that it meets the users' needs and remains up-to-date with the latest health-related technologies.

Conclusion

This case study highlights the potential benefits of using smart technology-based solutions for comprehensive family health monitoring. It emphasizes the importance of careful planning and execution, effective communication and training, and continuous evaluation and improvement. By addressing the challenges and leveraging the benefits of smart health monitoring solutions, Organizations can improve patient outcomes, increase engagement and satisfaction, and drive innovation in the healthcare industry.

INDUSTRY CONTEXT

The digital health technology market is rapidly expanding, with the development of smart solutions for comprehensive family health monitoring being one of the fastest-growing segments. The global digital health market size is expected to reach USD 640.2 billion by 2026, with the COVID-19 pandemic driving the growth of remote monitoring and telehealth technologies.

CHALLENGES

- Ensuring data privacy and security: Storing and sharing personal health data through smart devices requires high levels of data privacy and security to avoid data breaches and cyber-attacks.
- Designing a user-friendly interface: Smart solutions for comprehensive family health monitoring must be easy to use and navigate for users of all ages and technical abilities.
- Addressing technical issues: Smart devices and software may face technical issues that can impact their performance and disrupt the monitoring process, requiring timely resolution to ensure continued usage and user satisfaction.

LESSONS LEARNED

- Prioritize user experience: User experience is a critical factor in the success of smart solutions for comprehensive family health monitoring, and therefore, it is essential to design solutions that are user-friendly and easy to navigate.

- Data privacy and security should be a top priority: As these solutions involve the storage and sharing of personal health data, it is important to prioritize data privacy and security to protect users' information and avoid data breaches.

QUESTIONS

1. What are some potential benefits and drawbacks of smart solutions for comprehensive family health monitoring?
2. What strategies can Organizations use to ensure data privacy and security while implementing smart health solutions?
3. How can smart solutions for comprehensive family health monitoring be used to improve healthcare outcomes and reduce healthcare costs?

UN SDGs: Health and well-being (3); Industry, innovation, and infrastructure (9); Sustainable cities and communities (11)

RESOURCES

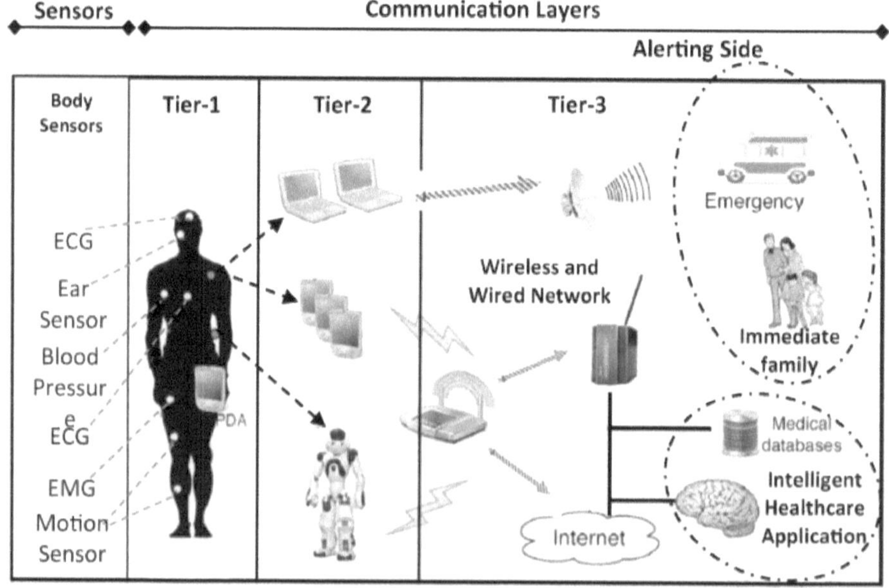

Source: AlBahri et al., 2018

REFERENCES

1. Lakshmi, G. J., Ghonge, M., & Obaid, A. J. (2021). Cloud-based IoT Smart Healthcare System for Remote Patient Monitoring. *EAI Endorsed Transactions on Pervasive Health and Technology*, e4.

2. Papaioannou, P., Tzanis, N., Tranoris, C., Denazis, S., & Birbas, A. (2021, June). A Prototype 5G/IoT Implementation for Transforming a Legacy Facility to a Smart Factory. In *IFIP International Conference on Artificial Intelligence Applications and Innovations* (pp. 52-61). Springer, Cham.

3. Rahaman, A., Islam, M. M., Islam, M. R., Sadi, M. S., & Nooruddin, S. (2019). Developing IoT Based Smart Health Monitoring Systems: A Review. *Rev. d'Intelligence Artif.*, *33*(6), 435-440.

Recycling Initiatives: Shaping the Future of Plastic Industry in UAE and Brunei

Themes: Recycling, Plastics, UAE, Markets, Emerging

TEACHING OBJECTIVES

The case study is intended to qualify students to:

- Recognize the significance of recycling initiatives in promoting environmental sustainability and circular economy.
- Analyze the economic, social, and environmental challenges faced by the plastic industry in adopting recycling initiatives.
- Evaluate the strategies and solutions implemented by the plastic industry in overcoming the challenges and achieving sustainable recycling practices.

SYNOPSIS

The plastic industry has been a significant contributor to environmental degradation, and it is increasingly becoming important for businesses and governments to focus on sustainable waste management practices. This has led to the adoption of recycling initiatives as a critical step towards creating a more sustainable future, particularly in emerging markets such as the UAE and Brunei. Recycling initiatives provide opportunities for businesses to create new markets and revenue streams, promote environmental responsibility, and improve their public image. However, the implementation of recycling initiatives in the plastic industry faces numerous challenges. These include limited infrastructure for recycling, a lack of awareness and incentives for businesses and consumers, and difficulty in sourcing high-quality materials for recycling. Businesses and governments must find innovative solutions to overcome these challenges and promote recycling as an essential part of waste management.

Advantages of Recycling Initiatives

Successful implementation of recycling initiatives can lead to numerous benefits for businesses, including reduced waste disposal costs, energy savings, and improved public image. It can also create new markets and revenue streams and meet increasing consumer demand for environmentally responsible practices.

Strategies and Solutions for Sustainable Recycling Practices

To overcome the challenges in adopting recycling initiatives, businesses and governments must find innovative solutions. These can include the development of recycling infrastructure, raising awareness about recycling, and offering incentives such as tax breaks. Businesses must also focus on sourcing high-quality materials for recycling and using sustainable waste management practices throughout their operations. Successful implementation of recycling initiatives can lead to reduced waste disposal costs, energy savings, and a more sustainable future. It can also help businesses to meet increasing consumer demand for environmentally responsible practices and align with the global movement towards sustainability. The plastic industry in emerging markets such as the UAE and Brunei must adopt recycling cultures to remain competitive and promote environmental responsibility. It is crucial to implement strategies that encourage and incentivize businesses to incorporate recycling initiatives into their operations. This can include the development of recycling infrastructure, raising awareness about recycling, and offering incentives such as tax.

Conclusion

Recycling initiatives are critical for promoting environmental sustainability and the circular economy in the plastic industry, particularly in emerging markets such as the UAE and Brunei. Despite the challenges, businesses and governments can implement innovative strategies and solutions to overcome these challenges and promote sustainable recycling practices. The successful implementation of recycling initiatives can lead to significant economic, social, and environmental benefits for businesses and society as a whole.

INDUSTRY CONTEXT

The plastic industry in the UAE and Brunei is expanding, driven by the increasing demand for plastic products. However, this growth also poses a significant challenge in managing plastic waste and reducing its impact on the environment.

CHALLENGES

- Limited infrastructure for plastic recycling, including collection and sorting facilities.
- Limited awareness and incentives for the adoption of recycling cultures among consumers and businesses.
- Difficulty in sourcing high-quality materials for recycling.

LESSONS LEARNED

- Collaboration between governments, businesses, and consumers is essential to the success of recycling initiatives.
- Investing in infrastructure and educating consumers and businesses can overcome challenges to the adoption of recycling cultures.

QUESTIONS

1. How can the plastic industry in the UAE and Brunei work towards a more sustainable future through recycling initiatives?
2. What incentives can be provided to consumers and businesses to promote the adoption of recycling cultures?
3. How can governments encourage and support the development of recycling infrastructure in the UAE and Brunei?

UN SDGs: Decent work and Economic Growth (8); Industry, innovation, and infrastructure (9)

RESOURCES

Source: EvoVend

REFERENCES

1. Ioannidis, A., Chalvatzis, K. J., Leonidou, L. C., & Feng, Z. (2021). Applying the reduce, reuse, and recycle principle in the hospitality sector: Its antecedents and performance implications. *Business Strategy and the Environment.*

2. de Campos, S. A. P., Gallon, S., & Becker, R. G. (2021). Intersectoral partnerships in the recycling sector. *Social Responsibility Journal.*

3. Salmenperä, H. (2021). Different pathways to a recycling society–Comparison of the transitions in Austria, Sweden and Finland. *Journal of cleaner production, 292,* 125986.

Turning Technology Pressures into Potential Opportunities

Themes: Technology, Strategy, Advance, Systems

TEACHING OBJECTIVES

The case study is intended to qualify students to:

- Analyze the potential challenges faced by organizations during the implementation of information technology
- Investigate the strategies employed by organizations to overcome IT-related challenges
- Assess the necessity of human involvement during the adoption of information technology

SYNOPSIS

Emerging technologies are laden with paradoxes. Often, we tend to focus solely on the issues or promises of technology, rarely examining both concurrently. Analyzing and monitoring the content and flow of information generated by these technologies can help understand how to prevent or mitigate violence. As a result, technology and the ensuing information can detect, monitor, or analyze ongoing or future conflict developments. Cutting-edge technology is revolutionizing every sector of the economy. Companies of all sizes feel compelled to incorporate them into every aspect of the value chain, from R&D and logistics to sales, marketing, and manufacturing. While advanced technologies unlock new opportunities, their implementation and value are fraught with challenges. Emerging technologies create new potentials, but their implementation and value are whisked with pitfalls. Advanced digital technologies provide developing multinationals with tools to produce, design, and market services and goods. Whereas the challenges are discomforting, they are likely to offer them new opportunities to disturb well-established competitors and generate value for customers worldwide.

Strategies for Overcoming Challenges

Organizations can overcome these challenges by developing a comprehensive strategy for technology adoption that includes clear goals, stakeholder engagement, and effective communication. Additionally, they can employ specialized talent to ensure that the technology is appropriately implemented, and leverage external expertise to ensure that data privacy and security concerns are addressed. Ongoing training and development programs can also help employees to adapt to new technologies and leverage them effectively.

Necessity of Human Involvement

Despite the many advantages of advanced technologies, human involvement remains critical to the successful implementation and adoption of technology. Organizations must balance the benefits of automation and AI with the importance of human judgment and expertise. Human involvement is necessary to ensure that technology is appropriately applied and that the risks and benefits of new technology are effectively evaluated.

Conclusion

The implementation of advanced technologies is a critical factor in driving business success, but it requires careful planning and execution. Organizations must identify and address the challenges associated with technology adoption, develop a comprehensive strategy for implementation, and ensure that human involvement remains an integral part of the process. By successfully navigating these challenges, companies can turn technology pressures into potential opportunities and gain a competitive advantage in their respective industries.

INDUSTRY CONTEXT

Advanced digital technologies provide emerging multinationals with the tools to create, design, and market products and services, offering new opportunities to disrupt established competitors and deliver value to customers worldwide.

CHALLENGES

- Overcoming resistance to adopting new technologies within the organization
- Ensuring seamless integration of advanced technologies into existing processes
- Addressing security and privacy concerns associated with implementing advanced technologies

LESSONS LEARNED

- An effective strategy for technology adoption can mitigate the challenges and pressures faced by organizations
- Human involvement remains crucial in the successful implementation and management of advanced technologies

QUESTIONS

1. How can organizations foster a culture that embraces and supports the adoption of new technologies?
2. What measures can companies take to address potential security and privacy concerns related to advanced technologies?
3. How can organizations strike a balance between human involvement and technology to maximize productivity and efficiency?

UN SDGs: Decent work and Economic Growth (8); Industry, innovation, and infrastructure (9)

RESOURCES

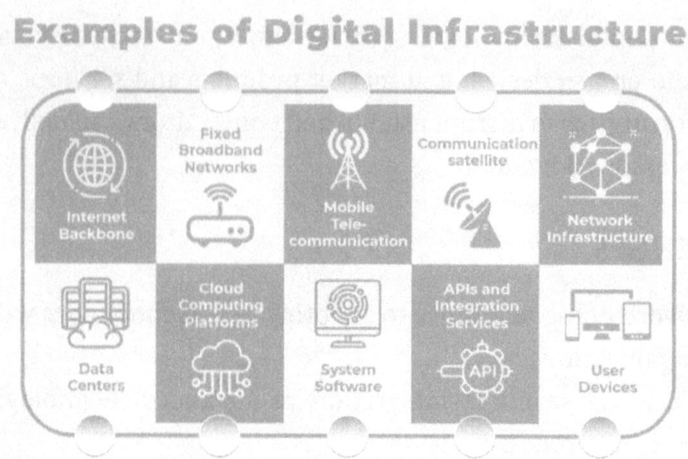

Source: IDC

REFERENCES

1. Barnes, S. J. (2020). Information management research and practice in the post-COVID-19 world. *International Journal of Information Management, 55*, 102175.

2. Bauer, M., & Erixon, F. (2020). *Europe's Quest for Technology Sovereignty: Opportunities and Pitfalls*. European Centre for International Political Economy.

3. Gupta, A., Ponticelli, J., & Tesei, A. (2020). *Information, technology adoption and productivity: The role of mobile phones in agriculture* (No. w27192). National Bureau of Economic Research.

Human Capital Management at Abu Dhabi Commercial Bank: Transitioning Efforts During the Pandemic

Themes: Banking, HRM, Transition, Pandemic

TEACHING OBJECTIVES

The case study is intended to qualify students to:

- Examine ADCB's HR management practices;
- Identify how ADCB responded to the threats and effects of the COVID-19 pandemic on its workforce;
- Discuss the key roles that ADCB's HRM strategies play in contributing to the company's competitive advantage and success

SYNOPSIS

Abu Dhabi Commercial Bank (ADCB) is one of the top banks in the United Arab Emirates with total assets of AED 395.82 billion. Since it was founded in 1985, the bank has been providing financial services in retail, commercial, Islamic banking, and more. In 2019, ADCB merged with Union National Bank. ADCB's business segments include consumer banking, wholesale banking, investment banking, property management, and treasury banking. Its headquarters is located in Abu Dhabi, with 72 branches and around 450 ATMs all over the UAE. It has around 5,000 people in its workforce. The company's mission statement is "Ensuring a stable foundation to allow responsible management, accountability, and decision-making through strong governance and the highest ethical practices." The bank upholds ethical practices and building an organization depends on leadership that has integrity, including its human resource management. ADCB considers its people as the success enablers. The bank's HR management practices are particularly crucial to the organization during the coronavirus (COVID-19) pandemic. Where many organizations were not able to survive the pandemic, those who managed to thrive owe much to their people. In times of crisis, HR managers need to find ways to rethink their programs and launch initiatives that will matter and make an impact. The bank attributed its ability to successfully navigate through the challenges of 2020 to its resilient culture and shared values.

ADCB's HR Management Practices

ADCB has a strong commitment to ethical practices and building an organization with strong governance and the highest ethical practices. The bank upholds these values through its HR management practices, which include talent acquisition and development, performance management, compensation and benefits, employee engagement, and diversity and inclusion. The bank's HR management practices have played a crucial role in its success in navigating the challenges posed by the COVID-19 pandemic.

ADCB's Response to the Pandemic

ADCB responded swiftly to the pandemic's challenges by implementing several measures to ensure the safety and well-being of its employees while maintaining its operations. The bank transitioned to remote work for non-branch employees and adopted strict safety protocols for employees working at branches. The bank also provided its employees with mental health support, financial assistance, and access to online learning and development programs. ADCB's response to the pandemic demonstrates the importance of effective HR management in crises.

Contributions of HRM Strategies to ADCB's Success

ADCB's HR management strategies have contributed significantly to the bank's competitive advantage and success. By prioritizing talent acquisition and development, the bank has built a strong workforce capable of navigating challenging situations like the COVID-19 pandemic. The bank's focus on employee engagement, diversity and inclusion, and compensation and benefits has also contributed to creating a positive workplace culture that attracts and retains top talent.

Conclusion

This case study highlights the critical role that HR management plays in organizations' success, particularly during crises like the COVID-19 pandemic. ADCB's HR management practices have been instrumental in enabling the bank to navigate the challenges posed by the pandemic successfully. By prioritizing talent acquisition and development, employee engagement, diversity and inclusion, and compensation and benefits, ADCB has created a positive workplace culture that attracts and retains top talent and contributes to the bank's competitive advantage and success.

INDUSTRY CONTEXT

Amid the COVID-19 pandemic, banks like Abu Dhabi Commercial Bank (ADCB) faced significant challenges in maintaining operations while ensuring the safety of their employees. Human resource management played a crucial role in navigating the crisis and ensuring business continuity.

CHALLENGES

- Adapting HR management practices to support remote working and ensure employee well-being during the pandemic
- Maintaining employee engagement and productivity amid the uncertainties and disruptions caused by COVID-19

- Implementing effective strategies to balance workforce costs and resource allocation while preserving jobs

LESSONS LEARNED

- A resilient organizational culture and shared values can help a company successfully navigate challenges and crises
- Agile HR management practices that focus on employee well-being and engagement are crucial to maintaining a strong workforce during uncertain times

QUESTIONS

1. How can HR management practices be adapted to better support employees during a crisis such as the COVID-19 pandemic?
2. What are some strategies that banks like ADCB can employ to maintain employee engagement and productivity amid disruptions?
3. How can organizations strike a balance between managing workforce costs and preserving jobs during a crisis?

UN SDGs: Decent work and Economic Growth (8); Industry, innovation, and infrastructure (9)

RESOURCES

OVERALL ENGAGEMENT SCORE	87%
COMMITMENT SCORE	86%
ENABLEMENT SCORE	87%
LINE MANAGER INDEX SCORE	89%
PARTICIPATION RATE	91%

ADCB EMPLOYEE ENGAGEMENT SURVEY RESULTS

Source: ADCB 2020 Annual Report

REFERENCES

1. Corporate Finance Institute. (2001). Top Banks in UAE. https://corporatefinanceinstitute.com/resources/careers/companies/top-banks-in-uae/.

2. Abu Dhabi Commercial Bank. (2020). 2020 Annual Report: Emerging Stronger. https://www.adcb.com/en/multimedia/pdfs/2021/march/annual-report-220321.pdf.

3. Cappelli, P. (2015, July-August). Why We love to Hate HR and What HR Can Do About It. Harvard Business Review.

Finding Ways: Banco De Oro's Human Capital Sustainability Strategy

Themes: BDO, HRM, Business Transformation, Funds

TEACHING OBJECTIVES

The case study is intended to qualify students to:

- Assess BDO's human capital management efforts;
- Discuss how BDO ensured employee health and safety during the pandemic;
- Examine how BDO strives to be a responsible employer and business

SYNOPSIS

Human resources are a critical aspect of any organization. They are the most important assets that help a business transform its strategies and goals into tangible results and provide a competitive advantage against competitors. For this reason, organizations must manage their human capital sustainably. Sustainability is paying attention to environmental, social, and governance (ESG) practices and integrating them into company strategies and operations. An organization that has strong ESG performance creates real value for its stakeholders and builds a strong foundation that allows it to withstand various challenges, including those that are beyond its control, such as a global pandemic and economic downturn. Banco De Oro (BDO) is a Philippine company that provides a full range of banking services and products, such as lending, deposit-taking, credit cards, leasing and finance, rural banking, brokering, trust, and investments.

BDO is the largest bank in the Philippines and has nearly 39,000 employees all over the country, including about 100 employees abroad. BDO provides a full range of banking services and products, such as lending, deposit-taking, credit cards, leasing and finance, rural banking, brokering, trust, and investments. BDO's Human Capital Management Efforts: BDO's human capital management efforts are designed to attract and retain top talent and to develop its employees' skills and capabilities. BDO's HR management practices include talent acquisition and development, performance management, employee engagement, diversity and inclusion, and compensation and benefits. BDO's HR management efforts have contributed to the bank's competitive advantage and success in the banking industry in the Philippines.

Ensuring Employee Health and Safety During the Pandemic

BDO prioritized employee health and safety during the COVID-19 pandemic by implementing several measures. The bank implemented work-from-home arrangements for non-branch employees, and for employees who needed to report to work, the bank implemented strict safety protocols to ensure their safety. The bank also provided employees with access to medical assistance, mental health support, and online learning and development programs. BDO's response to the pandemic demonstrates the importance of prioritizing employee health and safety during crises.

Striving to Be a Responsible Employer and Business

BDO strives to be a responsible employer and business by incorporating ESG practices into its strategies and operations. The bank's ESG practices include promoting financial inclusion, supporting micro, small, and medium-sized enterprises (MSMEs), supporting education and community development programs, promoting environmental sustainability, and advocating good governance. BDO's efforts to be a responsible employer and business have contributed to the bank's success in promoting financial inclusion, supporting MSMEs, and contributing to sustainable development.

Conclusion

This case study highlights the importance of managing human capital sustainably and prioritizing employee health and safety during crises. BDO's human capital sustainability strategy, which incorporates ESG practices into the company's strategies and operations, has contributed to the bank's competitive advantage and success. By prioritizing employee development and engagement, promoting financial inclusion, supporting MSMEs, and advocating good governance, BDO has demonstrated its commitment to being a responsible employer and business.

INDUSTRY CONTEXT

In the banking sector, human capital sustainability plays a critical role in ensuring business continuity and resilience, especially during challenging times like the COVID-19 pandemic. Banks like Banco De Oro (BDO) must adapt their human resources strategies to maintain employee well-being and engagement while ensuring operational efficiency.

CHALLENGES

- Implementing effective human capital management strategies in a rapidly changing business environment
- Ensuring employee health and safety during the pandemic while maintaining operational efficiency
- Integrating environmental, social, and governance (ESG) practices into company strategies to create long-term value for stakeholders

LESSONS LEARNED

- A sustainable human capital strategy is essential for building a resilient organization capable of withstanding various challenges
- An organization with strong ESG performance can create real value for its stakeholders and foster long-term business success

QUESTIONS

1. How can banks like BDO adapt their human capital management strategies to ensure sustainability and resilience during challenging times?
2. What measures can be implemented to prioritize employee health and safety while maintaining operational efficiency during a crisis?
3. How can integrating ESG practices into company strategies contribute to long-term business success and stakeholder value creation?

UN SDGs: Decent work and Economic Growth (8); Industry, innovation, and infrastructure (9)

RESOURCES

Employee Count by Location

Luzon	Visayas	Mindanao
30,568	3,680	4,526
2021	2021	2021
30,540	3,634	4,487
2020	2020	2020

Abroad

99	95
2021	2020

Source: 2021 BDO sustainability report

REFERENCES

1. M. (eds) Leadership, Innovation and Entrepreneurship as Driving Forces of the Global Economy. Springer Proceedings in Business and Economics. Springer, Cham. https://doi.org/10.1007/978-3-319-43434-6_38

2. Serafeim, G. (2022). Social-Impact Efforts That Create Real Value. Harvard Business Review. https://hbr.org/2020/09/social-impact-efforts-that-create-real-value

3. BDO. (2021). Finding Ways: Creating A Sustainable Future. 2021 Sustainability Report. https://www.bdo.com.ph/sites/default/files/pdf/BDO-2021-Sustainability-Report.pdf

Fostering Talent Management: Emaar Properties' People-Centric Strategies

Themes: Real estate, Inclusivity, Competitive Advantage, Pandemic

TEACHING OBJECTIVES

The case study is intended to qualify students to:

- Examine Emaar's commitment to its people by creating a diverse, inclusive, and rich work environment;
- Identify Emaar's human resource management strategies for attracting and retaining its talents;
- Discuss the key roles that Emaar's people play in contributing to the company's competitive advantage and success

SYNOPSIS

Dubai-based Emaar Properties is one of the largest real estate companies in the world. Its portfolio is comprised of over 1.6 billion square feet of properties, both commercial and residential, as well as retail and hospitality space, in various continents, such as Europe, North America, Africa, and Asia.

Emaar Properties' People-Centric Strategies

Emaar Properties' success is driven by its commitment to its people. The company's human resource management strategies are designed to create a diverse, inclusive, and rich work environment that attracts and retains top talent. Emaar's people-centric approach includes a focus on talent development, employee engagement, and diversity and inclusion. The company's talent development programs provide employees with opportunities for career growth and development, while its employee engagement initiatives aim to foster a positive workplace culture that promotes creativity, innovation, and collaboration. Emaar also prioritizes diversity and inclusion, recognizing that a diverse and inclusive workforce contributes to the company's competitive advantage and success.

Attracting and Retaining Top Talent

Emaar's human resource management strategies are designed to attract and retain top talent. The company offers competitive compensation and benefits packages, as well as opportunities for career growth and development. Emaar also prioritizes employee wellness and work-life balance, providing employees with access to health and wellness programs, as well as flexible work arrangements. The company's commitment to creating a positive workplace culture that promotes diversity and inclusion also contributes to its ability to attract and retain top talent.

Contributions of Emaar's People to the Company's Success

Emaar's people play a critical role in the company's competitive advantage and success. The company's talented workforce is responsible for creating innovative and world-renowned developments, such as the Burj Khalifa and The Dubai Mall. Emaar's focus on diversity and inclusion also allows the company to tap into a broad range of perspectives and ideas, contributing to its ability to innovate and remain competitive.

Impact of the COVID-19 Pandemic

The COVID-19 pandemic has had a significant impact on the construction industry, and Emaar Properties is no exception. The company has implemented several measures to ensure the safety and well-being of its employees while maintaining its operations. These measures include remote work arrangements, social distancing protocols, and regular health and wellness checks. Emaar's commitment to its people has enabled the company to navigate the challenges posed by the pandemic successfully.

Conclusion

Emaar Properties' people-centric strategies have been instrumental in the company's success as a globally admired lifestyle developer. By prioritizing talent development, employee engagement, and diversity and inclusion, Emaar has created a positive workplace culture that attracts and retains top talent and contributes to the company's competitive advantage and success. Despite the impact of the COVID-19 pandemic on the construction industry, Emaar's commitment to its people has enabled the company to navigate these challenges successfully.

INDUSTRY CONTEXT

In the competitive real estate industry, talent management plays a crucial role in driving success and innovation. Companies like Emaar Properties must prioritize a people-centric approach to attract, develop, and retain top talent while maintaining a diverse and inclusive work environment.

CHALLENGES

- Creating a diverse and inclusive work environment in a culturally diverse and dynamic industry
- Attracting and retaining top talent in the competitive real estate market
- Adapting human resource management strategies to navigate the challenges brought on by the COVID-19 pandemic

LESSONS LEARNED

- A strong talent management strategy is essential for driving success and innovation in the real estate industry

- Prioritizing a people-centric approach fosters a work environment that contributes to the company's competitive advantage and success

QUESTIONS

1. How can real estate companies like Emaar Properties create a diverse and inclusive work environment to drive innovation and success?
2. What strategies can be employed to attract and retain top talent in the competitive real estate market?
3. How can companies adapt their human resource management strategies to navigate the challenges brought on by the COVID-19 pandemic and ensure long-term success?

UN SDGs: Decent work and Economic Growth (8); Industry, innovation, and infrastructure (9)

RESOURCES

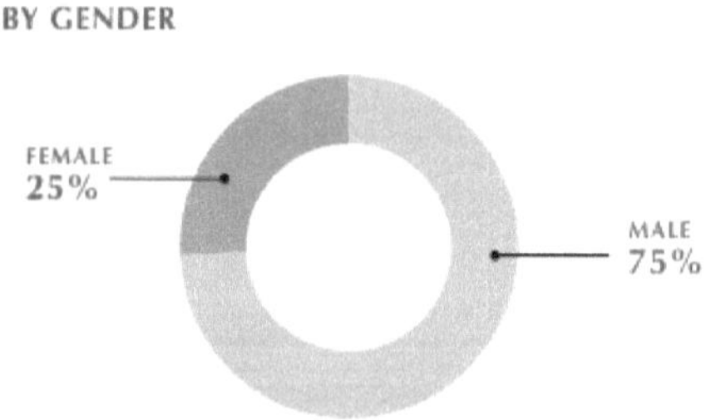

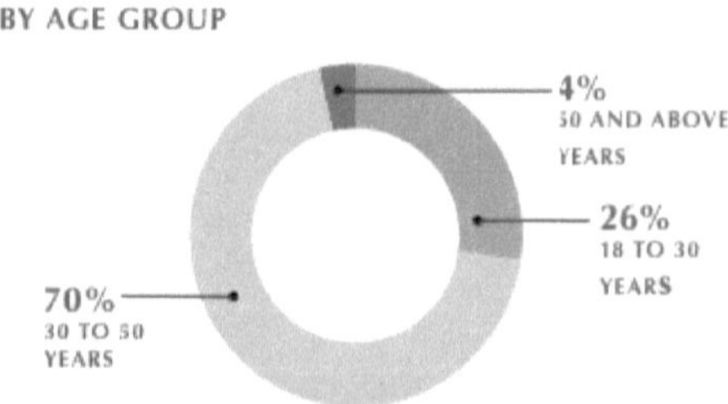

Source: Emaar Properties Sustainability Report 2020

REFERENCES

1. Emaar Properties. (n.d.) About Emaar. https://properties.emaar.com/en/about-emaar/.
2. Emaar Properties. (2021). Sustainability Report 2020. https://cdn.properties.emaar.com/wp-content/uploads/2021/07/EMAAR-PROPERTIES-ESG-2020.pdf.
3. Umar, T. (2022). The Impact of COVID-19 on the GCC Construction Industry. The International Journal of Service Science, Management, Engineering, and Technology (IJSSMET), 13(2), 17.

Quality and Affordable Errand Services: Tailored Solutions by Personal Assistant Service

Themes: Quality, Services, Business, Competition, Customers

TEACHING OBJECTIVES

The case study is intended to qualify students to:

- Analyze the factors contributing to the growth and demand for personal assistant service enterprises.
- Discuss the role of technology and digital platforms in shaping the errand services industry.
- Examine the challenges faced by personal assistant service companies in maintaining quality and affordability.

SYNOPSIS

This case study focuses on the personal assistant service industry and the factors contributing to its growth and demand. The industry has witnessed a surge in demand as busy professionals, households, and businesses require assistance in managing their daily tasks. Personal assistant service companies specialize in offering tailored errand solutions that cater to a variety of client needs, ranging from grocery shopping and appointment scheduling to travel planning and event coordination. This case study will analyze the role of technology and digital platforms in shaping the errand services industry, the challenges faced by personal assistant service companies in maintaining quality and affordability, and the strategies adopted by these companies to stay ahead in a competitive market landscape.

Factors Contributing to the Growth and Demand

The rise of the gig economy and the trend of outsourcing non-core tasks are some of the key factors contributing to the growth and demand for personal assistant service enterprises. Additionally, the increasing number of working professionals and households, especially in urban areas, has also led to a surge in demand for personal assistant services. The industry's growth is further fueled by the increasing adoption of digital platforms, making it easier for customers to access and avail of these services.

Role of Technology and Digital Platforms

Technology and digital platforms have played a significant role in shaping the personal assistant service industry. The advent of mobile applications and online platforms has made it easier for customers to book services and communicate with service providers. These platforms have also enabled personal assistant service companies to streamline their operations and enhance service delivery, resulting in increased efficiency and customer satisfaction.

Strategies Adopted by Personal Assistant Service Companies

To stay ahead in a competitive market landscape, personal assistant service companies have adopted innovative strategies. These include investing in staff training and development to enhance service quality, leveraging technology to streamline operations and enhance service delivery, and diversifying their service offerings to cater to evolving client demands. Additionally, personal assistant service companies need to continuously monitor customer feedback and adapt to changing market trends to remain relevant and competitive.

Conclusion

This case study highlights the factors contributing to the growth and demand for personal assistant service enterprises, the role of technology and digital platforms in shaping the industry, and the challenges faced by these companies in maintaining quality and affordability. To stay ahead in a competitive market landscape, personal assistant service companies need to adopt innovative strategies and continuously monitor customer feedback and changing market trends to remain relevant and competitive.

INDUSTRY CONTEXT

The personal assistant services industry is experiencing a boom in demand, driven by busy lifestyles and the growing desire for a work-life balance. This has resulted in a competitive market, where both large corporations and smaller local businesses offer tailored errand solutions to meet the needs of their clients. Technology is playing an increasingly important role in enhancing the efficiency and effectiveness of personal assistant services, further contributing to the industry's growth and evolution.

CHALLENGES

- Ensuring consistent service quality across diverse client needs.
- Adapting to changing client preferences and market trends.
- Attracting and retaining skilled professionals in a competitive industry.

LESSONS LEARNED

- Innovative strategies and technological integration can streamline operations and improve service delivery.
- Investing in staff training and development is crucial for maintaining high-quality services and retaining talented personnel.

QUESTIONS

1. How can personal assistant service companies differentiate themselves in a competitive market?
2. In what ways can technology be leveraged to enhance the efficiency of personal assistant services?
3. How can personal assistant service companies strike a balance between quality and affordability to attract a broader clientele?

UN SDGs: Decent work and Economic Growth (8); Industry, innovation, and infrastructure (9)

RESOURCES

Source: Zirtual

REFERENCES

1. Askheim, O. P. (2019). The Norwegian system of supporting people with disabilities in independent living, including assistant services.
2. Bryson, J. R., Sundbo, J., Fuglsang, L., & Daniels, P. (2020). Service Management. *Springer Books*.
3. Darling, A. R. (2018). *A Business Plan for Darling Suites: An Assisted Living Facility in Rock Island, IL*. California State University, Long Beach.

Career Reinvention for the Post-pandemic Workplace: Insights from UAE and Brunei

Themes: Technology, Invention, Reshaping, Ecosystem

TEACHING OBJECTIVES

The case study is intended to qualify students to:

- Investigate the potential obstacles organizations face as they navigate the post-pandemic world.
- Delve into the strategies organizations employ to reshape careers in response to the changing work environment.
- Assess the role of technology in facilitating career reinvention in the post-pandemic era.

SYNOPSIS

The pandemic has enhanced the future of work in the UAE and Brunei. As the pandemic resets significant work trends, human resource leaders must rethink employee and workforce planning, experience strategies, performance, and management. When COVID-19 forced much of the world, including the UAE and Brunei, quickly shut down offices, schools, restaurants, shops, and factories, and pushed millions of people unto makeshift workspaces, remote, no one knew how what would be the outcome. Now, it is known a lot more, and a lot of it is pretty positive. As the COVID-19 pandemic grows, firms should consider reshaping the work environment to ensure compliance with legal needs and guidelines, and secondly, to align the modifying requirements of their workforce both in the prompt and the longer term. Firms in the UAE and Brunei prioritize technology deployment and re-evaluate human resources policies and incentive plans. These can be classified into three areas that firms should consider when implementing new working ways.

Strategies for Reshaping Careers

Firms in the UAE and Brunei have adopted various strategies to reshape careers in response to the changing work environment. These include prioritizing technology deployment to facilitate remote work, re-evaluating human resources policies and incentive plans, and investing in employee training and development. Organizations have also focused on fostering a culture of adaptability and innovation to promote a smooth transition to the post-pandemic work environment.

The Role of Technology in Career Reinvention

Technology has played a significant role in facilitating career reinvention in the post-pandemic era. By embracing digital platforms, organizations have been able to facilitate remote work, maintain employee communication, and collaborate effectively. The use of technology has also allowed firms to automate repetitive tasks and streamline operations, improving productivity and efficiency.

Conclusion

The COVID-19 pandemic has forced organizations to adapt to a new work environment, and firms in the UAE and Brunei have responded by implementing strategies to reshape careers. These strategies have prioritized technology deployment, re-evaluated human resources policies and incentive plans, and invested in employee training and development. By embracing technology, organizations have been able to facilitate remote work, improve communication and collaboration, and streamline operations. As organizations navigate the post-pandemic world, they must continue to prioritize innovation and adaptability to remain competitive and successful.

INDUSTRY CONTEXT

The post-pandemic landscape has brought about significant changes in workforce management, highlighting the need for flexible working arrangements, technology integration, and revised HR policies to adapt to the evolving needs of employees and organizations alike.

CHALLENGES

- Adapting to new working models and remote work arrangements.
- Ensuring employee well-being and mental health support.
- Balancing productivity and work-life balance in a remote work setting.

LESSONS LEARNED

- The importance of proactive communication and collaboration in a remote work environment.
- The value of agility and adaptability in organizational structures and HR policies.

QUESTIONS

1. How can organizations effectively support employees during the transition to new working models in the post-pandemic world?
2. What role does technology play in enhancing employee engagement and collaboration in remote work settings?
3. How can organizations strike a balance between productivity and employee well-being in the post-pandemic landscape?

UN SDGs: Quality Education (5); Partnership for Goals (17)

RESOURCES

Five imperatives for resetting the future of work agenda

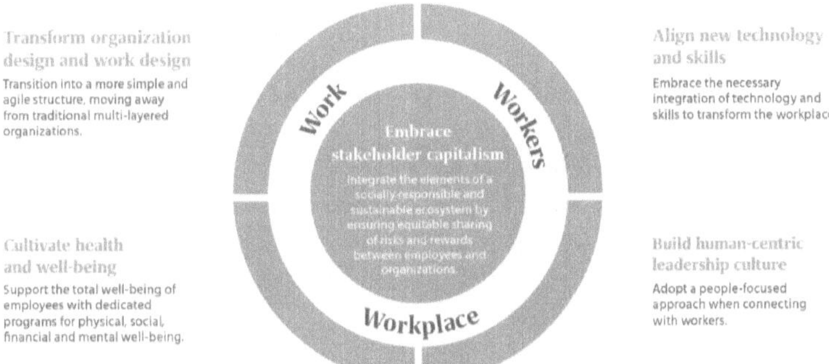

Source: World Economic Forum

REFERENCES

1. Agrawal, S., De Smet, A., Lacroix, S., & Reich, A. (2020). To emerge stronger from the COVID-19 crisis, companies should start reskilling their workforces now. *McKinsey Insights*.

2. Cukier, W. E. N. D. Y., MCCALLUM, K. E., EGBUNONU, P., & Bates, K. (2021). The mother of invention: Skills for innovation in the post-pandemic world. In *Public Policy Forum, Diversity Institute, Future Skills Centre. https://www. ryerson. ca/diversity/reports/MotherOfInvention_ EN. pdf*.

3. Fung, C. Y., & Gunasekara, A. (2021). Re-thinking post-COVID-19 career success: Insights from contemporary career approaches. *COVID-19, Business, and Economy in Malaysia*, 141-159.

DEWA's Sustainable Risk Management Strategy in IT Governance

Themes: IT, Risk, Management, Mitigation, Governance

TEACHING OBJECTIVES

The case study is intended to qualify students to:

- Understand the significance of sustainable risk management within IT Governance.
- Analyze the key elements that contribute to the successful implementation of sustainable risk management in IT governance.
- Investigate the journey towards achieving maturity in sustainable IT risk management practices.

SYNOPSIS

Dubai Electricity & Water Authority (DEWA) has grown significantly since its inception as a private entity, and its management team has crafted a strategy to enhance operations and optimize services to boost customer satisfaction throughout Dubai. However, the reengineering process encountered challenges from both internal and external stakeholders who resisted change. This case study explores how DEWA's sustainable risk management strategy has contributed to the successful implementation of IT governance and highlights the key elements that have enabled DEWA to achieve maturity in sustainable IT risk management practices.

Significance of Sustainable Risk Management within IT Governance

IT governance is critical to ensuring that organizations meet their objectives while managing risks and optimizing resources effectively. Sustainable risk management within IT governance enables organizations to maintain a proactive approach to identifying, assessing, and mitigating risks that may impact their operations. It involves a continuous process of risk assessment, monitoring, and mitigation to ensure that organizations are well-prepared to address potential risks and maintain resilience.

Key Elements for Successful Implementation

The successful implementation of sustainable risk management within IT governance requires several key elements, including evaluating information technology gaps, aligning the IT governance framework with best practices and standards, and articulating the risk appetite to influence the associated control and risk design. DEWA has also invested in resilient innovation, system automation, skill development, content management, talent management, decision support, data analysis, and collaboration networks to maintain IT risk management over time with limited investment methods of practice. By adopting a comprehensive and integrated approach to risk management, DEWA has been able to minimize the impact of risks and ensure continuity of operations.

Journey towards Achieving

DEWA has taken a proactive approach to achieving maturity in sustainable IT risk management practices by investing in employee training and development, fostering a culture of innovation and continuous improvement, and leveraging technology to streamline operations. DEWA has also collaborated with industry experts to stay updated on best practices and emerging risks, enabling the organization to anticipate potential threats and take appropriate actions to mitigate them. The journey towards achieving maturity in sustainable IT risk management practices is an ongoing process, and DEWA continues to explore new ways to enhance its risk management practices.

Conclusion

DEWA's sustainable risk management strategy has enabled the organization to maintain resilience in the face of potential risks and ensure continuity of operations. By adopting a comprehensive and integrated approach to risk management, DEWA has been able to minimize the impact of risks and achieve maturity in sustainable IT risk management practices. The successful implementation of sustainable risk management within IT governance requires a proactive approach to identifying, assessing, and mitigating risks and investing in employee training and development, fostering a culture of innovation and continuous improvement, and leveraging technology to streamline operations. As organizations navigate the complex and evolving risk landscape, they must continue to prioritize sustainable risk management practices to ensure resilience and continuity of operations.

INDUSTRY CONTEXT

The utility industry is becoming increasingly dependent on IT infrastructure, with growing complexity of IT systems and associated risks. As a result, there is a pressing need for robust IT governance to ensure efficient and secure operations within utility organizations.

CHALLENGES

- Resistance to change during the reengineering process.
- Alignment of the ICT department with the IT governance framework.
- Balancing IT risk management investment amidst budget constraints and fluctuating commodity prices.

LESSONS LEARNED

- Effective communication of risk appetite is crucial for the successful implementation of risk control measures.
- Investment in IT risk management can lead to long-term value enhancement and proactive risk identification.

QUESTIONS

1. How can DEWA effectively communicate its risk appetite and implement appropriate risk control measures?
2. What are the critical factors that contribute to the successful implementation of sustainable risk management in IT governance?
3. How can DEWA balance the need for investment in IT risk management with budget constraints and fluctuating commodity prices?

UN SDGs: Decent work and Economic Growth (8); Industry, innovation, and infrastructure (9)

RESOURCES

Source: MI-GSO

REFERENCES

1. AlSheibani, S., Messom, C., & Cheung, Y. (2020, January). Rethinking the competitive landscape of artificial intelligence. In *Proceedings of the 53rd Hawaii international conference on system sciences.*

2. Dewa, O., Makoka, D., & Ayo-Yusuf, O. (2022). A deliberative rural community consultation to assess support for flood risk management policies to strengthen resilience in Malawi. *Water, 14*(6), 874.

3. El Khatib, M., Al Zeyoudi, A., & Shaqar, S. B. (2020). The influence of integrating ISO and TQM on project risk management. *American Journal of Industrial and Business Management, 10*(12), 1886.

Public Sector Entrepreneurship: Unlocking Public-Private Partnership Models in UAE and Brunei

Themes: Public, Private, Models, Government, Partnership

TEACHING OBJECTIVES

The case study is intended to qualify students to:

- Understand the significance of implementing public-private partnerships to boost productivity.
- Analyze the potential obstacles organizations may encounter during the integration of public-private partnerships.
- Investigate the rationale behind government engagement in public-private partnerships.

SYNOPSIS

Public sector entrepreneurship has emerged as an effective way to boost economic success by transforming the financial ecosystem into one that is more advantageous to monetary entities engaged in creative activities amidst uncertainty. One way to achieve this is through public-private partnerships, which enhance the effectiveness of infrastructure projects through long-term collaborations between private enterprises and the public sector. This case study explores the potential obstacles that organizations may encounter during the integration of public-private partnerships and the rationale behind government engagement in such partnerships. It highlights the significance of implementing public-private partnerships to boost productivity.

Public-Private Partnerships

Public-private partnerships are built on principles such as payment upon delivery, risk allocation, whole-life costing, and competition to achieve the best value. They enable each party to excel in their respective domains, ultimately providing public infrastructure and services more efficiently. In the UAE and Brunei, public-private partnerships encompass a broad range of working arrangements, from strategic, and informal collaborations to design, build, finance, and operate (DBFO) service contracts and legal joint venture companies. These partnerships focus on delivering services and assets that support community outcomes and public services.

Potential Obstacles

One of the potential obstacles that organizations may encounter during the integration of public-private partnerships is a lack of trust between the public and private sectors. This may be due to the perception that the private sector is more focused on profit than public interest. Other challenges may include regulatory hurdles, funding constraints, and differences in organizational culture and priorities.

Government Engagement

Governments engage in public-private partnerships to leverage private sector resources, expertise, and technology to deliver public services more efficiently. By partnering with private enterprises, governments can access new sources of funding and expertise, reduce the burden on taxpayers, and increase transparency and accountability. Additionally, public-private partnerships can stimulate economic growth and job creation by promoting entrepreneurship and innovation.

Conclusion

Public-private partnerships have emerged as an effective way to boost productivity by enhancing the effectiveness of infrastructure projects through long-term collaborations between private enterprises and the public sector. Despite potential obstacles, governments engage in public-private partnerships to leverage private sector resources, expertise, and technology to deliver public services more efficiently. By partnering with private enterprises, governments can access new sources of funding and expertise, reduce the burden on taxpayers, and increase transparency and accountability. As organizations navigate the integration of public-private partnerships, they must continue to prioritize innovation and adaptability to remain competitive and successful.

INDUSTRY CONTEXT

Public-private partnerships are gaining increasing attention and importance in the context of the UAE and Brunei. These collaborations allow governments to leverage the expertise, resources, and innovation of the private sector to address various challenges, particularly in infrastructure development, service delivery, and technology implementation. As the need for efficient public services and sustainable development grows, public-private partnerships offer a promising solution to meet these demands while also promoting economic growth and diversification.

CHALLENGES

- Aligning the interests and objectives of both public and private partners
- Ensuring transparency, accountability, and fairness in partnership agreements
- Managing and mitigating risks associated with long-term collaborations

LESSONS LEARNED

- Clear communication and trust between partners are crucial for successful public-private partnerships.
- Effective risk management and a well-defined governance structure can greatly enhance the outcomes of such partnerships.

QUESTIONS

1. How can governments create an enabling environment for successful public-private partnerships in the UAE and Brunei?
2. What are some examples of successful public-private partnerships in the UAE and Brunei, and what factors contributed to their success?
3. How can the challenges faced by organizations during the adoption of public-private partnerships be overcome or minimized?

UN SDGs: Decent Work and Economic Growth (8); Industry, innovation, and Infrastructure (9); Partnership for Goals (17)

RESOURCES

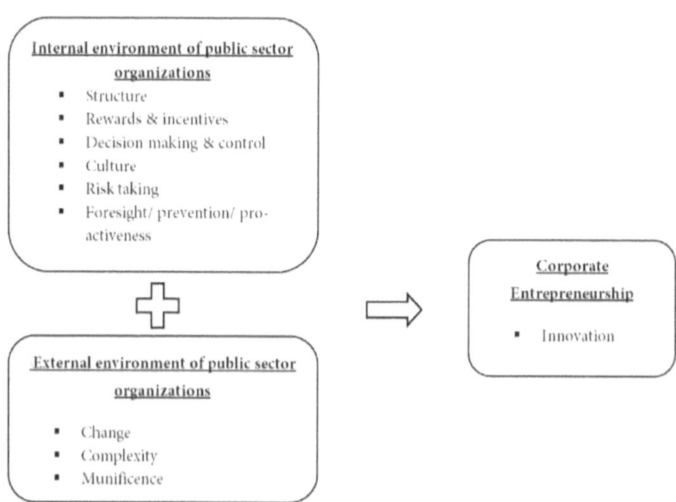

Source: Karyootakis et al.

REFERENCES

1. Castelblanco, G., Guevara, J., Mesa, H., & Flores, D. (2020). Risk allocation in unsolicited and solicited road public-private partnerships: Sustainability and management implications. *Sustainability*, *12*(11), 4478.
2. Cepparulo, A., Eusepi, G., & Giuriato, L. (2019). Public Private Partnership and fiscal illusion: A systematic review. *Journal of Infrastructure, Policy and Development*, *3*(2), 288-309.
3. Ermishina, A. V. (2018). Institutional Arrangements in Public Utilities and Public Management: Case of Russia Water Utilities. In *Handbook of Research on Urban Governance and Management in the Developing World* (pp. 84-99). IGI Global.

Artificial Intelligence and Machine Learning in Healthcare: Revolutionizing Patient Care

Themes: AI, Machine Learning, Patient Care, Quality

TEACHING OBJECTIVES

The case study is intended to qualify students to:

- Understand the impact of artificial intelligence (AI) and machine learning (ML) on healthcare and patient care.
- Examine the challenges and opportunities in implementing AI and ML solutions in healthcare settings.
- Analyze the ethical considerations and regulatory implications of AI and ML adoption in healthcare.

SYNOPSIS

Artificial intelligence (AI) and machine learning (ML) are at the forefront of a technological revolution within the healthcare industry, providing groundbreaking solutions to enhance patient care, medical diagnostics, and healthcare management. As these advanced technologies gain traction, they are transforming various aspects of healthcare in remarkable ways, including diagnostics, personalized medicine, drug discovery, and patient monitoring. In addition to these advancements, AI and ML are also proving invaluable in optimizing healthcare management by enhancing the efficiency of hospital operations, facilitating remote patient monitoring, and improving decision-making processes through the analysis of vast amounts of data.

Impact of AI and ML on Healthcare

AI and ML have transformed various aspects of healthcare, including medical diagnostics, personalized medicine, drug discovery, and patient monitoring. By analyzing vast amounts of data, these technologies can help healthcare providers make better decisions and improve patient outcomes. AI and ML can also optimize healthcare management by enhancing the efficiency of hospital operations and facilitating remote patient monitoring.

Ethical and Regulatory Considerations

As AI and ML are implemented in healthcare settings, it is critical to address ethical and regulatory considerations to ensure patient safety, data privacy, and responsible innovation. Interdisciplinary collaboration between healthcare professionals, data scientists, and technology experts is necessary to establish guidelines and safeguards for the safe and ethical use of these technologies. Regulatory bodies play a critical role in ensuring that these guidelines are established and adhered to.

Conclusion

AI and ML have the potential to transform healthcare, but their implementation presents challenges that must be addressed. By overcoming these challenges and addressing ethical and regulatory considerations, healthcare providers can reap the benefits of these technologies and improve patient outcomes. It is essential to approach AI and ML adoption in healthcare with a balanced approach, focusing on the benefits and risks and working together to ensure their safe and responsible use.

INDUSTRY CONTEXT

The healthcare industry has been rapidly adopting AI and ML technologies to address a growing demand for personalized care, improved diagnostics, and more efficient management of healthcare resources. As healthcare providers strive to meet the needs of an aging population and tackle complex health challenges, AI and ML offer the potential to revolutionize patient care and unlock new opportunities for innovation.

CHALLENGES

- Integrating AI and ML technologies into existing healthcare workflows and systems.
- Ensuring data privacy and security while leveraging AI and ML solutions.
- Addressing the potential biases and ethical concerns in AI and ML algorithms.

LESSONS LEARNED

- Successful implementation of AI and ML in healthcare requires interdisciplinary collaboration among healthcare professionals, data scientists, and technology experts.
- It is crucial to prioritize patient safety and data privacy while pursuing AI and ML innovations in healthcare.

QUESTIONS

1. How can healthcare providers overcome the challenges of integrating AI and ML technologies into their existing systems and workflows?
2. What role should regulatory bodies play in ensuring the safe and ethical use of AI and ML in healthcare?
3. How can AI and ML be leveraged to address health disparities and improve access to care for underserved populations?

UN SDGs: Industry, innovation, and infrastructure (9); Sustainable cities and communities (11)

RESOURCES

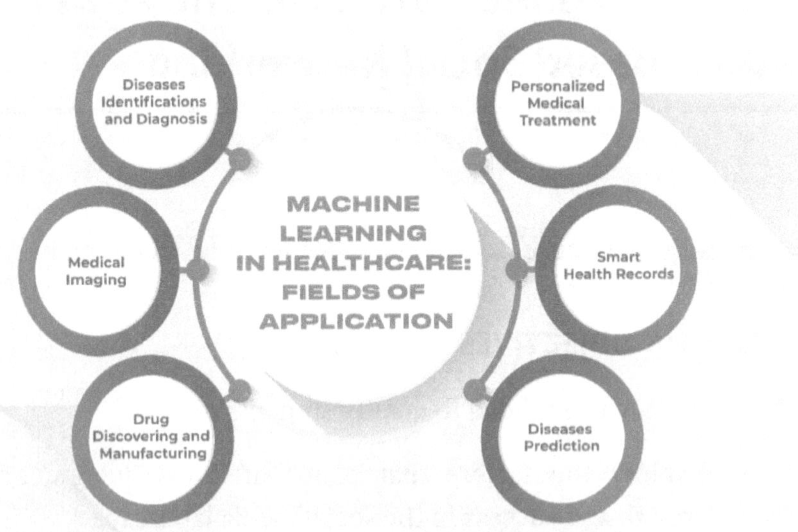

Source: Innovecs

REFERENCES

1. Futoma, J., Simons, M., Panch, T., Doshi-Velez, F., & Celi, L. A. (2020). The myth of generalisability in clinical research and machine learning in health care. *The Lancet Digital Health,* *2*(9), e489-e492.

2. Aung, Y. Y., Wong, D. C., & Ting, D. S. (2021). The promise of artificial intelligence: a review of the opportunities and challenges of artificial intelligence in healthcare. *British medical bulletin,* *139*(1), 4-15.

3. Shaw, J., Rudzicz, F., Jamieson, T., & Goldfarb, A. (2019). Artificial intelligence and the implementation challenge. *Journal of medical Internet research,* *21*(7), e13659.

Clubhouse's Meteoric Rise: The Power of Audio-Based Social Networking

Themes: Clubhouse, social media, Networking, Technology

TEACHING OBJECTIVES

The case study is intended to qualify students to:

- Explore the factors that contributed to Clubhouse's rapid growth and success in the social media landscape.
- Examine the unique value proposition of audio-based social networking and its implications for user engagement and content creation.
- Analyze the challenges and opportunities faced by Clubhouse as it competes with other social media platforms and adapts to changing user preferences and market conditions.

SYNOPSIS

Clubhouse, an invite-only, audio-based social networking app, made its debut in 2020, quickly garnering attention and creating a buzz in the tech world. The platform's meteoric rise can be attributed to its unique approach to social networking, which emphasizes authentic and spontaneous conversations over traditional text or image-based interactions. Users can join virtual "rooms" where they can engage in real-time discussions on various topics, with millions of users, including celebrities and influencers, already drawn to this innovative format. Clubhouse's success hinges on several key factors, including its air of exclusivity, user-friendly interface, and diverse array of content that caters to various interests and communities.

Clubhouse's Unique Value Proposition

Clubhouse's success can be attributed to its unique value proposition of offering an innovative approach to social networking. By focusing on audio-based conversations, the app provides users with a space to engage in authentic and spontaneous conversations on various topics. The app's exclusivity, user-friendly interface, and diverse array of content have also contributed to its growth.

Strategies

Clubhouse must also grapple with issues surrounding content moderation to ensure that the platform remains a safe space for users while preserving its open and spontaneous nature. Scaling its user base to maintain momentum and keep users engaged as the novelty wears off will be crucial for the platform's long-term success.

Conclusion

Clubhouse's success in the social media landscape can be attributed to its unique approach to social networking. The app's focus on audio-based conversations and real-time discussions has created a space for authentic and spontaneous interactions among users. However, the app must continue to adapt to changing user preferences and market conditions while addressing the challenges it faces to remain competitive in the long run.

INDUSTRY CONTEXT

In recent years, the social media landscape has become increasingly saturated, with numerous platforms vying for users' attention. Amidst this fierce competition, Clubhouse managed to carve out a niche by offering an audio-only format that fosters real-time conversations and promotes genuine connections among users. This innovative approach sets Clubhouse apart from the heavily visual and curated nature of most social media platforms and has resonated with users seeking more authentic interactions.

CHALLENGES

- Competition from established social media platforms, such as Facebook and Twitter, which are launching their audio-based features.
- Maintaining user interest and engagement as the novelty of the platform wears off.
- Ensuring effective content moderation to prevent the spread of misinformation and harmful content while preserving the platform's open and spontaneous nature.

LESSONS LEARNED

- The importance of differentiating a platform in a crowded social media landscape by offering a unique value proposition and user experience.
- The power of exclusivity and word-of-mouth marketing in generating buzz and driving early adoption.

QUESTIONS

1. What factors contributed to Clubhouse's rapid growth, and how can the platform maintain its momentum in the face of competition from other social media giants?
2. How do you think Clubhouse's audio-based format will influence the future of social media and user engagement?
3. What strategies should Clubhouse adopt to address the challenges it faces, such as content moderation and maintaining user interest?

UN SDGs: Industry, innovation, and infrastructure (9); Sustainable cities and communities (11)

RESOURCES

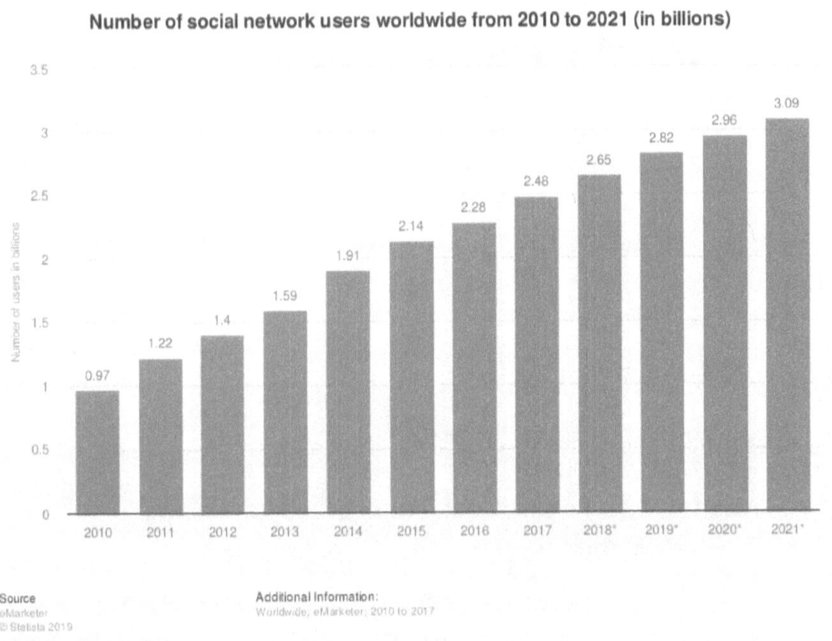

Source: Emarketer

REFERENCES

1. Pribila, M. Š. K. Clubhouse Application as an Effective Tool for Media Students.
2. Rahy, P. B. (2022). Social Media Business Models: an Analysis of the Prevailing Models and Kult's Proposal of Monetizing Human Curation.
3. Olanrewaju, A. S. T., Hossain, M. A., Whiteside, N., & Mercieca, P. (2020). Social media and entrepreneurship research: A literature review. *International Journal of Information Management*, 50, 90-110.

Peloton's At-Home Fitness Revolution: Reshaping the Exercise Industry

Themes: Home Fitness, Covid-19 Pandemic, Competitive Advantage, Consumer Market

TEACHING OBJECTIVES

The case study is intended to qualify students to:

- Analyze the factors that contributed to Peloton's success in revolutionizing the at-home fitness industry.
- Evaluate the impact of the COVID-19 pandemic on Peloton's growth and the broader fitness industry.
- Examine the challenges faced by Peloton in maintaining its competitive edge and adapting to the evolving consumer demands and market trends.

SYNOPSIS

Peloton, a pioneer in the at-home fitness revolution, has transformed the way people exercise by combining cutting-edge technology, live-streamed classes, and a sense of community to create a seamless and engaging workout experience. Founded in 2012, the company has rapidly grown, catering to an increasingly health-conscious and time-strapped consumer base seeking convenient fitness options without sacrificing quality. Peloton's innovative approach of integrating hardware, software, and content into a cohesive ecosystem has disrupted the traditional fitness industry, driving competitors to adapt or risk obsolescence.

Peloton has revolutionized the at-home fitness industry by offering a seamless and engaging workout experience through its combination of cutting-edge technology, live-streamed classes, and a sense of community. The company's rapid growth and success in the highly competitive fitness industry have been attributed to its innovative approach of integrating hardware, software, and content into a cohesive ecosystem that caters to an increasingly health-conscious and time-strapped consumer base. This case study explores the factors that contributed to Peloton's success, the impact of the COVID-19 pandemic on its growth and the broader fitness industry, and the challenges faced by the company in maintaining its competitive edge in the face of evolving consumer demands and market trends.

Factors Contributing to Peloton's Success

Peloton's success can be attributed to several factors, including its innovative approach to integrating hardware, software, and content, which offers a seamless and engaging workout experience to users. The company has also created a sense of community among its users through its live-streamed classes, allowing individuals to connect and support each other in their fitness journeys. Additionally, Peloton has leveraged data analytics to customize workout recommendations to individual users, further enhancing the personalized and convenient nature of the service.

Impact of COVID-19 on Peloton and the Fitness Industry

The COVID-19 pandemic had a significant impact on Peloton's growth, as gym closures prompted many consumers to seek out at-home workout options. Peloton's success in providing a high-quality workout experience at home positioned the company to take advantage of this trend, resulting in a significant increase in demand for its products and services. The pandemic also accelerated the shift towards at-home fitness solutions, with many traditional fitness companies launching digital offerings to remain competitive.

Conclusion

Peloton has revolutionized the at-home fitness industry through its innovative approach of integrating hardware, software, and content into a cohesive ecosystem that offers a seamless and engaging workout experience to users. The company's rapid growth and success have been fueled by a highly engaged and tech-savvy user base, as well as the acceleration of the trend toward at-home fitness solutions due to the COVID-19 pandemic. Peloton faces challenges in maintaining its competitive edge in the face of evolving consumer demands and market trends, but its success in disrupting the traditional fitness industry suggests that the company is well-positioned to continue driving innovation and growth in the at-home fitness market.

INDUSTRY CONTEXT

The fitness industry has experienced significant disruption in recent years, driven by advancements in technology and shifting consumer preferences towards more personalized, convenient, and engaging workout experiences. Peloton has capitalized on these trends by offering a comprehensive at-home fitness solution that combines state-of-the-art equipment, an extensive library of live and on-demand classes, and a strong sense of community.

CHALLENGES

- Facing increased competition from both traditional fitness companies and new market entrants offering similar at-home workout solutions.
- Ensuring the scalability and sustainability of Peloton's business model while maintaining the quality and uniqueness of its offerings.

- Adapting to potential shifts in consumer preferences and behaviors as the COVID-19 pandemic subsides and gyms reopen.

LESSONS LEARNED

- Emphasizing the importance of innovation and a customer-centric approach in creating a differentiated product and service offering that resonates with consumers.
- Demonstrating the power of community-building and social engagement in driving customer loyalty and retention in the digital age.

QUESTIONS

1. How can Peloton continue to differentiate itself from competitors and maintain its market position in the face of increasing competition?
2. What are the potential long-term impacts of the at-home fitness trend on traditional gyms and fitness centers?
3. As Peloton expands its product and service offerings, how can the company ensure it retains its core values and unique brand identity?

UN SDGs: Good Health and Well-Being (3); Climate Action (13)

RESOURCES

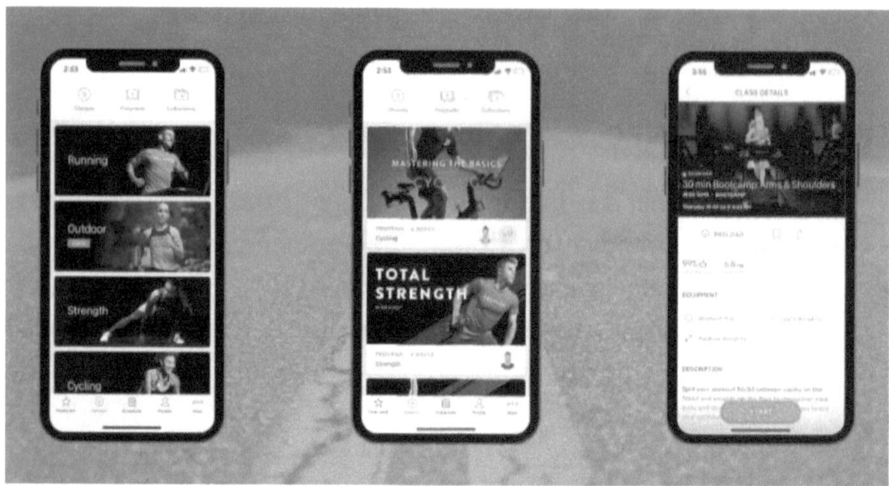

Source: Peloton

REFERENCES

1. https://www.washingtonpost.com/road-to-recovery/2021/01/07/home-fitness-boom/
2. https://www.businessinsider.com/complete-guide-to-the-rise-of-the-digital-fitness-industry-2021-8
3. https://www.vox.com/recode/22925513/peloton-recall-gyms-nordictrack-mirror

Vertical Farming Innovations: The Case of AeroFarms

Themes: Vertical farming, Innovation, Sustainability,

TEACHING OBJECTIVES

The case study is intended to qualify students to:

- Understand the concept of vertical farming and its role in addressing global food security and sustainability challenges.
- Analyze the factors contributing to AeroFarms' success in pioneering innovative vertical farming techniques and technologies.
- Evaluate the potential impact of vertical farming on traditional agriculture and explore opportunities for growth and expansion in the future.

SYNOPSIS

AeroFarms, a leading vertical farming company, is at the forefront of innovative and sustainable agricultural practices. By growing crops in vertically stacked layers using hydroponic systems and LED lighting, AeroFarms can produce food with minimal land, water, and energy resources. This method of farming has the potential to address global food security concerns and environmental issues, while also contributing to local food systems and reducing food transportation costs. This case study explores the concept of vertical farming and its potential impact on traditional agriculture. It focuses on AeroFarms, a leading vertical farming company, and its innovative and sustainable farming practices.

Factors Contributing to AeroFarms' Success

AeroFarms has achieved success by pioneering innovative vertical farming techniques and technologies. The company's commitment to sustainability and efficient use of resources has enabled it to produce food with minimal land, water, and energy resources. AeroFarms uses aeroponics, a form of hydroponics that sprays the roots of plants with a nutrient-rich mist, which uses less water and nutrients than traditional hydroponics, reducing waste and improving efficiency. The company also uses LED lighting that can be customized to specific wavelengths, resulting in faster growth and higher yields. AeroFarms' focus on innovation and sustainability has allowed it to achieve significant growth and establish itself as a leader in the vertical farming industry.

Impact of Vertical Farming on Traditional Agriculture

Vertical farming has the potential to address some of the challenges faced by traditional agriculture, including limited land, water scarcity, and the adverse environmental impact of farming practices. By growing crops in controlled environments, vertical farming reduces the use of pesticides and herbicides and reduces water usage. However, vertical farming is not intended to replace traditional agriculture entirely. Traditional agriculture will continue to play an important role in providing a diverse range of crops and supporting rural communities. Vertical farming can complement traditional agriculture by providing locally grown produce, reducing transportation costs, and improving the sustainability of the food system.

Opportunities for Growth and Expansion

The demand for food is expected to rise by 70% by 2050, as the global population continues to grow. This presents significant opportunities for the vertical farming industry to expand and address food security and sustainability challenges. The case study analyzes the potential for growth and expansion in the vertical farming industry and explores opportunities for innovation and collaboration with traditional agriculture. The success of AeroFarms and other vertical farming companies is likely to inspire further innovation and investment in the industry.

Conclusion

Vertical farming has the potential to transform the food system by addressing global food security and sustainability challenges. AeroFarms is a leading player in the vertical farming industry, with its innovative and sustainable farming practices. While vertical farming is not intended to replace traditional agriculture entirely, it can complement it by providing locally grown produce, reducing transportation costs, and improving the sustainability of the food system. As the demand for food continues to rise, the vertical farming industry is poised for significant growth and expansion.

INDUSTRY CONTEXT

The agriculture industry is under increasing pressure to meet the demands of a growing global population while simultaneously addressing environmental concerns such as land use, water scarcity, and climate change. Vertical farming has emerged as a promising solution to these challenges, offering the potential for higher crop yields, resource efficiency, and reduced environmental impact. Companies like AeroFarms are pioneering advancements in vertical farming techniques, leveraging data-driven approaches and state-of-the-art technology to optimize crop growth and reduce resource consumption.

CHALLENGES

- Overcoming the high initial investment costs associated with establishing vertical farming facilities.

- Scaling the vertical farming model to meet increasing global food demand.
- Ensuring the economic viability of vertical farming and competing with traditional agriculture in terms of cost and profitability.

LESSONS LEARNED

- Innovative technologies and sustainable agricultural practices have the potential to revolutionize the way we produce food, addressing both food security and environmental challenges.
- Collaboration between technology companies, agricultural experts, and policymakers is crucial for fostering the growth of vertical farming and integrating it into the global food system.

QUESTIONS

1. How can vertical farming companies like AeroFarms overcome the high initial investment costs and ensure long-term profitability?
2. In what ways can vertical farming contribute to local food systems and help reduce the environmental impact of food transportation?
3. What role can governments and policymakers play in supporting the growth and adoption of vertical farming practices?

UN SDGs: Health and well-being (3); Sustainable cities and communities (11)

RESOURCES

Source: AeroFarms

REFERENCES

1. https://www.aerofarms.com/
2. https://www.greenbiz.com/article/aerofarms-trying-cultivate-future-vertical-farming
3. http://wam.ae/en/details/1395303129346

The Digital Transformation of Education: The Success of EdTech Startups like Coursera

Themes: Digital Transformation, Business, Innovation, EdTech

TEACHING OBJECTIVES

The case study is intended to qualify students to:

- Examine the digital transformation of education and the role of EdTech startups like Coursera in shaping the industry.
- Analyze the factors contributing to Coursera's success and competitive advantage in the online learning space.
- Evaluate the challenges faced by EdTech startups and the future outlook for the industry.

SYNOPSIS

The education industry has undergone significant changes in recent years, with the emergence of new technologies and digital platforms transforming the way students learn and acquire knowledge. This case study explores the impact of EdTech startups like Coursera in disrupting traditional education models, the challenges and opportunities faced by these companies, and their potential to shape the future of education.

The Rise of EdTech Startups

EdTech startups have revolutionized the education industry by leveraging technology to provide innovative learning solutions. Coursera, one of the leading players in this space, has disrupted traditional education models by offering online courses from top universities and experts around the world. Coursera's platform has democratized education by providing access to high-quality learning materials to anyone with an internet connection, regardless of their geographical location or financial means.

The Benefits of EdTech

EdTech has several advantages over traditional education models. For students, it offers flexibility, convenience, and accessibility, allowing them to learn at their own pace and on their own schedule. For institutions, EdTech can improve efficiency and reduce costs by automating administrative tasks and enabling online collaboration. Additionally, EdTech can provide insights into student performance and engagement, allowing instructors to personalize their teaching and improve learning outcomes.

Conclusion

The success of EdTech startups like Coursera has prompted a shift towards digital and online learning, signaling a fundamental transformation of the education industry. While traditional education models will continue to play a critical role in providing a comprehensive and well-rounded education, EdTech will become increasingly integrated into the educational landscape. This transformation will require collaboration and innovation from both traditional educational institutions and EdTech companies to provide students with a holistic and effective learning experience.

INDUSTRY CONTEXT

The digital transformation of education has been underway for several years, with EdTech startups like Coursera at the forefront of this revolution. Coursera was founded in 2012 with the mission to provide universal access to world-class education. The company offers over 4,000 courses and 400 specializations in a variety of subjects, ranging from computer science to social sciences. Coursera has partnered with top universities and institutions worldwide, enabling learners to earn degrees, certificates, and other credentials online. The EdTech market has grown exponentially in recent years, driven by the increasing demand for flexible and affordable learning solutions. According to research, the global EdTech market is expected to reach $252 billion by 2025, with online learning being a significant contributor to this growth.

CHALLENGES

- Ensuring the quality and relevance of online courses and programs
- Addressing issues related to access and equity, such as the digital divide and language barriers
- Overcoming the resistance of traditional academic institutions to embrace EdTech and online learning solutions

LESSONS LEARNED

- Providing a diverse range of courses and programs that cater to the needs and interests of learners
- Building strong partnerships and collaborations with top universities and institutions to enhance the credibility and quality of online courses and programs

QUESTIONS

1. How has the rise of EdTech startups like Coursera changed the landscape of education, and what are the implications for traditional academic institutions?
2. What are some potential drawbacks and limitations of online learning, and how can these be addressed to ensure equitable access and high-quality education?
3. What role should regulatory bodies and governments play in the regulation and oversight of EdTech startups, and what impact could this have on the industry's growth and development?

UN SDGs: Decent Work and Economic Growth (8); Industry, innovation, and Infrastructure (9);

RESOURCES

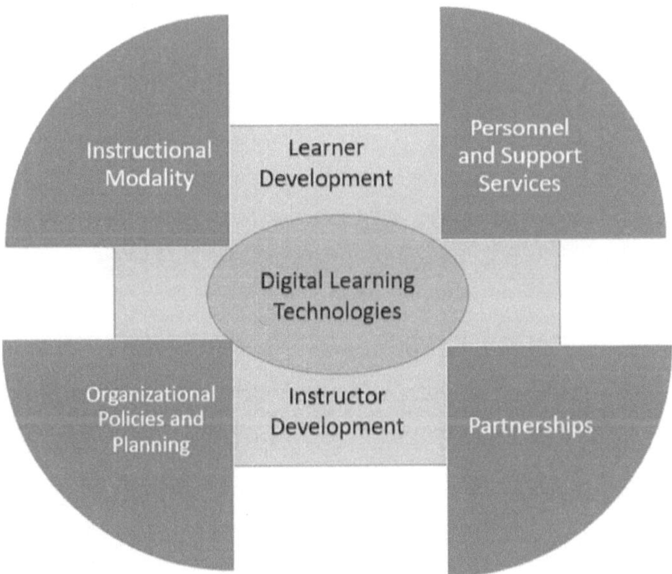

Source: Educase

REFERENCES

1. Tojimamatovich, J. V. (2023). Digital Transformation of Educational Management System. *Web of Semantic: Universal Journal on Innovative Education, 2*(4), 202-206.
2. Testov, V. A. (2019). On some methodological problems of digital transformation of education. *Informatics and education,* (10), 31-36.
3. Uvarov, A. Y. (2019). From computer literacy to digital transformation of education. *Informatics and education,* (4), 5-11.

Robotic Process Automation (RPA): UiPath's Journey to Automate the World

Themes: Innovation, Automation, Resources, Robotics

TEACHING OBJECTIVES

The case study is intended to qualify students to:

- Understand the importance of recycling used oils.
- Examine the probable challenges faced by the waste management hierarchy during the recycling of used oils.
- Explore the strategies used by waste management authorities to handle the oil recycling challenges.

SYNOPSIS

Robotic Process Automation (RPA) is transforming the business landscape, allowing organizations to automate repetitive, rule-based tasks and free up valuable time and resources. UiPath, a leading RPA provider, has played a critical role in driving the adoption of this technology, offering innovative solutions to businesses across a range of industries. This case study explores UiPath's journey to automate the world, including its advantages, strategies, challenges, and lessons learned.

Advantages of RPA

RPA offers numerous advantages to businesses, including increased efficiency, accuracy, and productivity. By automating repetitive tasks,

RPA frees up employees' time to focus on more complex and strategic work. RPA can also reduce errors and improve compliance, as bots follow predefined rules and workflows. Additionally, RPA can be deployed quickly and scaled up or down as needed, making it a flexible and cost-effective solution for businesses of all sizes.

UiPath's Strategies

UiPath has been successful in driving RPA adoption through its innovative solutions and strategic partnerships. The company offers a user-friendly platform that enables businesses to easily create, manage, and deploy bots. UiPath also provides a range of training and certification programs to help businesses upskill their employees in RPA technology. Furthermore, UiPath has formed strategic partnerships with leading technology companies and service providers to expand its reach and offer integrated solutions to customers.

Conclusion

UiPath's journey to automate the world has taught several important lessons. Firstly, it is crucial to focus on customer needs and provide user-friendly solutions that address their pain points. Secondly, partnerships and collaborations can be instrumental in expanding the reach and capabilities of RPA solutions. Finally, effective change management and employee engagement are critical to successfully implementing RPA and realizing its full potential.

INDUSTRY CONTEXT

Robotic Process Automation (RPA) is a technology that enables businesses to automate repetitive, rule-based tasks previously done by humans. This technology has been rapidly gaining popularity in recent years as businesses seek to improve efficiency, reduce errors, and cut costs. UiPath is a leading RPA company that has revolutionized the industry with its platform that allows businesses to automate a wide range of tasks using software robots. UiPath's platform is designed to be user-friendly, making it accessible to businesses of all sizes and industries. As a result, UiPath has become the market leader in RPA with a significant market share.

CHALLENGES

- Resistance to change: Some employees may resist the adoption of RPA technology as they fear it will replace their jobs.
- Lack of skilled workers: The demand for skilled RPA workers has outpaced the supply, making it challenging for businesses to find qualified workers.
- Integration challenges: Integrating RPA technology with existing systems can be difficult and time-consuming.

LESSONS LEARNED

- Educating employees on the benefits of RPA technology and involving them in the implementation process can help reduce resistance to change.
- Investing in training and development programs can help businesses build a skilled workforce and address the shortage of qualified RPA workers.

QUESTIONS

1. How can businesses ensure a smooth integration of RPA technology with existing systems and workflows?
2. What role do education and training play in the successful adoption of RPA technology?
3. What are the potential ethical considerations of using RPA technology to replace human workers?

UN SDGs: Industry, innovation, and infrastructure (9); Sustainable cities and communities (11)

RESOURCES

Business Processes in which RPA can be used

Take over repetitive tasks that employees carry out **50-60** times a day

Periodic reporting, data entry and **data analysis**

Mass email generation, archiving, extracting

Conversion of data formats and graphics

ERP transactions

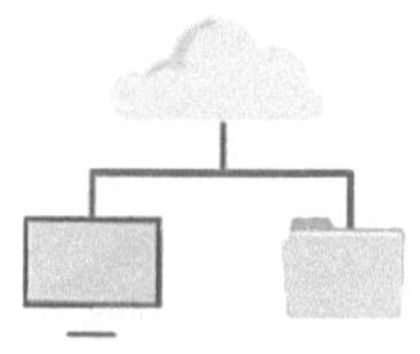

Process lists and **file storage**

Source: UiPath

REFERENCES

1. https://www.uipath.com/rpa/robotic-process-automation#:~:text=Robotic%20process%20automation%20(RPA)%20is,with%20digital%20systems%20and%20software.
2. https://www.techtarget.com/searchcio/definition/RPA
3. https://www.gartner.com/reviews/market/robotic-process-automation-software

The Impact of 5G Technology on IoT: A Look at Qualcomm's Innovations

Themes: SMART, Products, Revolution, Business, Innovation, Technology, Intelligent

TEACHING OBJECTIVES

The case study is intended to qualify students to:

- Understand the transformative potential of 5G technology in the realm of the Internet of Things (IoT) and its potential to reshape industries.
- Examine Qualcomm's leading role in 5G development and its applications in IoT.
- Identify the challenges that come with the implementation of 5G technology in IoT and explore potential solutions.

SYNOPSIS

The dawn of 5G, the fifth generation of wireless communication, has been hailed as a transformational development in the technological landscape. Offering vast improvements in speed, latency, and network capacity, 5G is projected to revolutionize the Internet of Things (IoT) by enhancing connectivity and enabling an extensive range of innovative applications, from smart cities and autonomous vehicles to advanced manufacturing and healthcare.

In the vanguard of 5G development is Qualcomm, a trailblazing innovator in wireless technology. Qualcomm's pioneering advancements in this field, including the development of comprehensive modem-to-antenna solutions and cutting-edge chipsets, have been instrumental in catalyzing the global transition to 5G. By harnessing the potential of 5G to bolster the IoT, Qualcomm is accelerating digital transformation, facilitating the rise of a more connected, efficient, and intelligent world.

Advantages of 5G and IoT integration

The advantages of integrating 5G with IoT are multifold. By vastly improving data transfer rates and reducing latency, 5G facilitates real-time data analytics and enables the seamless functioning of critical IoT applications, such as remote surgery and autonomous driving, which demand instant data transmission. Furthermore, 5G's capacity to connect a massive number of devices simultaneously makes it a pivotal enabler of large-scale IoT networks in smart cities and industrial IoT environments.

Qualcomm's strategies

However, Qualcomm's pioneering journey into the 5G-IoT landscape isn't without challenges. Security concerns, infrastructure readiness, and regulatory hurdles present significant obstacles that need to be navigated effectively. Qualcomm's approach to addressing these issues combines continual technological innovation, active collaboration with other industry players, and robust engagement with policymakers.

Conclusion

Qualcomm's innovative work in merging 5G and IoT holds immense promise for the future, transforming how we live, work, and interact with the world. However, it is vital to address the associated challenges head-on to harness the full potential of this technology fusion and pave the way for the next wave of digital revolution.

INDUSTRY CONTEXT

The telecommunications industry is on the brink of a monumental shift with the global rollout of 5G networks. Coupled with the IoT, 5G is set to change how we live, work, and interact with the world around us. Qualcomm, renowned for its technology innovations, is a pivotal player in this transformative era.

CHALLENGES

- Addressing security vulnerabilities that might arise with the increased connectivity and complexity brought by 5G and IoT integration.
- Ensuring the infrastructure is in place to handle the significant increase in data traffic.
- Overcoming technical and regulatory hurdles related to 5G deployment and spectrum allocation.

LESSONS LEARNED

- Continued innovation and advancement in wireless communication technologies are integral to realizing the full potential of the IoT.
- Collaboration among tech companies, telecom operators, policymakers, and other stakeholders is key to addressing the challenges associated with 5G implementation and maximizing its benefits.

QUESTIONS

1. What strategies can companies like Qualcomm employ to address potential security vulnerabilities in 5G-enabled IoT systems?
2. How can tech companies, network providers, and policymakers work together to ensure the infrastructure is ready for the data demands of 5G and IoT?

3. In what ways might the integration of 5G and IoT transform industries such as healthcare, transportation, and manufacturing?

UN SDGs: Industry, innovation, and infrastructure (9); Sustainable cities and communities (11)

RESOURCES

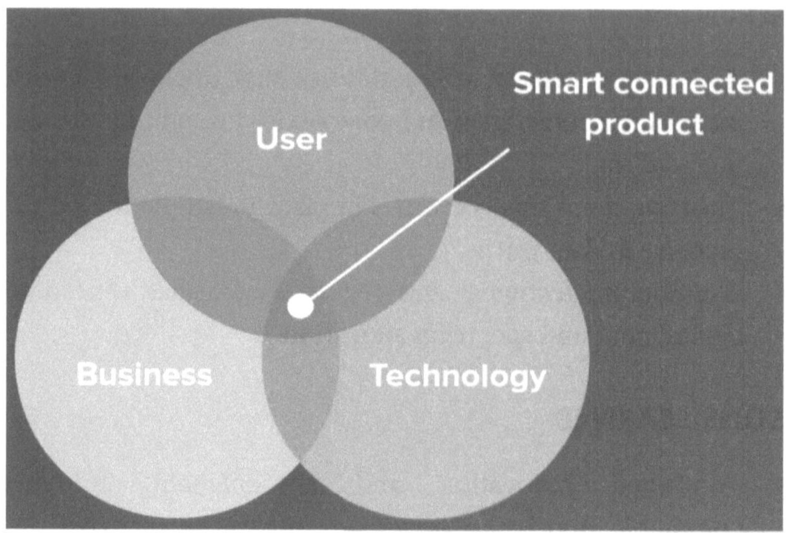

Source: sirris.com

REFERENCES

1. Chettri, L., & Bera, R. (2019). A comprehensive survey on Internet of Things (IoT) toward 5G wireless systems. *IEEE Internet of Things Journal, 7*(1), 16-32.

2. Pisarov, J., & Mester, G. (2020). The impact of 5G technology on life in 21st century. *IPSI BgD Transactions on Advanced Research (TAR), 16*(2), 11-14.

3. Painuly, S., Sharma, S., & Matta, P. (2021, April). Future trends and challenges in next generation smart application of 5G-IoT. In *2021 5th international conference on computing methodologies and communication (ICCMC)* (pp. 354-357). IEEE.

Harnessing AI to Cultivate Emotionally Intelligent Employees

Themes: Artificial Intelligence, Emotional intelligence, Employees management, Human resources, Technology

TEACHING OBJECTIVES

The case study is intended to qualify students to:

- Explain the importance of adopting artificial intelligence to enhance the emotional intelligence of employees.
- Explore the probable challenges faced by people while using artificial intelligence.
- Propose strategies used by firms to handle the AI implementation challenges for emotional intelligence.

SYNOPSIS

As the world continues to navigate the complexities of the digital age, one trend that has emerged is the increasing convergence of artificial intelligence (AI) and emotional intelligence (EI). Emotional intelligence refers to the ability to recognize, understand, and manage our own emotions and the emotions of others. On the other hand, AI involves the simulation of human intelligence processes by machines, especially computer systems. This case study examines how AI can be harnessed to cultivate emotionally intelligent employees, focusing on the importance of emotional intelligence in the workplace, the role of AI in enhancing EI, and the challenges and opportunities that this convergence presents.

AI and benefits of emotional intelligence

Emotionally intelligent employees are critical to the success of any organization. They can understand and manage their own emotions, demonstrate empathy for others, and navigate social networks effectively. This leads to improved teamwork, better decision-making, and a more positive workplace culture. The ability of employees to understand and respond to their emotions and those of their colleagues can greatly influence an organization's productivity, morale, and overall workplace environment.

Strategies and opportunities

With the advent of AI, new opportunities have emerged to enhance emotional intelligence in the workplace. Advances in machine learning, natural language processing, and computer vision have enabled the development of AI tools that can analyze various aspects of human communication, including tone of voice, facial expressions, and even the choice of words. These tools can provide real-time feedback, helping employees to become more aware of their emotional states and how they are perceived by others. As such, AI has the potential to transform emotional intelligence training, making it more personalized, efficient, and effective.

Conclusion

However, the integration of AI into emotional intelligence training is not without challenges. There are issues related to data privacy and user acceptance that need to be carefully addressed. Furthermore, while AI tools can analyze communication cues, accurately interpreting these cues can be difficult due to their subjective nature.

INDUSTRY CONTEXT

In an increasingly automated world, the role of emotional intelligence (EI) in the workplace has gained heightened importance. Emotional intelligence, a set of skills that influence the way we perceive and express ourselves, develop and maintain social relationships, cope with challenges, and use emotional information effectively, has become a key determinant of employee effectiveness, leadership, and resilience.

CHALLENGES

- User Acceptance: Despite its benefits, using AI to cultivate emotional intelligence can be met with resistance from employees due to a lack of understanding or fear of job replacement.
- Data Privacy: To operate effectively, AI tools require access to personal and sensitive data, posing potential privacy concerns.
- Accuracy and Reliability: While AI algorithms can analyze verbal and non-verbal cues, interpreting them correctly and consistently across diverse individuals and contexts can be a significant challenge.

LESSONS LEARNED

1. The Power of Synergy: Harnessing AI to cultivate emotional intelligence illustrates how technology and human skills can complement each other. Rather than replacing humans, AI can be used as a tool to improve human abilities and outcomes.
2. Importance of Training: To address resistance and enhance user acceptance, organizations must invest in training and change management initiatives to educate employees about the benefits of AI and how it can support their development.

QUESTIONS

1. What strategies can be used to ensure the accuracy and reliability of AI tools used for cultivating emotional intelligence?
2. What are some potential ethical considerations when using AI to analyze employees' emotional states, and how can they be mitigated?
3. How can companies ensure that AI is used responsibly and ethically when it comes to improving the emotional intelligence of employees?

UN SDGs: Good health and well-being (3); Industry, innovation, and infrastructure (9); Sustainable cities and communities (11)

RESOURCES

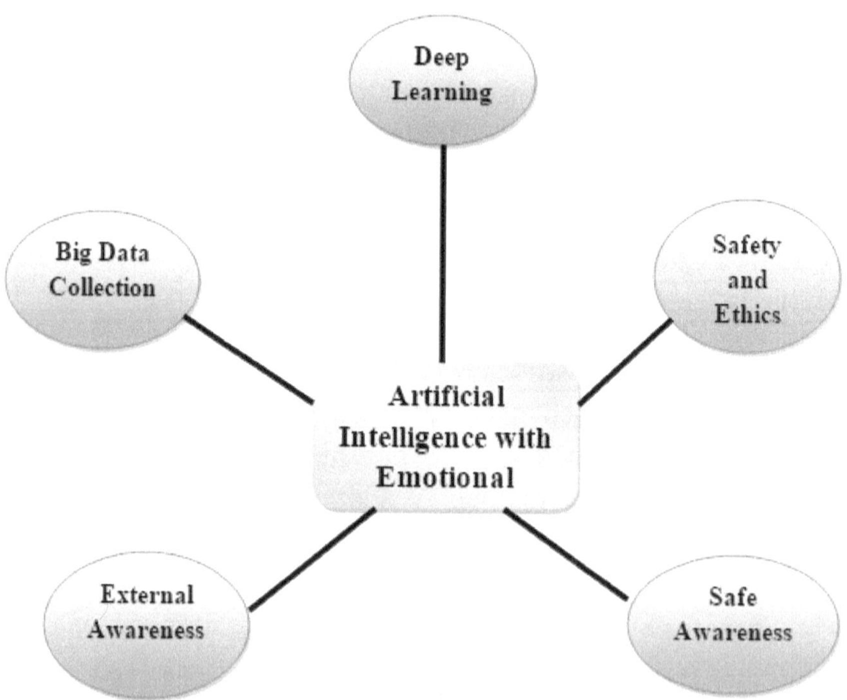

Source: datascience.foundation

REFERENCES

1. Arslan, A., Cooper, C., Khan, Z., Golgeci, I., & Ali, I. (2021). Artificial intelligence and human workers interaction at the team level: a conceptual assessment of the challenges and potential HRM strategies. *International Journal of Manpower.*

2. Bayighomog, S. W., & Arasli, H. (2022). Reviving employees' essence of hospitality through spiritual well-being, spiritual leadership, and emotional intelligence. *Tourism Management, 89*, 104406.

3. Bhargava, A., Bester, M., & Bolton, L. (2021). Employees' perceptions of the implementation of robotics, artificial intelligence, and automation (RAIA) on job satisfaction, job security, and employability. *Journal of Technology in Behavioral Science, 6*(1), 106-113.

Blockchain in Supply Chain Management: The Walmart-IBM Collaboration

Themes: Blockchain, Supply Chain, Collaboration, Strategy, Operations

TEACHING OBJECTIVES

The case study is intended to qualify students to:

- Understand the application and benefits of blockchain technology in supply chain management, using the Walmart-IBM collaboration as an example.
- Explore the strategies and techniques used by Walmart and IBM in implementing blockchain technology for improving supply chain transparency and efficiency.
- Evaluate the challenges faced and solutions implemented during the application of blockchain technology in a real-world setting.

SYNOPSIS

This case study explores the pioneering collaboration between Walmart and IBM to incorporate blockchain technology into supply chain management. With an expansive global reach, Walmart, one of the world's leading retail giants, identified the need to improve its supply chain's transparency, traceability, and efficiency. To this end, Walmart teamed up with IBM, renowned for its advanced technological solutions, to leverage the power of blockchain technology.

Blockchain technology's fundamental features

Decentralization, immutability, and transparency – offered a powerful solution for Walmart's supply chain management. Through a shared, immutable ledger, blockchain could store product information at each stage of the supply chain, from production to delivery. This ensured unparalleled traceability of each product, allowing the retailer to quickly pinpoint any quality or safety issues, thereby significantly improving their response to potential product recalls.

Moreover, the enhanced transparency offered by blockchain was instrumental in bolstering consumer trust. Walmart's customers could access a product's complete history, gaining detailed insights about its origin, handling, quality, and more. In an era where consumers are increasingly mindful of the ethical sourcing and quality of the products they purchase, such transparency offered Walmart a significant edge in the highly competitive retail market.

Opportunities

The collaboration leveraged IBM's "IBM Food Trust," a blockchain-based platform designed to promote transparency and collaboration across food supply networks. This platform integrated various stakeholders – including producers, suppliers, and regulators – into the supply chain, offering a holistic view of each product's journey from farm to store. This holistic approach was crucial in streamlining operations, improving communication, reducing waste, and ensuring safety standards across the board.

This innovative application of blockchain technology opened a plethora of opportunities not just for Walmart, but for the entire retail industry. It set a precedent for harnessing blockchain for enhancing product safety, improving inventory management, reducing wastage, and ultimately driving operational efficiency. Moreover, it showcased the potential of blockchain to revolutionize supply chain management across different industries, paving the way for more secure, transparent, and efficient supply chain operations.

Conclusion

Walmart-IBM collaboration underlined the transformative potential of blockchain in redefining supply chain management. It served as a beacon for other businesses to follow, highlighting the benefits of transparency, collaboration, and advanced technological adoption. However, it also underscored the challenges of implementing such a complex system, emphasizing the need for comprehensive planning, stakeholder integration, and sustained management to reap blockchain's benefits fully.

INDUSTRY CONTEXT

Supply chain management is a complex process involving numerous stakeholders and transactions. Traditional methods often struggle with issues such as lack of transparency, inefficiency, and vulnerability to fraud. With the advent of blockchain technology, there is an opportunity to address these issues. Blockchain can provide a decentralized, secure, and transparent platform for recording transactions, enabling real-time tracking of products and facilitating trust and collaboration among stakeholders.

CHALLENGES

- Achieving cooperation and integration among various stakeholders in the supply chain, each with their own systems and interests.
- Addressing the technical complexities and resource requirements associated with implementing and maintaining a blockchain system.
- Ensuring data security and privacy in a system where information is widely shared.

LESSONS LEARNED

- Effective implementation of blockchain in supply chain management requires not just technical solutions but also collaboration and alignment among all stakeholders.
- Blockchain technology has the potential to greatly enhance transparency and efficiency in supply chain management, but its success depends on careful planning, execution, and ongoing management.

QUESTIONS

1. How can blockchain technology address the traditional challenges faced in supply chain management?
2. What factors should be considered when implementing blockchain technology in a supply chain setting?
3. How might the Walmart-IBM collaboration influence other industries to adopt blockchain technology in their supply chain management?

UN SDGs: Industry, innovation, and infrastructure (9); Sustainable cities and communities (11)

RESOURCES

Key actors in a blockchain-based supply chain

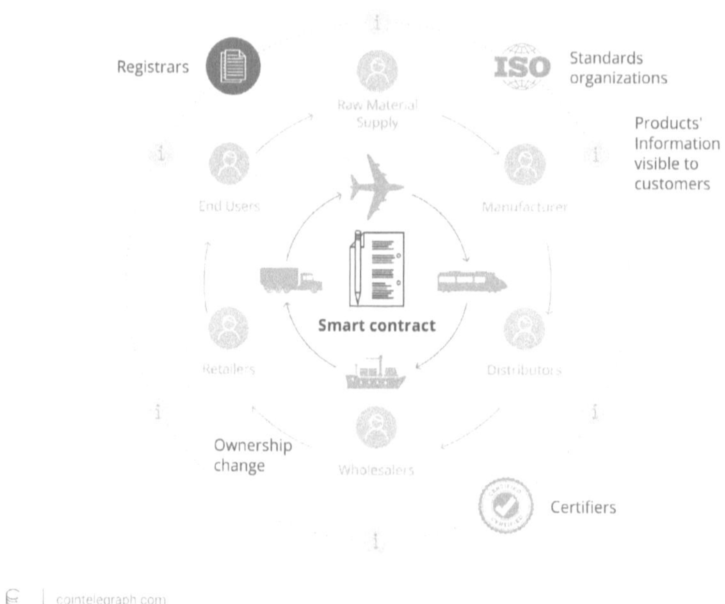

Source: Cointelegraph

REFERENCES

1. Chang, S. E., & Chen, Y. (2020). When blockchain meets supply chain: A systematic literature review on current development and potential applications. *Ieee Access, 8*, 62478-62494.

2. Moosavi, J., Naeni, L. M., Fathollahi-Fard, A. M., & Fiore, U. (2021). Blockchain in supply chain management: A review, bibliometric, and network analysis. *Environmental Science and Pollution Research*, 1-15.

3. Lu, Y., Xu, X., & Wang, L. (2020). Smart manufacturing process and system automation–a critical review of the standards and envisioned scenarios. *Journal of Manufacturing Systems, 56*, 312-325.

The Role of Robotics in Post-Pandemic Healthcare: Boston Dynamics' Spot Robot

Themes: Robotics, Post-Pandemics, Healthcare, Boston, Experience

TEACHING OBJECTIVES

The case study is intended to qualify students to:

- Understand the role of robotics technology in the healthcare industry, with a particular focus on the post-pandemic era.
- Explore the application, advantages, and potential challenges of Boston Dynamics' Spot Robot in healthcare services.
- Discuss the strategies and opportunities for robotics application in healthcare moving forward.

SYNOPSIS

In a world that is continually advancing, the field of healthcare is not left untouched. With the advent of technology, there has been a notable transformation in the way healthcare services are delivered, and robotics has emerged as one of the key components in this evolution. The COVID-19 pandemic further emphasized the importance of robotic intervention in healthcare as a vital tool in reducing human-to-human contact, thus minimizing the spread of the virus. A notable example of this is the adaptation and deployment of the Spot Robot by Boston Dynamics.

Advantages

The development and introduction of Boston Dynamics' Spot Robot have brought a new perspective to the advantages of robotics in healthcare. Spot is a versatile and autonomous robot originally designed for industrial inspections and public safety applications. However, with the onslaught of the COVID-19 pandemic, its utility found a significant place in healthcare. Boston Dynamics equipped Spot with an iPad and a two-way radio, transforming it into a mobile telemedicine platform. It was able to facilitate remote patient consultations, allowing healthcare providers to interact with patients from a distance. This capacity to minimize exposure while maintaining patient interaction has presented a substantial advantage in managing the healthcare crisis and ensuring the safety of healthcare professionals.

Strategies

The agility and innovation of Boston Dynamics were put to the test during the COVID-19 pandemic. They strategically modified their existing Spot robot to meet the pressing demands of the healthcare sector. In particular, their use of readily available digital tools such as iPads and two-way radios as a part of the robot's interface was a practical and cost-effective solution. This showcased how flexible adaptation and repurposing of existing technology can effectively meet emergent needs.

Opportunities

With the successful adaptation and deployment of Spot in healthcare settings, the realm of possibilities for robotics in this sector has broadened. Opportunities now extend beyond telemedicine to include potential applications like delivery of medical supplies, disinfection of hospital spaces, direct patient care tasks such as taking vital signs, or even assisting with mobility. As the healthcare industry grapples with ongoing challenges, including staffing shortages and infection control, the role of robotics in addressing these issues continues to grow.

Conclusion

In conclusion, Boston Dynamics' Spot Robot has served as a prime example of the transformative potential of robotics in healthcare, particularly in times of crises such as the COVID-19 pandemic. The application of robotics in healthcare has demonstrated its ability to augment healthcare services while ensuring the safety and well-being of healthcare professionals. While there are indeed challenges to address, including safety, regulatory compliance, and acceptance by healthcare professionals and patients, the opportunities for innovative solutions and improvement in patient care are immense and encouraging. The Spot Robot case thus leaves us with valuable insights into the future of robotics in healthcare, a future that holds the promise of increased efficiency, safety, and adaptability.

INDUSTRY CONTEXT

The healthcare industry is increasingly turning to technology to solve its most pressing problems. With the advent of COVID-19, the need for contactless, efficient solutions has driven the rapid adoption of robotics. Robots like Spot from Boston Dynamics represent the intersection of innovation and necessity, offering a glimpse into the future of healthcare.

CHALLENGES

- Ensuring the safety and accuracy of robotics in performing healthcare tasks.
- Navigating regulatory and compliance issues in healthcare applications.
- Overcoming resistance from healthcare professionals and patients towards robotics.

LESSONS LEARNED

- Flexibility and adaptability are crucial for technology companies in responding to evolving healthcare needs.
- Successful integration of robotics in healthcare requires collaboration and acceptance from healthcare professionals.

QUESTIONS

1. How can the application of robotics in healthcare be expanded beyond pandemic response?
2. What strategies can be employed to overcome resistance towards robotics in healthcare?
3. How can regulatory bodies ensure the safety and efficacy of robotics in healthcare applications?

UN SDGs: Good health and well-being (3); Sustainable cities and communities (11); Partnership for goals (17)

RESOURCES

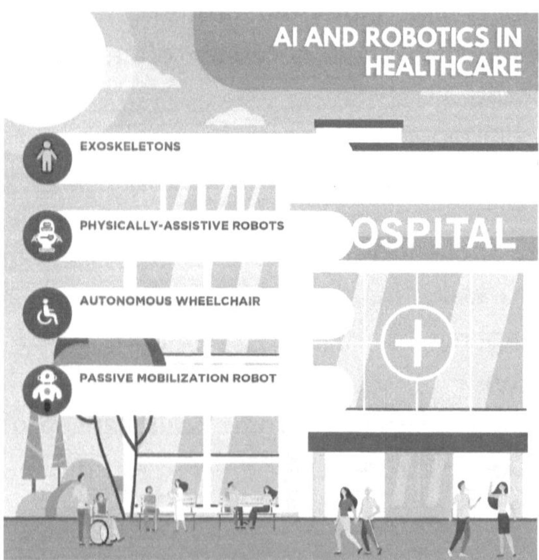

Source: Forbes

REFERENCES

1. Kim, D. K. D., Kreps, G. L., & Ahmed, R. (2021). Communicative development and diffusion of humanoid AI robots for the post-pandemic health care system. *Human-Machine Communication, 3*, 65-82.

2. Fikry, A., Shafie, I. S. M., Yusof, Y. L. M., Mahamood, S. F., & Jamil, N. (2023). When Contactless Service Matters: The Use of Robotic Services in the Healthcare Sector. *IEEE Engineering Management Review*.

3. Lee, S. M., & Lee, D. (2021). Opportunities and challenges for contactless healthcare services in the post-COVID-19 Era. *Technological Forecasting and Social Change, 167*, 120712.

The Relevance of NFTs in Art and Collectibles: The Beeple Phenomenon

Themes: NFTs, Art, Innovation, Solutions, Challenges

TEACHING OBJECTIVES

The case study is intended to qualify students to:

- Understand the concept of NFTs (Non-Fungible Tokens) and their impact on the art and collectibles industry, using the Beeple phenomenon as a case study.
- Explore the advantages and opportunities presented by NFTs for artists and collectors alike, with a focus on digital ownership, monetization, and accessibility.
- Evaluate the challenges and ethical considerations related to NFTs, including issues of copyright, environmental impact, and market volatility.

SYNOPSIS

Non-fungible tokens, or NFTs, have revolutionized the art and collectibles industry in recent years, creating a new market for digital ownership. NFTs are blockchain-based tokens that represent ownership of a unique digital asset, such as a piece of art, a song, or a tweet. The Beeple phenomenon, which saw digital artist Mike Winkelmann, aka Beeple, sell an NFT of his work for $69 million at Christie's auction house, highlights the immense potential of this technology.

Advantages

NFTs present several advantages, particularly for creators. They allow artists to monetize their work in new ways, providing them with more control over their art and a cut of any future resales. For collectors, NFTs offer the chance to own unique digital assets and potentially profit from their increase in value. The transparency and immutability of blockchain technology also ensure the authenticity and provenance of NFTs.

Strategies

Beeple capitalized on the potential of NFTs by embracing this technology early on and leveraging his existing popularity in the digital art world. His strategy was to create unique, provoking digital art pieces and tokenize them on the blockchain, essentially creating an unforgeable certificate of authenticity for each piece.

Opportunities

The rise of NFTs has opened up new opportunities for artists and collectors. For artists, NFTs can serve as a new revenue stream, allowing them to profit directly from their art. The technology also has the potential to democratize art, making it more accessible to a global audience. For collectors, NFTs provide a new class of digital assets to invest in, with the potential for high returns.

Conclusion

The Beeple phenomenon serves as a striking example of the transformative potential of NFTs in the art and collectibles industry. While the market is still in its early stages and challenges remain, the opportunities for artists and collectors are vast. The case study serves as a starting point for exploring the wider implications of NFTs, not only in the art world but also in other areas of society where digital ownership could play a significant role.

INDUSTRY CONTEXT

The art and collectibles industry has traditionally relied on physical ownership and the provenance of items. With the advent of blockchain technology and NFTs, digital ownership has become a reality, shaking up the industry. The high-profile sale of Beeple's artwork has brought significant attention to this emerging market, raising questions about the future of art and collectibles in the digital age.

CHALLENGES

- The environmental impact of NFTs, given the high energy consumption of blockchain transactions.
- Copyright and intellectual property issues, as there are currently no clear regulations governing the sale and ownership of NFTs.
- Market volatility and the risk of a speculative bubble, as the NFT market has seen dramatic price fluctuations.

LESSONS LEARNED

- The Beeple case shows that early adoption of emerging technology, coupled with a strong creative vision, can lead to significant success.
- It also highlights the importance of understanding the technology and the market when entering the NFT space, due to its volatility and the complex issues involved.

QUESTIONS

1. How do you see the role of NFTs in the art and collectibles industry evolving in the future?
2. What measures could be taken to address the environmental impact of NFTs?
3. How can the issue of copyright and intellectual property be effectively managed in the NFT space?

UN SDGs: Industry, innovation, and infrastructure (9); Sustainable cities and communities (11)

RESOURCES

Source: Bloomberg

REFERENCES

1. Kumar, S. (2022). Strategic management of carbon footprint using carbon collectible nonfungible tokens (NFTS) on blockchain. *Academy of Strategic Management Journal, 21*, 1-9.
2. Trautman, L. J. (2022). Visual Art, Galleries, Collectibles, and NFTs. *Visual Art, Galleries, Collectibles, and NFTs, In The Cambridge Handbook on Law and Policy for NFTs (Nizan Geslevich Packin, Ed.),*
3. Allen, S., Juels, A., Khaire, M., Kell, T., & Shrivastava, S. (2022). NFTs for art and collectables: Primer and outlook.

Public-Private Partnership (PPP) Models Driving Corporate Entrepreneurial Outcomes: Nigeria's Lekki-Epe Expressway Project

Themes: Innovation, Public, Private, Partnerships, Financial, PPP

TEACHING OBJECTIVES

The case study is intended to qualify students to:

- Understand the role of public-private partnership (PPP) models in fostering corporate entrepreneurial outcomes, using the Lekki-Epe Expressway Project in Nigeria as a case study.
- Explore the advantages and challenges of PPP models in infrastructural development.
- Evaluate strategies and opportunities in PPP models for infrastructure and the lessons learned from their implementation.

SYNOPSIS

Public-Private Partnerships (PPPs) represent a collaborative approach between government entities and private-sector businesses to fund and operate projects that benefit society. The Lekki-Epe Expressway Project in Nigeria, a prime example of such a collaboration, aimed to resolve the chronic transportation challenges in the rapidly developing Lekki-Epe region.

Advantages

PPP models offer several benefits. They allow the public sector to leverage private-sector expertise and efficiency, leading to potentially higher quality and cost-effective infrastructure projects. Furthermore, by involving private investors, public resources can be allocated to other pressing needs. In the case of the Lekki-Epe Expressway, the PPP model aimed to fast-track infrastructural development, addressing the pressing need for a robust transportation network to support the area's rapid growth.

Strategies

The Nigerian government adopted a strategy of cooperation with private entities, granting them the rights to design, finance, construct, operate, and maintain the expressway for a set period. The agreement was based on a revenue-sharing model, with the private entities expected to recoup their investments through toll collections. This strategy aimed to ensure the sustainability of the project, addressing long-term infrastructure and maintenance needs.

Opportunities

The successful implementation of PPP models can lead to improved public services and infrastructure, driving economic growth and improving quality of life. Additionally, these partnerships offer private entities an opportunity to invest in large-scale infrastructure projects, opening up new revenue streams.

Conclusion

The Lekki-Epe Expressway case illustrates the potential of PPP models to drive corporate entrepreneurial outcomes and deliver critical infrastructure projects. Despite the challenges, the lessons learned from this case offer valuable insights into how PPP models can be effectively employed in developing nations to address infrastructural gaps.

INDUSTRY CONTEXT

Infrastructure development is a critical need in emerging economies, with a significant investment gap hindering growth. PPP models present an innovative solution to this challenge, enabling governments to leverage private sector resources and expertise to deliver large-scale projects.

CHALLENGES

- Achieving a fair balance of risks and rewards between the public and private partners.
- Ensuring transparency and accountability in the project implementation.
- Managing potential social resistance to aspects of the project, such as the introduction of tolls.

LESSONS LEARNED

- Effective planning and clear contractual agreements are critical in PPP models to ensure all stakeholders understand their roles and responsibilities.
- Transparent and regular communication with the public can help manage social resistance and ensure community support for the project.

QUESTIONS

1. How can the risks associated with PPP models be effectively managed?
2. What are the key factors that contribute to the success of a PPP model in infrastructure development?
3. How can PPP models be used to drive corporate entrepreneurial outcomes in other sectors?

UN SDGs: Industry, innovation, and infrastructure (9); Climate action (13); Partnership for goals (17)

RESOURCES

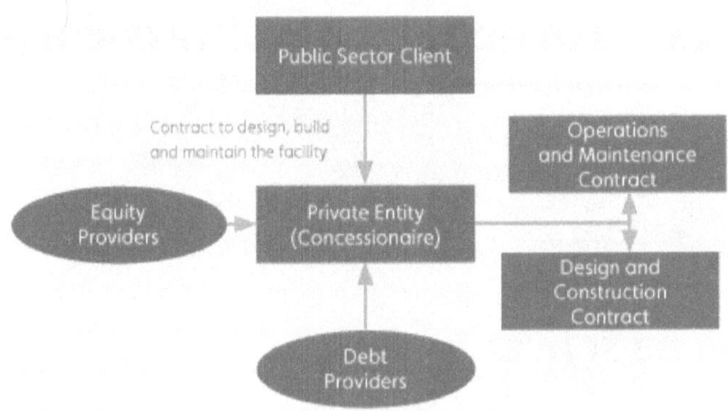

Source: nzsif.co.nz

REFERENCES

1. Arimoro, A. E. (2018). The role of law in the successful completion of public-private partnership projects in Nigeria: lessons from South Africa.

2. Cherkos, F. D., & Jha, K. N. (2021). Drivers of Road Sector Public-Private Partnership Adoption in New and Inexperienced Markets. *Journal of Construction Engineering and Management, 147*(3), 04020186.

3. Demeke Cherkos, F., & Jha, K. N. (2020). Enabling successful application of PPPs in new (inexperienced) markets: Implications of PPPs' success and failure in toll roads. *Journal of Legal Affairs and Dispute Resolution in Engineering and Construction, 12*(4), 05020015.

The Gig Economy and its Challenges: Uber's Controversial Labor Practices

Themes: Gig economy, challenges, Labor Practices, Uber

TEACHING OBJECTIVES

The case study is intended to qualify students to:

- Understand the workings of the gig economy, its benefits, and challenges, with a specific focus on Uber's business model.
- Analyze the controversy surrounding Uber's labor practices and its implications for workers in the gig economy.
- Evaluate the strategies and adjustments made by Uber in response to legal, societal, and competitive pressures, and consider potential future developments in the gig economy.

SYNOPSIS

Uber, one of the most prominent faces of the gig economy, has drastically transformed the transportation sector. Since its inception, Uber has consistently pioneered new paradigms in the industry by connecting drivers and riders through a simple, intuitive app. This platform-based model, which fundamentally hinges on the use of independent contractors rather than employing drivers in the traditional sense, has revolutionized transportation. It has not only provided unparalleled convenience to customers but also opened avenues for flexible income-earning opportunities for individuals from various walks of life.

Advantages

Uber's gig economy model presents numerous benefits to its participants. For drivers, the freedom to choose when, where, and how often they work marks a sharp departure from traditional employment constructs, providing them with a degree of autonomy rarely seen in other industries. This flexibility can lead to a more favorable work-life balance, making it a preferred choice for many. For riders, Uber's app stands as a beacon of convenience, offering swift, on-demand access to transportation that was previously dominated by less efficient taxi systems. The competitive pricing provided by Uber, primarily due to lower operational costs, offers an affordable alternative to traditional transportation services.

Strategies

Central to Uber's strategy has been its relentless pursuit of expansion and user growth, sometimes sidestepping traditional labor norms. By categorizing drivers as independent contractors, Uber avoids several costs associated with traditional employment, including providing health insurance, overtime, paid leave, and minimum wage assurances. This approach has enabled Uber to scale rapidly and operate more affordably, undercutting existing taxi services in the process.

Opportunities

The gig economy's ongoing evolution presents various opportunities for Uber. For instance, the company could further diversify its service offerings or improve its existing relationships with drivers by exploring new driver benefits or protections. Additionally, Uber could cultivate new partnerships that would enrich its platform and potentially attract more drivers. Expansion into new markets, especially those with inefficient public transportation systems, also offers potential growth opportunities.

Conclusion

Despite facing a plethora of challenges and controversies, most notably around its labor practices, Uber remains a prominent player in the gig economy. The company's journey, filled with both victories and missteps, offers invaluable insights for other businesses seeking to navigate this new economic landscape. Furthermore, Uber's experiences also provide important lessons for regulators, workers, and consumers who must traverse the complexities of this ever-evolving ecosystem. Their collective experiences will continue to shape the future direction of the gig economy and the policies that govern it.

INDUSTRY CONTEXT

CHALLENGES

- Controversies and legal battles over driver classification (independent contractors vs. employees).
- Maintaining competitive pricing for customers while ensuring fair earnings for drivers.
- Reputation and trust issues due to controversies and high-profile incidents.

LESSONS LEARNED

- Companies operating in the gig economy need to carefully balance growth and profitability with fair treatment and compensation for their workers.
- Legal, societal, and competitive pressures can force companies to adapt their strategies and policies, even after achieving significant success.

QUESTIONS

1. What are the pros and cons of Uber's approach to labor practices, and how might these impact the future of the gig economy?
2. How can companies like Uber balance the need for flexibility and scalability with the need to provide fair compensation and protections for workers?
3. What potential strategies could Uber employ to address its labor controversies and improve its relationship with drivers?

UN SDGs: Decent work and Economic Growth (8); Industry, innovation, and infrastructure (9)

RESOURCES

RISE OF THE GIG WORKERS

Source: PwC

REFERENCES

1. Duggan, J., Sherman, U., Carbery, R., & McDonnell, A. (2020). Algorithmic management and app-work in the gig economy: A research agenda for employment relations and HRM. *Human Resource Management Journal, 30*(1), 114-132.
2. Graham, M., & Anwar, M. (2019). The global gig economy: Towards a planetary labour market?. *First Monday, 24*(4).
3. Pichault, F., & McKeown, T. (2019). Autonomy at work in the gig economy: analysing work status, work content and working conditions of independent professionals. *New Technology, Work and Employment, 34*(1), 59-72.

Case Study **58**

Leveraging Digital Transformation to Enhance Hospital Decision-Making

Themes: Digital, Transformation, Decision-making, Operations, Hospital, Artificial intelligence

TEACHING OBJECTIVES

The case study is intended to qualify students to:

- Understand the concept and process of digital transformation and its impact on hospital decision-making processes.
- Explore the advantages, strategies, and opportunities offered by digital transformation in the healthcare sector.
- Analyze the challenges associated with implementing digital transformation in hospitals and learn from past lessons.

SYNOPSIS

Hospitals face the challenge of balancing the need to provide individualized patient care with managing hospital resources efficiently. As the healthcare industry rapidly evolves, hospitals worldwide are increasingly leveraging digital transformation to enhance their decision-making processes. Digital transformation, involving the integration of digital technology into all areas of a hospital, fundamentally changes how the institution operates and delivers value to its patients. It's more than just a technological shift—it represents a cultural change that requires hospitals to continually challenge the status quo, experiment often, and get comfortable with failure.

Advantages

Digital transformation offers multiple advantages for hospitals. These include improved operational efficiency, enhanced patient experience, and better-informed decision-making. It allows hospitals to utilize data in unprecedented ways, leading to improved patient outcomes, reduced errors, and more efficient resource allocation.

Strategies

Successful digital transformation requires a strategic approach, which includes a clear vision, leadership buy-in, and a focus on change management. Hospitals need to identify areas where digital technology can have the most significant impact and start their digital journey there. Additionally, a culture of continuous learning and adaptation is vital for success in the digital age.

Opportunities

As technology continues to advance, the opportunities for digital transformation in hospitals are vast. Potential avenues include implementing AI in diagnosis and treatment, utilizing telemedicine for remote patient care, integrating IoT devices for real-time monitoring, and using blockchain for secure patient data management.

Conclusion

Despite numerous challenges, the benefits of digital transformation for hospitals are clear. As healthcare continues to evolve, hospitals that effectively leverage digital transformation will be well-positioned to improve patient care, optimize operations, and make better-informed decisions.

INDUSTRY CONTEXT

In today's digital age, the healthcare industry is experiencing an unprecedented shift. As technology continues to evolve at a rapid pace, hospitals are under increasing pressure to adapt and innovate. Digital transformation has become a strategic imperative for hospitals as they strive to meet changing patient expectations, improve care outcomes, and maintain operational efficiency.

CHALLENGES

- Resistance to change from staff who are comfortable with traditional ways of doing things.
- Ensuring data privacy and security in the face of increasing cyber threats.
- The high cost of implementing and maintaining digital technologies.

LESSONS LEARNED

- Digital transformation is not just about implementing new technologies—it's about changing organizational culture.
- Patient-centricity is key; any digital transformation initiative should aim to improve patient care and experience.

QUESTIONS

1. What are some specific examples of how digital transformation can improve hospital decision-making?
2. How can hospitals overcome resistance to change when implementing digital transformation initiatives?
3. What steps can hospitals take to ensure the privacy and security of patient data during digital transformation?

UN SDGs: Health and well-being (3); Industry, innovation, and infrastructure (9); Partnership for goals (17)

RESOURCES

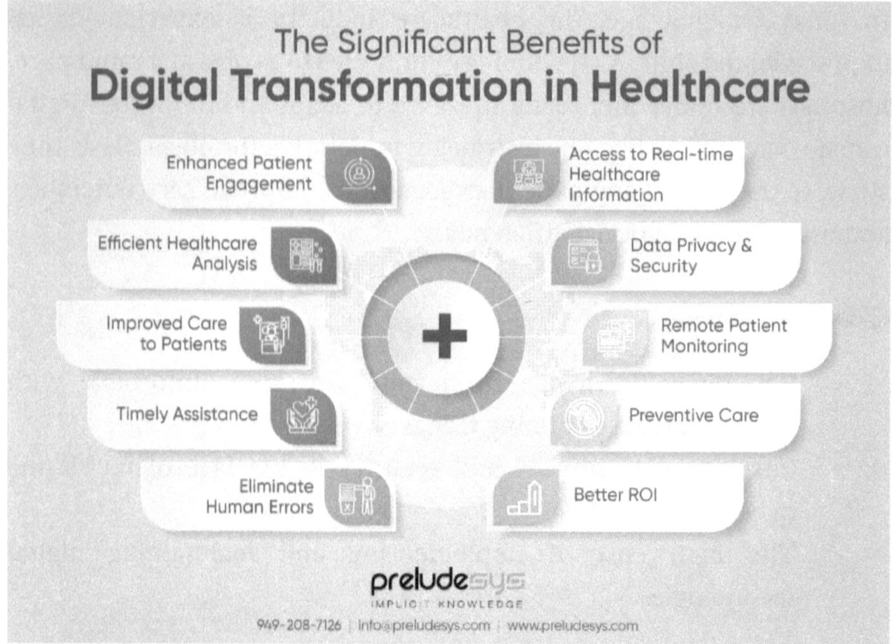

Source: preludesys.com

REFERENCES

1. Akter, S., Michael, K., Uddin, M. R., McCarthy, G., & Rahman, M. (2020). Transforming business using digital innovations: The application of AI, blockchain, cloud, and data analytics. *Annals of Operations Research*, 1-33.

2. Bieser, J., & Hilty, L. (2018). Indirect Effects of the Digital Transformation on Environmental Sustainability: Methodological Challenges in Assessing the Greenhouse Gas Abatement Potential of ICT. *EPiC Series in Computing*, (52), 68-81.

3. Brock, J. K. U., & Von Wangenheim, F. (2019). Demystifying AI: What digital transformation leaders can teach you about realistic artificial intelligence. *California Management Review*, 61(4), 110-134.

Intelligent Process Automation: Unlocking Competitive Superiority for Modern Enterprises

Themes: Process, Automation, Competitive, Firms, Change, Management

TEACHING OBJECTIVES

The case study is intended to qualify students to:

- Understand the concept of Intelligent Process Automation (IPA) and its role in creating a competitive edge for modern enterprises.
- Analyze the advantages, strategies, and opportunities related to the deployment of IPA in the business environment.
- Identify and explore challenges that come with implementing IPA and draw lessons from the experiences of businesses that have successfully deployed it.

SYNOPSIS

Intelligent Process Automation (IPA), a blend of artificial intelligence (AI) and Robotic Process Automation (RPA), is revolutionizing the way modern enterprises conduct business. By automating repetitive tasks and improving the efficiency of complex processes, IPA has the potential to unlock a new level of competitive superiority for organizations across various industries. This transformation is more than just a technological shift; it signifies a strategic evolution in operational management, with the potential to drastically boost productivity, accuracy, and cost-efficiency.

Advantages

IPA offers several significant advantages, including reduced operational costs due to less manual labor, increased productivity, minimized errors, and enhanced decision-making due to the real-time, data-driven insights it provides. The ability of IPA to integrate seamlessly with existing systems allows organizations to increase their process efficiency without a significant overhaul of the current operational structure.

Strategies

The successful implementation of IPA requires a clear strategic approach. This involves identifying and understanding the processes that would most benefit from automation, securing leadership buy-in, investing in staff training to ensure a smooth technological transition, and adopting an iterative, agile approach to implementation. Furthermore, organizations need to develop robust data governance policies to ensure data accuracy and compliance with privacy laws.

Opportunities

The advent of IPA opens up new opportunities for businesses to redefine their operational models, improve customer service, and gain an edge over competitors. By harnessing the power of IPA, businesses can focus more on innovation and value-creating tasks, thus moving up the value chain.

Conclusion

In a business environment that's becoming increasingly digital, the deployment of IPA can lead to a significant competitive advantage. However, realizing its full potential requires not just an investment in technology, but also a strategic focus on people, process, and change management.

INDUSTRY CONTEXT

In the age of digital transformation, businesses across all industries are facing pressure to innovate and improve efficiency. With rising labor costs and increasing competition, more and more enterprises are turning to Intelligent Process Automation to streamline operations and drive competitive advantage.

CHALLENGES

- The high initial cost of implementing IPA technology.
- Resistance to change from employees, particularly fear of job loss due to automation.
- Technical challenges in integrating IPA with existing IT infrastructure.

LESSONS LEARNED

- Successful IPA implementation requires a holistic approach that includes technology, people, and process management.
- Despite the potential job displacement, IPA can also lead to job enrichment by freeing up employees from repetitive tasks and enabling them to focus on more strategic, value-adding tasks.

QUESTIONS

1. What are the key considerations for businesses planning to implement IPA?
2. How can businesses address employee fears about job loss due to IPA?
3. What are some potential ethical issues related to the use of IPA, and how can businesses mitigate them?

UN SDGs: Decent work and economic growth (8); Industry, innovation, and infrastructure (9)

RESOURCES

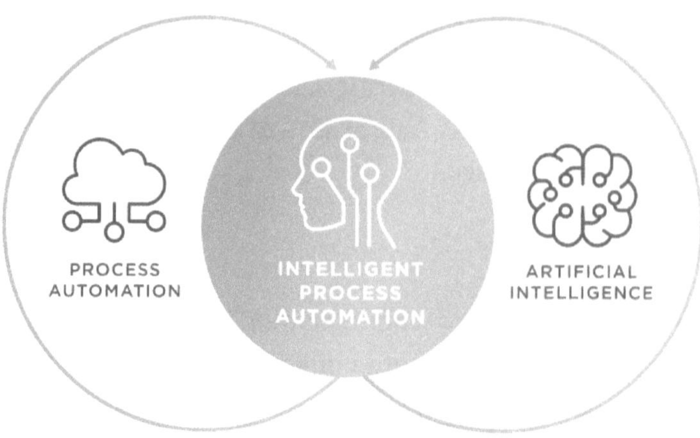

Source: tibcosoftware.com

REFERENCES

1. Evtodieva, T. E., Chernova, D. V., Ivanova, N. V., & Wirth, J. (2020). The internet of things: possibilities of application in intelligent supply chain management. *Digital transformation of the economy: Challenges, trends and new opportunities*, 395-403.

2. Kiani Mavi, R., & Standing, C. (2018). Cause and effect analysis of business intelligence (BI) benefits with fuzzy DEMATEL. *Knowledge Management Research & Practice, 16*(2), 245-257.

3. Kiani Mavi, R., & Standing, C. (2018). Cause and effect analysis of business intelligence (BI) benefits with fuzzy DEMATEL. *Knowledge Management Research & Practice, 16*(2), 245-257.

Virtual Reality in Real Estate: Zillow's 3D Home Tour Feature

Themes: Virtual Reality, Advertisements, Customers, Technology, Applications, Productivity

TEACHING OBJECTIVES

The case study is intended to qualify students to:

- Evaluate the requirements of human involvement while using technological apps.
- Understand the implications of virtual reality (VR) technology in the real estate industry, particularly focusing on Zillow's 3D Home Tour Feature.
- Discuss the advantages, strategies, and opportunities associated with implementing VR in the real estate sector.
- Examine the challenges posed by VR implementation and extract lessons from Zillow's experiences.

SYNOPSIS

In today's digitally-driven world, industries across the board are adopting cutting-edge technologies to remain competitive and meet their customer's evolving expectations. A pivotal example of this can be seen in the real estate industry, specifically through Zillow's use of virtual reality (VR) technology. Zillow, a leading online real estate marketplace, has capitalized on VR to create an immersive home viewing experience for its users through its 3D Home Tour Feature. This feature, which enables potential buyers to explore listed properties via a virtual walkthrough, stands as a testament to the transformative potential of VR in real estate.

Advantages

The integration of VR technology into the real estate sector presents numerous advantages for both consumers and realtors. For potential buyers, it provides the convenience of viewing properties remotely, saving time and resources otherwise spent on physical visits. It also enables them to make more informed decisions by offering an immersive and realistic view of the property. For realtors, VR allows for showcasing properties innovatively and engagingly, which can attract a larger audience and potentially accelerate sales.

Strategies

Zillow's strategic implementation of the 3D Home Tour Feature demonstrates their foresight in acknowledging the potential of VR technology. They understood the need to elevate their users' property browsing experience and responded by offering a virtual, interactive home touring option. This decision necessitated meticulous planning and execution, involving the creation of a user-friendly interface and the production of high-quality 3D visuals to deliver a realistic virtual experience resembling an actual in-person tour.

Opportunities

The advancement of VR technology presents promising opportunities for the real estate industry. Beyond merely providing virtual tours, future applications could include the virtual staging of properties, allowing potential buyers to visualize how a furnished version of the property would look. This could extend to customizable virtual staging, enabling buyers to arrange virtual furniture according to their preferences. Additionally, there is potential for further advancements in 3D mapping technologies, promising even more realistic and immersive VR experiences.

Conclusion

The case of Zillow's 3D Home Tour Feature underscores the significance of embracing technological innovation in the evolving real estate landscape. While VR technology poses its own set of challenges, the potential benefits and opportunities it offers outweigh the hurdles. By enhancing customer experience and efficiency, VR serves as a powerful tool for real estate businesses to differentiate themselves and achieve sustainable growth in an increasingly digital world.

INDUSTRY CONTEXT

The real estate industry has been increasingly digitized over the past decade, with online property listings becoming the norm. The next frontier is enhancing these digital interactions with immersive experiences, such as VR home tours, which are set to redefine how properties are bought and sold.

CHALLENGES

- High development and implementation costs associated with VR technology.
- Possible technical difficulties for users unfamiliar with VR.
- Limitations of VR experience compared to physical property visits.

LESSONS LEARNED

- The integration of VR into real estate platforms can significantly enhance the property viewing experience, providing a competitive advantage.
- User-friendly design and high-quality visuals are crucial for the successful implementation of VR in real estate.

QUESTIONS

1. How might VR technology further evolve and impact the real estate industry in the future?
2. What are the implications of VR for other stakeholders in the real estate industry, such as property developers and interior designers?
3. How might Zillow further leverage VR technology to enhance its platform and services?

UN SDGs: Industry, innovation, and infrastructure (9); Sustainable cities and communities (11)

RESOURCES

Source: GeekWire

REFERENCES

1. https://www.zillow.com/z/3d-home/
2. https://www.zillow.com/sellers-guide/how-to-make-a-virtual-tour-for-real-estate/
3. https://www.cnet.com/tech/gaming/zillow-3d-home-uses-vr-make-online-real-estate-more-authentic/

Case Study **61**

Embracing the Future of Contactless Business Operations

Themes: Technology, Business, Contactless payments, Artificial Intelligence, Virtual

TEACHING OBJECTIVES

The case study is intended to qualify students to:

- Understand the concept of contactless business operations and their importance in the current digital and pandemic era.
- Identify the advantages of implementing contactless business operations and strategies for their successful implementation.
- Evaluate the opportunities presented by contactless operations and how businesses can navigate the challenges they pose.

SYNOPSIS

In an age where digital technology continues to shape business landscapes, coupled with the paradigm shift caused by the COVID-19 pandemic, companies are progressively transitioning towards contactless business operations. This approach has become paramount for organizations seeking to maintain operational efficiency, customer engagement, and business continuity during periods of physical distancing and beyond. The concept of contactless operations extends beyond merely enabling remote work; it encompasses all aspects of business, including contactless customer service, digital payments, remote collaboration, and virtual product/service delivery.

Advantages

Contactless operations provide numerous benefits for businesses and customers alike. For businesses, they allow for cost reduction, increased operational efficiency, improved customer service, and enhanced flexibility. They also facilitate remote work, helping to maintain productivity even during unpredictable circumstances like the ongoing pandemic. For customers, contactless operations provide convenience, speed, and safety, thus improving their overall experience and engagement with the business.

Strategies

Implementing contactless operations successfully requires a strategic approach. This includes investing in the right digital infrastructure and tools, training employees to adapt to new ways of working, and continually updating business processes to maximize efficiency and customer satisfaction. It also involves maintaining robust cybersecurity measures, as contactless operations often involve handling sensitive data remotely.

Opportunities

The shift towards contactless operations presents ample opportunities for business innovation and growth. It allows businesses to reimagine their service delivery, operational processes, and customer engagement methods, making them more aligned with the digital era's demands. It also opens up possibilities for reaching a broader, global customer base, as geographical boundaries become less relevant in a contactless operational environment.

Conclusion

Embracing contactless business operations has moved from being a futuristic concept to an essential business survival strategy, fueled by technological advancements and recent global events. While it comes with its own set of challenges, the benefits it offers make it a worthwhile pursuit for businesses willing to innovate and adapt in the face of changing business landscapes.

INDUSTRY CONTEXT

Contactless operations have become increasingly relevant in various industries due to the advancements in digital technology and the necessity imposed by the COVID-19 pandemic. From retail to banking to healthcare, businesses across sectors are leveraging technologies like AI, cloud computing, and IoT to transform their operations, making them more resilient, efficient, and customer-centric.

CHALLENGES

- Transitioning to contactless operations involves significant initial investment and could face resistance from employees accustomed to traditional ways of working.
- Ensuring robust data security can be challenging in a contactless operational setup, especially with employees working remotely.
- Maintaining the personal touch and human connection, a key aspect of customer service can be difficult in a fully contactless operation.

LESSONS LEARNED

- Contactless operations, while offering numerous benefits, require careful planning and execution, considering the organization's specific needs and the readiness level of employees and customers.
- As contactless operations often involve handling sensitive data remotely, prioritizing cybersecurity is essential to protect customer trust and business integrity.

QUESTIONS

1. How can businesses maintain the personal touch in customer service in a contactless operational setup?
2. How should businesses train their employees to effectively adapt to contactless operations?
3. How can small businesses with limited resources transition to contactless operations, and what specific strategies could they use?

UN SDGs: Health and well-being (3); Industry, innovation, and infrastructure (9); Sustainable cities and communities (11)

RESOURCES

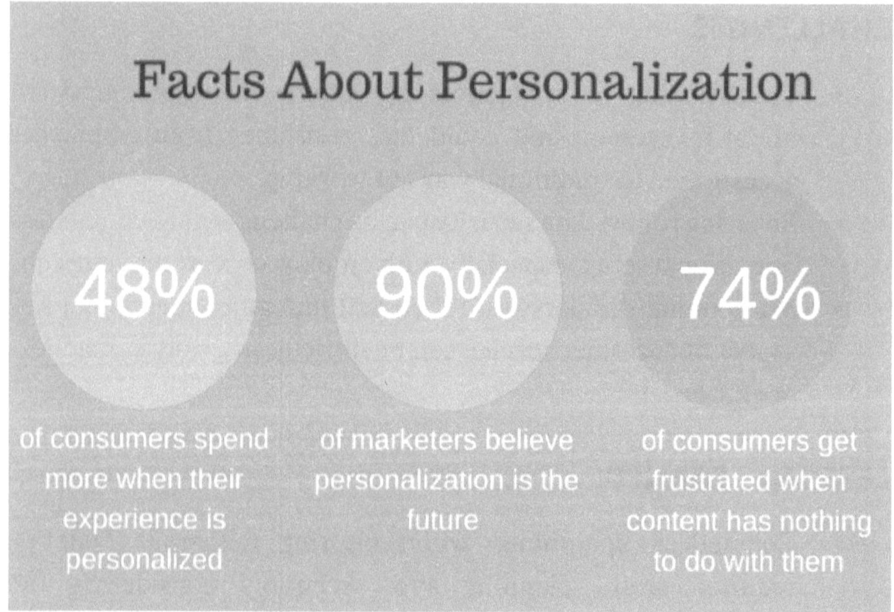

Source: smartinsights.com

REFERENCES

1. Alam, M. M., Awawdeh, A. E., & Muhamad, A. I. B. (2021). Using e-wallet for business process development: challenges and prospects in Malaysia. Business Process Management Journal.
2. Bradford, T. (2021). Are Contactless Payments Finally Poised for Adoption? Payments System Research Briefing, 1-6.
3. Dube, K. (2021). Implications of COVID-19 induced lockdown on the South African tourism industry and prospects for recovery. African Journal of Hospitality, Tourism, and Leisure, 10(1), 270-287.

Agile Cloud: Business Improvement Strategy Execution

Themes: Business, Cloud, Migration, Strategy, Culture, Start-up, Agile

TEACHING OBJECTIVES

The case study is intended to qualify students to:

- Understand the concept of Agile Cloud and how it can be leveraged for business improvement strategy execution.
- Analyze the advantages of Agile Cloud for modern enterprises and the key strategies for effective implementation.
- Examine the opportunities and challenges associated with Agile Cloud adoption, and understand lessons learned from real-world examples.

SYNOPSIS

In today's digital age, the need for flexible and efficient IT infrastructure is paramount for organizations to stay competitive. Agile Cloud, a term that marries two key technological trends - Agile methodologies and Cloud computing, offers such a solution. It combines the iterative, quick-to-change nature of Agile with the scalability, accessibility, and cost-effectiveness of Cloud computing to execute business improvement strategies.

Advantages

Adopting Agile Cloud offers several benefits to businesses. It supports continuous integration and delivery, allowing teams to develop, test, and deploy software quickly and efficiently. Agile Cloud also provides scalability to handle variable workloads, improves collaboration among teams, and reduces time to market. Moreover, its pay-as-you-go model leads to cost optimization by eliminating the need for extensive upfront capital investments in IT infrastructure.

Strategies

Implementing Agile Cloud involves the alignment of business and IT strategies, investment in the right tools and technologies, and an organizational culture that embraces change. Businesses need to foster collaboration among cross-functional teams, apply automation where beneficial, and maintain a customer-centric focus. It's also crucial to provide training and support to employees for a successful transition.

Opportunities

With the increasing demand for real-time data processing and insights, Agile Cloud presents numerous opportunities for businesses. It enables the rapid deployment of new features or services, facilitating innovation and a competitive edge. It also supports remote work, a trend further accelerated by the COVID-19 pandemic, by providing anytime, anywhere access to business resources.

Conclusion

The Agile Cloud is transforming the way businesses operate, offering a path to improved efficiency, agility, and cost savings. Despite the challenges, its adoption is crucial for businesses aiming to stay ahead in the fast-paced digital landscape.

INDUSTRY CONTEXT

In the current industry context, businesses across sectors are moving towards digital transformation, and Agile Cloud is playing a pivotal role in this transition. It's especially prevalent in industries such as software development, e-commerce, finance, and telecommunication, where the need for fast, efficient, and scalable solutions is of utmost importance.

CHALLENGES

- Ensuring data security and compliance in the cloud can be challenging, given the increased risk exposure.
- Migrating existing applications and data to the cloud may pose technical difficulties.
- Achieving an organizational culture shift towards agility and continuous learning could be a complex process.

LESSONS LEARNED

- Agile Cloud implementation is not just a technological shift but also requires a cultural change toward embracing agility and continuous improvement.
- The selection of the right service model (IaaS, PaaS, SaaS) and the provider is crucial in determining the success of Agile Cloud implementation.

QUESTIONS

1. How can businesses overcome the challenges related to data security and compliance in Agile Cloud?
2. What role does an organization's culture play in the successful implementation of Agile Cloud?
3. How can small and medium enterprises (SMEs) leverage Agile Cloud for their business improvement strategies?

UN SDGs: Health and well-being (3); Industry, innovation, and infrastructure (9); Sustainable cities and communities (11)

RESOURCES

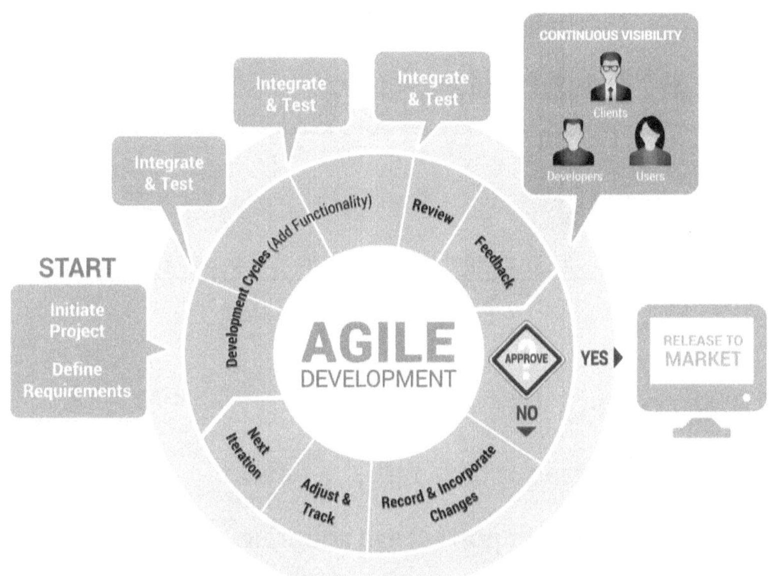

Source: CustomizeWindows

REFERENCES

1. Khan, M. O., Jumani, A. K., & Farhan, W. A. (2020). Fast delivery, continuously build, testing, and deployment with DevOps pipeline techniques on the cloud. Indian Journal of Science and Technology, 13(05), 552-575.

2. Kirchmer, M., Franz, P., & Gusain, R. (2018, June). Digitalization for Agile Business Process Management: The BPM-D® Application. In Conference: Seventh International Symposium on Business Modeling and Software Design. June.

3. Krishnaiyer, K., Chen, F. F., & Bouzary, H. (2018). Cloud Kanban framework for service operations management. Procedia Manufacturing, 17, 531-538.

Artificial Intelligence: Pioneering the Future of Smart Banking

Themes: Artificial Intelligence, Innovation, SMART, Banking, Digital

TEACHING OBJECTIVES

The case study is intended to qualify students to:

- Understand the importance of adopting artificial intelligence to improve bank operations.
- Examine the probable challenges faced by banks during the adoption of artificial intelligence.
- Explore the strategies used by banks to handle artificial intelligence implementation challenges.
- Evaluate the requirements of human involvement while adopting artificial intelligence in banks.

SYNOPSIS

Technologies based on artificial intelligence are becoming increasingly essential in the present world, and banks must implement these technologies at scale to remain persistent. Banks should take an all-inclusive approach to avoid the risks restricting the firm-wide implementation of artificial intelligence technologies. Banks should make investments in the transformation of abilities across all four layers of the combined ability stack to become AI-first: the involvement layer, the AI-powered decision layer, the prime technology and data layer, and the operating framework.

Artificial Intelligence (AI) has rapidly become a significant catalyst for change in the banking industry, creating new opportunities to streamline operations, improve customer experiences, and reduce costs. By leveraging AI, banks can automate processes, gain insights from data, and offer personalized services. This shift toward smart banking is poised to revolutionize the financial sector.

Advantages

AI offers myriad advantages for the banking industry. From enhancing customer service through chatbots and virtual assistants to detecting and preventing fraud through machine learning algorithms, AI helps banks optimize their operations. It also enables banks to personalize their services, providing customers with tailored products, recommendations, and financial advice.

Strategies

Successful implementation of AI in banking requires a strategic approach. Banks must start by identifying areas where AI can create the most value, such as customer service, risk management, or back-office operations. They must also invest in the right technologies and talent, and foster a culture of innovation and continuous learning.

Opportunities

The rise of AI in banking presents numerous opportunities. By leveraging AI, banks can enhance their decision-making processes, improve risk assessments, and increase operational efficiency. AI can also help banks stay competitive by driving innovation and enabling them to offer new, value-added services.

Conclusion

AI is pioneering the future of smart banking, offering significant benefits for banks and their customers. Despite the challenges it presents, AI is becoming an indispensable tool for banks that want to remain competitive in a rapidly evolving industry.

INDUSTRY CONTEXT

The banking industry has traditionally been slow to adopt new technologies, often due to regulatory concerns and the need to maintain the security and trust of their customers. However, with the rise of fintech and the increasing demand for digital services, banks have been forced to innovate. AI has emerged as a key technology in this context, offering solutions that enhance customer experience, streamline operations, and improve security.

CHALLENGES

- Ensuring the security and privacy of customer data is a major concern when implementing AI.
- The lack of regulatory clarity around the use of AI in banking can present challenges.
- Building AI models that accurately reflect complex financial systems can be difficult.

LESSONS LEARNED

- Implementing AI in banking is not just a technological shift, but also requires a cultural and strategic shift within the organization.
- AI is a tool that can enhance human capabilities, not replace them. Successful AI implementations often involve human-AI collaboration.

QUESTIONS

1. How can banks ensure the security and privacy of customer data when implementing AI?
2. What role does regulation play in the adoption of AI in banking?
3. How can banks effectively integrate human and AI capabilities to maximize the benefits of AI?

UN SDGs: Industry, innovation, and infrastructure (9); Sustainable cities and communities (11)

RESOURCES

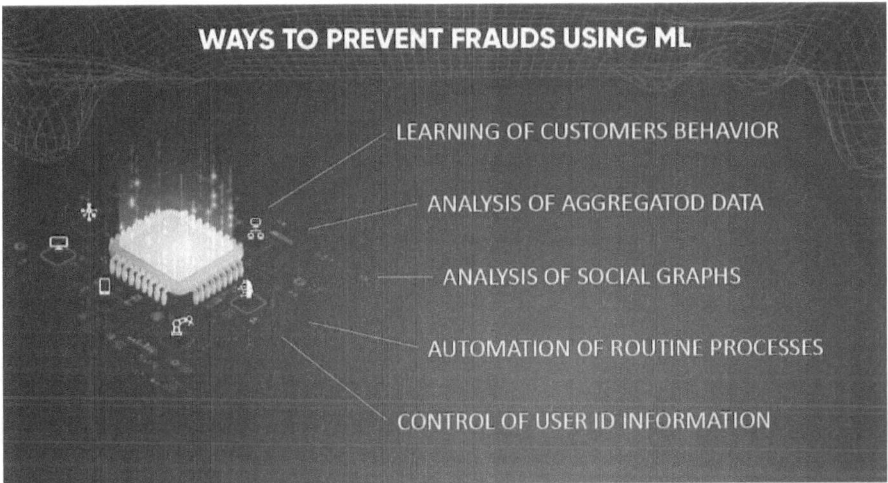

Source: spd.group

REFERENCES

1. Crosman, P. (2018). How Artificial Intelligence is reshaping jobs in banking. *American Banker, 183*(88), 1.
2. Gallego-Gomez, C., & De-Pablos-Heredero, C. (2020). Artificial Intelligence as an Enabling Tool for the Development of Dynamic Capabilities in the Banking Industry. *International Journal of Enterprise Information Systems (IJEIS), 16*(3), 20-33.

3. Golubev, A., Ryabov, O., & Zolotarev, A. (2020, September). Digital transformation of the banking system of Russia with the introduction of blockchain and artificial intelligence technologies. In *IOP Conference Series: Materials Science and Engineering* (Vol. 940, No. 1, p. 012041). IOP Publishing.

Sustainable Packaging Solutions: Ecoware's Biodegradable Packaging Initiative

Themes: Innovation, Ecoware, Applications, Recycling, Packaging

TEACHING OBJECTIVES

The case study is intended to qualify students to:

- Understand the importance and benefits of sustainable packaging solutions, specifically biodegradable packaging, in addressing environmental concerns.
- Analyze the strategies used by Ecoware in implementing its biodegradable packaging initiative.
- Evaluate the opportunities and challenges that Ecoware faced during this initiative, and understand the lessons learned.

SYNOPSIS

In recent years, sustainable packaging has become an important focus for businesses worldwide, driven by growing environmental concerns and increasing consumer demand for eco-friendly products. Ecoware, a New Zealand-based company, is at the forefront of this shift, with a strong commitment to developing biodegradable packaging solutions. Their initiative is not just a business strategy, but a response to a global environmental issue – reducing packaging waste and its impact on the environment.

Advantages

Biodegradable packaging offers several advantages. It reduces the amount of waste that ends up in landfills and the ocean, decreasing pollution and its harmful effects on biodiversity. For businesses, adopting sustainable packaging can enhance their corporate social responsibility profile, strengthen their brand image, and attract environmentally conscious customers.

Strategies

Ecoware adopted several key strategies for its biodegradable packaging initiative. First, they invested in research and development to create packaging that is both functional and eco-friendly. Second, they established transparent supply chains to ensure that their raw materials are sustainably sourced. Third, they engaged in extensive communication and education efforts to inform customers about the benefits of their products.

Opportunities

The shift towards sustainable packaging opens up numerous opportunities for businesses. It can stimulate innovation, help companies differentiate themselves in the market, and generate customer loyalty. For Ecoware, their initiative has helped them establish themselves as leaders in the sustainable packaging market, creating opportunities for growth and expansion.

Conclusion

Ecoware's biodegradable packaging initiative offers a prime example of how businesses can contribute to environmental sustainability while also gaining competitive advantages. Despite the challenges, their success highlights the potential of sustainable business practices in today's market.

INDUSTRY CONTEXT

Packaging plays a significant role in the global waste problem, with plastics being a major contributor. Increasing awareness about the environmental impact of packaging waste has led to growing demand for sustainable alternatives. As a result, the packaging industry is undergoing a significant transformation, with businesses increasingly exploring and adopting eco-friendly packaging solutions.

CHALLENGES

- The cost of sustainable materials and processes can be higher than traditional packaging.
- Finding the right balance between functionality, aesthetics, and sustainability in packaging design can be challenging.
- Customer acceptance and willingness to pay for sustainable packaging can vary.

LESSONS LEARNED

- Sustainability is not just an environmental obligation, but can also provide strategic business advantages.
- Transparency and education are key to gaining customer support for sustainable initiatives.

QUESTIONS

1. How can companies balance the higher costs of sustainable packaging with the need for profitability?
2. What role do consumers play in driving the shift toward sustainable packaging?
3. How can companies overcome the challenges associated with implementing sustainable packaging solutions?

UN SDGs: Decent work and Economic Growth (8); Industry, innovation, and infrastructure (9); Sustainable cities and communities (11)

RESOURCES

Source: ToscheSupply

REFERENCES

1. https://www.expo2020dubai.com/en/understanding-expo/expo-initiatives/expo-live/global-innovators/ecoware
2. https://ecoware.in/tag/sustainable-packaging/
3. https://unreasonablegroup.com/ventures/ecoware/

The Transformation of Traditional Retail: Target's Drive Up Service

Themes: Technology, Transformation, Retail, Drive Up service

TEACHING OBJECTIVES

The case study is intended to qualify students to:

- Understand the impact of digital transformation on traditional retail, with a specific focus on Target's Drive Up service.
- Examine the strategic approaches employed by Target to integrate this new service and the advantages it offers to customers and the business.
- Assess the opportunities and challenges of implementing such a service and identify key lessons from Target's experience.

SYNOPSIS

The retail industry is undergoing a profound transformation, spurred by digital innovation and changing consumer expectations. One manifestation of this change is Target's Drive Up service, which allows customers to order items via Target's app and have them delivered directly to their car at a nearby Target store. This case study focuses on the strategic execution of this service and its implications for the broader retail industry.

Advantages

The Drive Up service offers several advantages. For customers, it combines the convenience of online shopping with the immediacy of in-store purchasing, eliminating the need to navigate store aisles or wait for home delivery. Target leverages existing store infrastructure and inventory minimizes delivery costs, and encourages impulse purchases as customers receive their items quicker than standard online orders.

Strategies

Target's successful execution of the Drive Up service can be attributed to several strategic decisions. First, it fully integrated the service into its existing app, ensuring a seamless user experience. Second, it meticulously planned and implemented a system for processing Drive Up orders efficiently within stores. Finally, it leveraged its widespread store footprint to make the service widely available, thereby gaining a competitive advantage.

Opportunities

The Drive Up service presents several opportunities. It offers a platform for Target to further personalize and enhance customer service. It also allows for integration with other services, such as same-day delivery. More broadly, it provides a model for other retailers to follow as they seek to innovate and meet evolving customer expectations.

Conclusion

Target's Drive Up service illustrates how traditional retailers can effectively leverage digital technologies to improve customer experience and operational efficiency. The case provides valuable insights for retailers seeking to navigate the ongoing digital transformation of the industry.

INDUSTRY CONTEXT

The rise of e-commerce has significantly impacted the retail industry, leading to a decline in traditional brick-and-mortar stores. However, many retailers are responding by integrating digital technologies into their operations, thereby creating an 'omnichannel' shopping experience that combines the best aspects of online and in-store shopping.

CHALLENGES

- Balancing the high demand for the Drive Up service with store operations and staff workload.
- Ensuring fast and efficient fulfillment of Drive Up orders to maintain customer satisfaction.
- Continuously enhancing the app and service in response to customer feedback and technological advancements.

LESSONS LEARNED

- Innovative use of digital technologies can breathe new life into traditional retail operations.
- A seamless and convenient customer experience is key to the success of omnichannel retail strategies.

QUESTIONS

1. What other opportunities could Target explore to further leverage its Drive Up service?
2. How can traditional retailers strike a balance between their in-store operations and digital services like Drive Up?
3. What are some of the potential risks that Target and other retailers face in implementing services like Drive Up?

UN SDGs: Industry, innovation, and infrastructure (9); Sustainable cities and communities (11)

RESOURCES

Source: Traget

REFERENCES

1. https://www.grocerydive.com/news/5-ways-target-is-pushing-customer-driven-innovations-in-omnichannel-grocer/640577/
2. https://d3.harvard.edu/platform-digit/submission/hitting-the-target-in-retail/
3. https://www.supplychaindive.com/news/target-roll-out-curbside-drive-up-returns-nationwide/644144/

Re-Engaging Customers with Digital Technology in a Post-COVID World

Themes: Pandemic, Health, Safety, Consumer, Strategies

TEACHING OBJECTIVES

The case study is intended to qualify students to:

- Understand the significance of digital technology in re-engaging customers in a post-COVID world.
- Analyze the strategies and advantages of using digital technology to enhance customer engagement.
- Evaluate the challenges and opportunities that businesses face in deploying digital technologies for customer re-engagement.

SYNOPSIS

The COVID-19 pandemic has drastically impacted customer behavior, with a significant shift towards online and digital platforms. As the world gradually emerges from the pandemic, businesses are tasked with the challenge of re-engaging customers in this new digital reality. This case study explores how digital technology can be leveraged to effectively reconnect with customers in a post-COVID world.

Advantages

Utilizing digital technology to re-engage customers offers several benefits. It can provide personalized experiences, making customers feel valued and understood. Digital technology can also facilitate greater communication and interaction, leading to stronger customer relationships. Moreover, it allows businesses to gather valuable data, which can be used to further refine and improve customer engagement strategies.

Strategies

There are several strategies that businesses can adopt to harness the power of digital technology for customer re-engagement. These include deploying omnichannel marketing strategies to reach customers on multiple platforms, utilizing data analytics to understand customer preferences and behaviors, and investing in digital innovations like AR, VR, and AI to create unique and immersive customer experiences.

Opportunities

The post-COVID world presents various opportunities for businesses to leverage digital technology. The increased acceptance and use of digital platforms by customers open new avenues for businesses to engage and interact with them. Additionally, advancements in digital technology offer the possibility of creating innovative and novel experiences that can set a business apart from its competitors.

Conclusion

Re-engaging customers in a post-COVID world requires a robust and strategic utilization of digital technology. Businesses that can effectively leverage these tools and strategies are likely to have a competitive edge in this new era of customer engagement.

INDUSTRY CONTEXT

The COVID-19 pandemic has accelerated the digital transformation across industries. As businesses adapted to lockdowns and social distancing measures, the digital engagement of customers became paramount. As we transition into the post-COVID world, businesses are presented with the challenge of retaining digitally engaged customers while also attracting those who prefer traditional methods.

CHALLENGES

- Adapting to rapidly evolving digital trends and customer preferences.
- Managing data privacy and security issues associated with increased digital interactions.
- Integrating new digital tools and platforms with existing business operations.

LESSONS LEARNED

- The COVID-19 pandemic has highlighted the importance of digital platforms in customer engagement.
- Personalization and innovation are key components of successful digital customer engagement strategies.

QUESTIONS

1. How can businesses balance digital and traditional methods of customer engagement in a post-COVID world?
2. What are some of the ethical considerations businesses must keep in mind while utilizing digital technologies for customer re-engagement?
3. How can small businesses with limited resources effectively use digital technology for customer re-engagement?

UN SDGs: Health and well-being (3); Reduced inequalities (10); Sustainable cities and communities (11)

RESOURCES

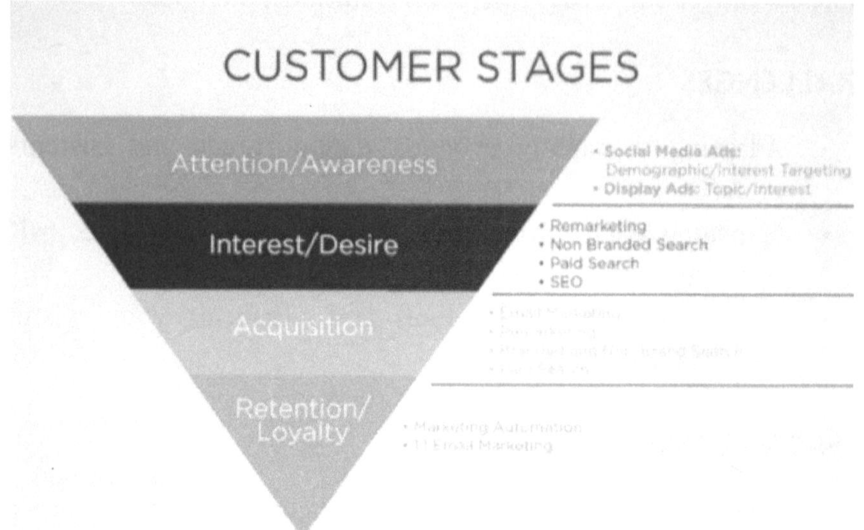

Source: digitalschoolofmarketing.co.za

REFERENCES

1. Friend, S. B., Malshe, A., & Fisher, G. J. (2020). What drives customer Re-engagement? The foundational role of the sales-service interplay in episodic value co-creation. *Industrial Marketing Management*, 84, 271-286.

2. Ho, M. H. W., Chung, H. F., Kingshott, R., & Chiu, C. C. (2020). Customer engagement, consumption and firm performance in a multi-actor service eco-system: The moderating role of resource integration. *Journal of Business Research*, 121, 557-566.

3. Ho, R. C. (2021). Chatbot for online customer service: Customer engagement in the era of artificial intelligence. In *Impact of globalization and advanced technologies on online business models* (pp. 16-31). IGI Global.

AI in Agriculture: The Case of Blue River Technology's See & Spray

Themes: Artificial Intelligence, Technology, Agriculture, Application, Innovation

TEACHING OBJECTIVES

The case study is intended to qualify students to:

- Understand the application of AI in agriculture, particularly focusing on Blue River Technology's See & Spray.
- Analyze the advantages and strategic implications of AI technology in modern farming practices.
- Discuss the opportunities and challenges presented by AI technology in agriculture.

SYNOPSIS

As technology continues to advance, one sector that has experienced significant changes due to these advancements is agriculture. Blue River Technology, a pioneering company in the agritech industry, has created a compelling niche for itself through the development and implementation of a groundbreaking product known as 'See & Spray'. This advanced technological tool harnesses the power of artificial intelligence (AI) and machine learning to transform traditional weed control strategies in farming, thus signaling a new era of agriculture that is more sustainable, cost-effective, and efficient.

Advantages

Incorporating AI into the agricultural process brings several advantages that were unattainable with traditional farming methods. Blue River's See & Spray is an embodiment of such benefits. This system uses cutting-edge AI technology to discern weeds from crops and selectively sprays only the unwanted plants. Consequently, it leads to significant reductions in the quantities of herbicides used, which is both economically beneficial for farmers and reduces the environmental footprint of farming activities. Furthermore, this system allows for real-time decision-making with unparalleled precision, improving crop yield and quality, and mitigating the risk of human error.

Strategies

Blue River Technology's primary strategy is to infuse advanced technology into farming practices for improved outcomes. At the heart of their innovative approach lies the See & Spray technology, which successfully integrates machine learning with high-resolution imaging. By training the system to differentiate between crops and weeds, the company has introduced a novel method for weed control that is precise and eco-friendly, a significant step forward in sustainable farming.

Opportunities

The successful deployment and acceptance of AI technologies in agriculture open doors to myriad opportunities. These encompass possible expansion into diverse farming operations such as pest and disease identification, crop health monitoring, and accurate yield forecasting. Additionally, the vast amounts of data gathered through these AI-driven systems could be harnessed to gain crucial insights about farming practices and consequently used to augment both farming strategies and agricultural policies.

Conclusion

The implementation of Blue River Technology's See & Spray presents an enlightening case study of the potential of AI in the agriculture sector. While it's true that challenges continue to persist, the far-reaching opportunities for refining efficiency, enhancing sustainability, and boosting productivity in farming via AI are immense and waiting to be fully tapped.

INDUSTRY CONTEXT

The agriculture industry is undergoing a digital transformation as farmers increasingly turn to technology to improve efficiency and sustainability. AI, in particular, has emerged as a game-changer, offering solutions to some of the industry's most pressing challenges, such as weed control, resource management, and yield optimization.

CHALLENGES

- The high cost of AI technology can be a barrier for small-scale farmers.
- Integrating AI technology into traditional farming practices requires significant training and adaptation.
- Technical issues, such as software glitches or hardware malfunctions, can affect the reliability and effectiveness of AI solutions.

LESSONS LEARNED

- AI can significantly improve efficiency and sustainability in agriculture when appropriately implemented.
- Successful integration of AI in agriculture requires a balance between technological innovation and understanding of agricultural practices.

QUESTIONS

1. How can the benefits of AI in agriculture be made more accessible to small-scale farmers?
2. What are the ethical considerations related to the use of AI and data collection in agriculture?
3. How might AI technologies like See & Spray reshape the future of farming practices and policies?

UN SDGs: Decent work and Economic Growth (8); Industry, innovation, and Infrastructure (9)

RESOURCES

Source: See & Spray

REFERENCES

1. https://bluerivertechnology.com/our-products/
2. https://www.globalagtechinitiative.com/market-watch/how-blue-rivers-see-spray-technology-could-change-agriculture-forever/
3. https://www.deere.com/en/news/all-news/see-spray-ultimate/

The Rise of Regenerative Medicine: BioLife4D's 3D Bioprinting Innovations

Themes: Technology, Medicine, Regenerative, Innovation, 3D-printing

TEACHING OBJECTIVES

The case study is intended to qualify students to:

- To understand the impact and possibilities of regenerative medicine, specifically focusing on the innovations in 3D bioprinting by BioLife4D.
- To discuss the advantages, strategies, and potential opportunities of 3D bioprinting in healthcare.
- To explore the challenges faced in the adoption of this cutting-edge technology and lessons learned from BioLife4D's approach.

SYNOPSIS

Regenerative medicine has emerged as a promising field that has the potential to revolutionize the healthcare industry. The advent of 3D bioprinting technology has further accelerated this shift, enabling the creation of patient-specific tissues and organs. One company leading this innovative charge is BioLife4D, which has been breaking ground in the development of 3D bioprinted human organs for transplant.

Advantages

The use of 3D bioprinting in medicine, specifically in creating patient-specific organs, comes with numerous advantages. The technology could potentially eliminate the organ shortage crisis, reduce organ rejection rates, and remove the need for anti-rejection drugs post-transplant. BioLife4D is advancing this technique to successfully 3D print a mini human heart, a significant step towards 3D printing fully functional human hearts suitable for transplantation.

Strategies

BioLife4D is capitalizing on 3D bioprinting and regenerative medicine to realize its ambitious goal of making organ transplant waitlists a thing of the past. The company uses a patient's own cells to create biocompatible cardiac tissue, reducing the risk of organ rejection. Moreover, BioLife4D is heavily investing in research and development to refine and improve its bioprinting capabilities.

Opportunities

The success of BioLife4D opens up tremendous opportunities in the field of regenerative medicine. The possibility of creating a wide range of patient-specific organs and tissues not only revolutionizes organ transplantation but also holds promise for pharmaceutical testing and disease modeling.

Conclusion

BioLife4D's pioneering work in 3D bioprinting underlines the immense potential of regenerative medicine. Although significant hurdles remain, the progress made by BioLife4D provides valuable lessons and inspires optimism for the future of healthcare.

INDUSTRY CONTEXT

The healthcare industry is undergoing a paradigm shift, with regenerative medicine at the forefront of this transformation. The advent of 3D bioprinting has introduced the possibility of creating functional human organs, significantly impacting organ transplantation and pharmaceutical testing. With innovators like BioLife4D leading the way, this technology has the potential to solve some of the most pressing healthcare challenges.

CHALLENGES

- Technical challenges of creating complex organs with functional vascularization and cellular arrangements.
- Ethical and regulatory issues surrounding the use of 3D bioprinting in creating human organs.
- High cost of 3D bioprinting technology, making it currently inaccessible to many healthcare providers and patients.

LESSONS LEARNED

- Pioneering new technology requires significant investment in research and development to overcome technical and ethical challenges.
- The potential of 3D bioprinting and regenerative medicine reaffirms the importance of cross-disciplinary collaboration in healthcare innovations.

QUESTIONS

1. How can we address the ethical and regulatory challenges surrounding the use of 3D bioprinting in medicine?
2. What impact could the widespread use of 3D bioprinting technology have on the organ donation system?
3. How can we make innovations like 3D bioprinted organs more accessible to a wider population?

UN SDGs: Industry, innovation, and infrastructure (9); Sustainable cities and communities (11)

RESOURCES

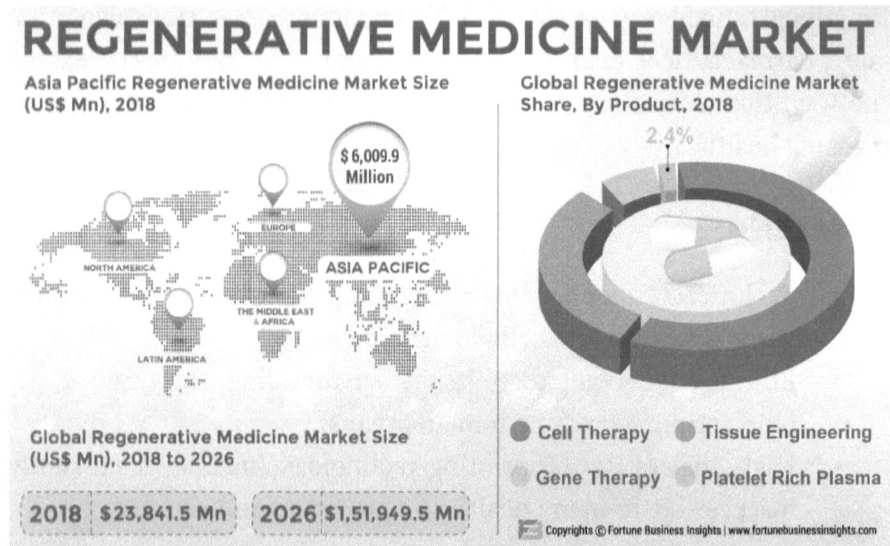

Source: Medgadget

REFERENCES

1. https://www.ncbi.nlm.nih.gov/pmc/articles/PMC7214652/
2. https://www.sec.gov/Archives/edgar/data/1714919/000147793219002927/biolife_1k.htm
3. https://www.biopharminternational.com/view/gaining-ground-the-rise-of-regenerative-medicines

Fintech Revolution: TransferWise's Impact on International Money Transfers

Themes: Fintech, Revolution, TransferWise, Economics, Finance

TEACHING OBJECTIVES

The case study is intended to qualify students to:

- Understand the concept of fintech and its impact on traditional banking, focusing on the case of TransferWise and international money transfers.
- Analyze the strategies employed by TransferWise to disrupt the banking industry and the advantages that this presents to consumers.
- Explore the challenges faced by TransferWise and other fintech startups, the lessons learned, and the future opportunities in this rapidly evolving sector.

SYNOPSIS

Fintech has significantly transformed the financial industry over the past decade, with startups like TransferWise leading the charge. TransferWise, a London-based fintech company, has reinvented international money transfers by offering lower fees and transparent pricing, thereby challenging the traditional banking sector.

Advantages

TransferWise provides a cheaper, faster, and more transparent service for international money transfers than traditional banks. By employing a peer-to-peer system and optimizing currency routes, the company has managed to drastically cut costs and pass these savings on to its customers. Moreover, TransferWise's user-friendly digital platform offers convenience and accessibility, further enhancing customer experience.

Strategies

TransferWise's strategy has been to prioritize transparency and customer-centricity. Unlike traditional banks, TransferWise clearly discloses its fees upfront and uses the real mid-market exchange rate for conversions. They've also focused on making their services easy to use and understand, and have expanded their offerings to include a multi-currency account and a debit card.

Opportunities

With its disruptive model, TransferWise has ample opportunities for growth and expansion. These include diversifying its product offerings, entering new geographical markets, and forming strategic partnerships. As the world becomes increasingly digital and interconnected, the demand for affordable and efficient international money transfer services is set to rise.

Conclusion

TransferWise's successful disruption of the international money transfer market highlights the potential of fintech to revolutionize traditional banking. While challenges persist, the lessons learned and the opportunities presented by this rapidly evolving sector make it a compelling area for study and exploration.

INDUSTRY CONTEXT

The financial industry has seen significant disruption with the advent of fintech, or financial technology. Startups like TransferWise are leveraging technology to offer more efficient, cost-effective, and user-friendly alternatives to traditional banking services. This has led to heightened competition in the industry and forced legacy banks to rethink their strategies and adapt to this new digital landscape.

CHALLENGES

- Regulatory hurdles and compliance requirements in different jurisdictions.
- Building trust with customers who might be wary of using a digital platform for financial transactions.
- Competition from both other fintech startups and traditional banks that are launching their digital solutions.

LESSONS LEARNED

- Transparency and customer-centricity are key to disrupting entrenched industries like banking.
- Despite the promise of technology, trust remains a crucial factor in the financial sector.

QUESTIONS

1. How has TransferWise's strategy allowed it to disrupt the international money transfer market?
2. What challenges might TransferWise face as it seeks to further grow and expand its services?
3. How can traditional banks respond to the disruption caused by fintech startups like TransferWise?

UN SDGs: Decent Work and Economic Growth (8); Sustainable Cities and Communities (11)

RESOURCES

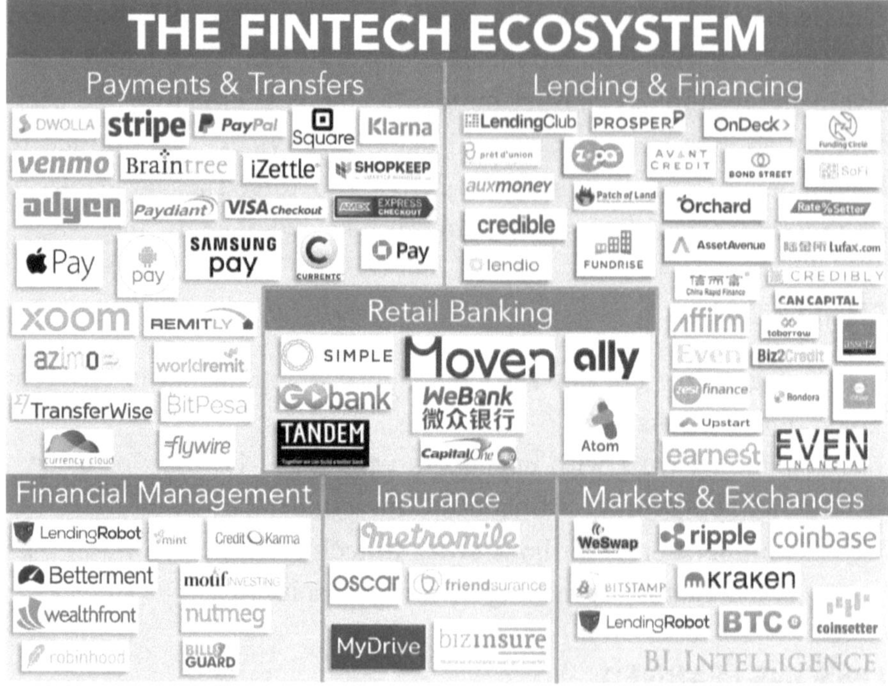

Source: Business Insider

REFERENCES

1. https://d3.harvard.edu/platform-rctom/submission/transferwise-the-money-transfer-revolution/

2. https://medium.com/@StartUpSelfie/startupselfie-26-fintech-revolution-with-transferwise-148042403454

3. https://www.jobstreet.com.my/career-resources/plan-your-career/5-ways-fintech-redefining-financial-services-paying-attention/

AI in Drug Discovery: The Story of DeepMind's AlphaFold

Themes: Service, Artificial Intelligence, Drug Market, Innovation

TEACHING OBJECTIVES

The case study is intended to qualify students to:

- Understand the role and potential of AI in drug discovery, focusing on DeepMind's AlphaFold's breakthroughs.
- Analyze the strategies used by DeepMind to develop AlphaFold and the advantages it brings to the pharmaceutical industry.
- Explore the challenges, opportunities, and lessons learned in integrating AI into drug discovery.

SYNOPSIS

Artificial Intelligence (AI) is revolutionizing numerous industries, including pharmaceuticals and biotechnology. In particular, DeepMind's AlphaFold, a cutting-edge AI system, has made substantial breakthroughs in the realm of protein folding - a complex problem that has perplexed scientists for decades. Understanding protein structure is critical to drug discovery as it enables researchers to discern disease mechanisms better and develop more targeted therapies.

Advantages

AlphaFold's ability to predict protein structure with unprecedented accuracy can potentially speed up drug discovery, lowering costs and reducing the time-to-market for new therapies. Moreover, it can help avoid 'dead-end' research paths by providing early indications of whether a drug target is viable, leading to more efficient use of resources.

Strategies

DeepMind has harnessed the power of deep learning, training AlphaFold on vast datasets of known protein structures. Furthermore, they've embraced an open science philosophy, sharing AlphaFold's findings with the broader scientific community, fostering collaboration, and accelerating scientific progress.

Opportunities

AlphaFold presents exciting opportunities for personalized medicine, as it could help understand individual protein mutations and develop tailored treatments. Also, the technology could have broad applications beyond drug discovery, such as designing enzyme catalysts for use in sustainable manufacturing.

Conclusion

While AlphaFold's accomplishments are groundbreaking, they represent just the tip of the iceberg in AI's potential to revolutionize drug discovery. The case of DeepMind and AlphaFold underscores the promise, challenges, and critical lessons inherent in leveraging AI for scientific and medical breakthroughs.

INDUSTRY CONTEXT

The pharmaceutical industry is under growing pressure to increase the efficiency and productivity of drug discovery, given the soaring costs and lengthy timelines associated with bringing new drugs to market. In this context, AI, particularly machine learning, is being increasingly harnessed to streamline various aspects of the drug discovery process, from target identification to clinical trial design.

CHALLENGES

- Despite its accuracy, AI systems like AlphaFold still have limitations and cannot replace the nuanced understanding that human researchers bring.
- Maintaining a balance between open-source knowledge sharing and intellectual property protection.
- Ensuring ethical use of AI and managing issues around data privacy and security.

LESSONS LEARNED

- Collaboration and openness in scientific research can accelerate progress and lead to ground-breaking discoveries.
- Technology should serve as a tool that complements human expertise, not as a replacement.

QUESTIONS

1. How is AlphaFold's breakthrough in protein structure prediction likely to impact drug discovery?
2. What are the ethical considerations to keep in mind when using AI in drug discovery?
3. What can other industries learn from the use of AI in drug discovery?

UN SDGs: Health and well-being (3); Industry, innovation, and infrastructure (9)

RESOURCES

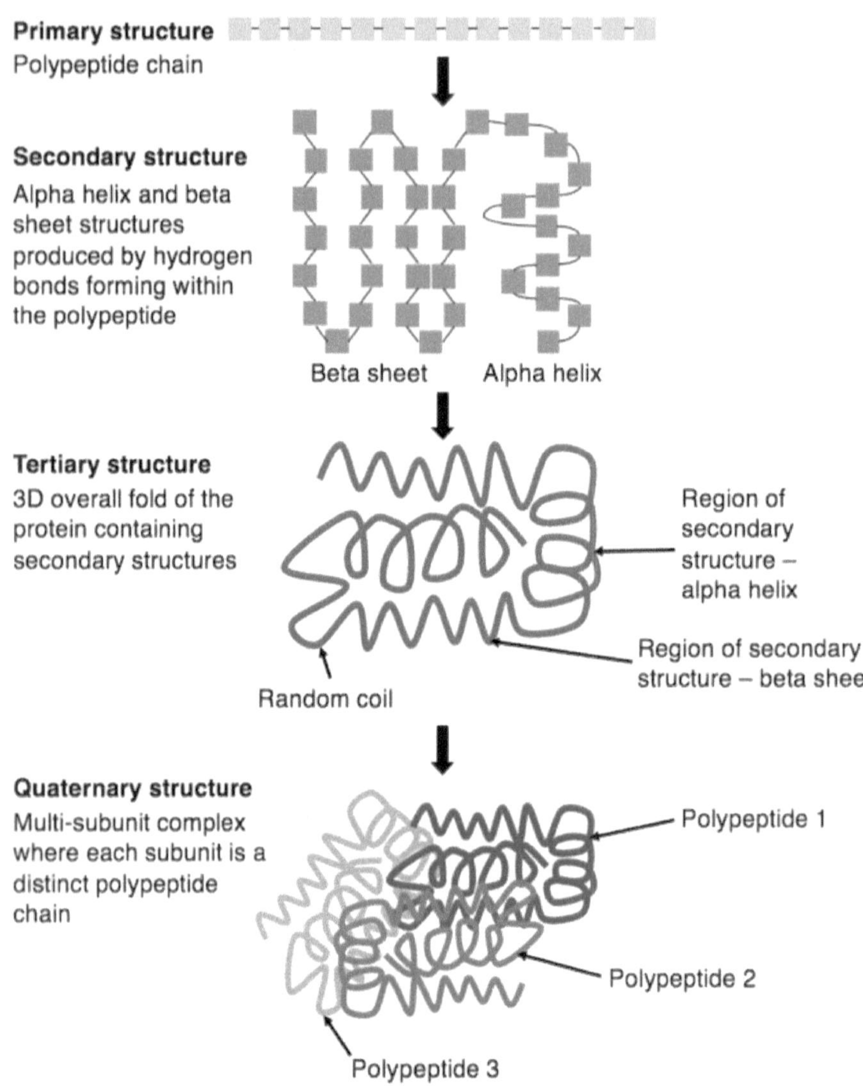

Source: AlphaFold

REFERENCES

1. https://www.nature.com/articles/s41586-021-03819-2#:~:text=The%20AlphaFold%20network%20directly%20predicts,of%20homologues%20as%20inputs%20(Fig.
2. https://www.deepmind.com/research/highlighted-research/alphafold
3. https://journals.plos.org/plosone/article?id=10.1371/journal.pone.0282689

Case Study **71**

Real-time Streaming Analytics: The Success of Stream Processing with Flink

Themes: Technology, Analytics, Stream, Real-time

TEACHING OBJECTIVES

The case study is intended to qualify students to:

- Understand the fundamentals of real-time streaming analytics, with an emphasis on stream processing using Flink.
- Evaluate the advantages and strategies that Flink provides for handling large-scale, real-time data streams.
- Identify the challenges, opportunities, and key lessons from Flink's successful implementation of streaming analytics.

SYNOPSIS

In the age of big data, the ability to process large volumes of data in real time is a significant advantage for businesses across industries. Apache Flink is an open-source stream processing framework that has gained recognition for its ability to handle real-time streaming analytics effectively. It allows companies to harness actionable insights from vast amounts of data as they are generated, facilitating quicker, more informed business decisions.

Advantages

Flink provides several advantages, such as its ability to process boundless and bounded data streams, fault tolerance, and scalability. This makes it suitable for various use cases, ranging from event-driven applications, real-time analytics, and large-scale machine learning tasks. It is optimized for high throughput and low latency, which is crucial for real-time analytics applications.

Strategies

Flink's success can be attributed to its stateful computations over data streams and its powerful windowing mechanism. This, coupled with a robust and flexible API, has made it a versatile tool for different real-time processing needs. Additionally, Flink's active community engagement and open-source development model have contributed to its widespread adoption.

Opportunities

Flink's scalable architecture and powerful computation capabilities provide opportunities to expand its application to various fields, including real-time recommendation systems, fraud detection, and Internet of Things (IoT) analytics. It can also play a crucial role in edge computing, where real-time processing is often required.

Conclusion

As businesses continue to rely on real-time insights to drive decision-making, tools like Flink that offer robust, scalable, and efficient stream processing capabilities will play a pivotal role. The case of Flink demonstrates the immense potential of real-time streaming analytics, while also highlighting the challenges and lessons learned in this evolving field.

INDUSTRY CONTEXT

The exponential growth of data and the need for real-time insights have made streaming analytics crucial across industries. Industries like finance, healthcare, transportation, and e-commerce extensively use real-time analytics for use cases like fraud detection, real-time recommendations, and predictive maintenance.

CHALLENGES

- Ensuring data privacy and security while processing real-time data streams.
- Managing the complexity of setting up and maintaining a Flink cluster for large-scale data processing.
- Balancing between the latency, throughput, and accuracy of real-time analytics.

LESSONS LEARNED

- The power of an open-source development model in driving innovation and adoption.
- The importance of scalability and fault tolerance in handling large-scale, real-time data streams.

QUESTIONS

1. How can businesses effectively leverage real-time streaming analytics using tools like Flink?
2. What are the considerations when choosing a stream processing framework for real-time analytics?
3. How can we address the challenges related to data privacy and security in real-time analytics?

UN SDGs: Industry, innovation, and infrastructure (9); Sustainable cities and communities (11)

RESOURCES

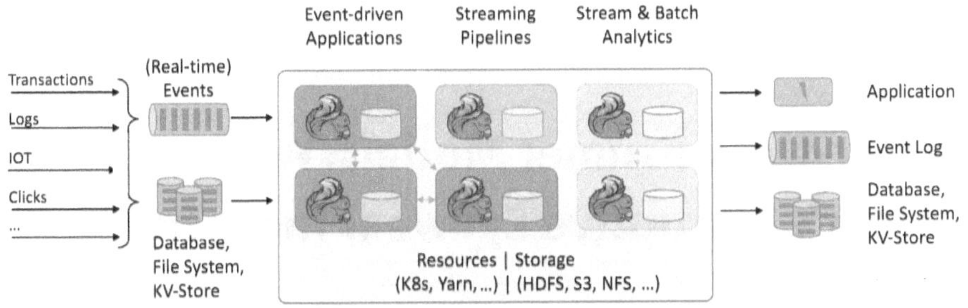

Source: Apache Flink

REFERENCES

1. https://flink.apache.org/
2. https://medium.com/big-data-processing/apache-flink-getting-started-stream-processing-377b06d6aec4
3. https://towardsdatascience.com/an-introduction-to-stream-processing-with-apache-flink-b4acfa58f14d

Direct-to-Consumer Models: Warby Parker's Disruptive Eyewear Industry Approach

Themes: Models, Eyewear, Challenges, Strategies, Startup

TEACHING OBJECTIVES

The case study is intended to qualify students to:

- Understand the principles of the Direct-to-Consumer (DTC) model
- Evaluate the advantages and strategic implications of the DTC model for both startup ventures and established industries.
- Identify and discuss the challenges faced and opportunities available to businesses that employ the DTC model.

SYNOPSIS

The introduction to this case study focuses on the transformative journey of Warby Parker, a revolutionary business in the eyewear industry. With a unique Direct-to-Consumer (DTC) business model, Warby Parker entirely bypassed traditional retail channels, dealing directly with customers. This approach provided a platform for the firm to present high-quality and fashionable eyewear at significantly lower prices than traditional eyewear retailers. The company's ability to re-engineer the eyewear supply chain, minimize unnecessary costs, and deliver value to consumers brought a paradigm shift in the industry, which was traditionally dominated by a small number of large corporations.

Advantages

Warby Parker's DTC model brings several advantages to the table. The control over the entire customer experience, ranging from design to manufacturing, marketing, and direct sales, allows the firm to build robust customer relationships. It bolsters the brand's identity, maintains firm control over its pricing strategy, and ensures quality at every touchpoint. The online home try-on program has been a game-changer. By allowing customers to try five frames at home for free before buying, Warby Parker mitigates the risk associated with online eyewear shopping, thereby revolutionizing the customer experience.

Strategies

In terms of strategy, Warby Parker has stuck to its core principle of disrupting the eyewear industry by offering exceptional value and convenience to customers. The company exploited technology to facilitate a seamless online shopping experience, backed by a network of stylish physical showrooms that blend the digital and physical shopping experiences. An integral part of their business strategy is rooted in social consciousness. Warby Parker's "Buy a Pair, Give a Pair" program ensures that for every pair of glasses sold, another pair is donated to someone in need through non-profit partners.

Opportunities

The success of Warby Parker has set the stage for numerous expansion opportunities. The company can consider extending its product range or even leverage its DTC expertise to venture into new sectors. The application of the DTC model extends beyond Warby Parker, providing other businesses with an opportunity to learn and adapt the DTC model to fit their industries.

Conclusion

Warby Parker's journey offers profound insights into how the DTC model can cause significant disruption in a traditional industry. Despite the inherent challenges linked with this model, the potential for enhanced customer relationships, control over pricing, and opportunities for market disruption present significant incentives for both entrepreneurs and existing businesses. The DTC model, pioneered by firms like Warby Parker, has demonstrated the feasibility and success of reimagining traditional business models and consumer relationships, leading to a more competitive and diverse marketplace.

INDUSTRY CONTEXT

The DTC model is transforming various industries by eliminating intermediaries and enabling companies to interact directly with customers. This model leverages the power of digital channels to streamline operations, offer competitive pricing, and deliver a personalized customer experience. The success of DTC companies like Warby Parker indicates a growing trend of customers preferring these models due to their convenience, cost-effectiveness, and unique brand experiences.

CHALLENGES

- Building a trusted and recognizable brand without the benefit of traditional retail exposure.
- Managing the complete customer experience, from product design to post-sale service.
- Scaling operations while maintaining product quality and customer service levels.

LESSONS LEARNED

- The power of disrupting traditional business models through direct engagement with customers.

- The importance of a socially conscious business model in building a strong brand image.

QUESTIONS

1. How did Warby Parker's DTC model enable it to disrupt the traditional eyewear industry?
2. What challenges might a business face when adopting a DTC model, and how could they overcome these?
3. How might established industries respond to the disruption caused by DTC models?

UN SDGs: Decent work and economic growth (8); Industry, innovation, and infrastructure (9)

RESOURCES

Source: Warbys

REFERENCES

1. https://www.businessofbusiness.com/articles/history-of-warby-parker-jobs-data/
2. https://blog.experiencepoint.com/warby-parker-disruption-design-thinking
3. https://www.cnbc.com/2019/12/12/warby-parker-how-a-lost-pair-of-glasses-disrupted-the-eyewear-industry.html

The Future of Autonomous Delivery: The Success of Nuro's Self-Driving Delivery Vehicles

Themes: Autonomous, Driverless, Robotics, Business Model

TEACHING OBJECTIVES

The case study is intended to qualify students to:

- Understand the evolution and potential impact of autonomous vehicles on the delivery industry.
- Evaluate the business model, strategies, and innovations driving the success of Nuro's self-driving delivery vehicles.
- Analyze the challenges and opportunities in the autonomous delivery market and the broader implications for logistics and supply chain management.

SYNOPSIS

The case study commences with an exploration of Nuro, an American robotics company that is redefining the concept of delivery through its groundbreaking autonomous delivery vehicles. Nuro, established by two former Google engineers, has secured robust financial backing and initiated strategic collaborations with large-scale retail brands, propelling a revolutionary shift in the last-mile delivery industry. The company's uniquely designed, slow-moving vehicles, intended solely for carrying goods, are projected to significantly reduce delivery costs, diminish environmental harm, and enhance efficiency and convenience for consumers. With the case of Nuro, the future of autonomous delivery unfolds, bringing to light the potential upsides and hurdles in the journey toward an automated future in delivery and logistics. It also provides a thought-provoking discussion on the broader implications for the workforce, city infrastructure, and the future of personal transport.

Advantages

The advantages conferred by Nuro's autonomous delivery vehicles are manifold. They promise to drastically cut delivery costs, as there's no need for a human driver, which implies lower labor expenses. Nuro's vehicles also have the potential to decrease carbon emissions significantly due to their optimized design for minimal energy consumption. Their ability to operate continuously offers the possibility of improving delivery efficiency, enabling a faster and more reliable service for consumers. These vehicles, designed exclusively for deliveries, maximize cargo capacity while minimizing the vehicle's size, as they need no space for a driver or passengers.

Strategies

Nuro's strategic approach to gaining a competitive edge in the market is rooted in its exclusive focus on autonomous delivery, which contrasts with many competitors also targeting passenger transportation. This specific focus allows Nuro to navigate regulatory challenges more smoothly and to optimize the design of its vehicles for their purpose, which is solely delivery. Moreover, Nuro has been successful in creating and maintaining key partnerships with major food delivery and grocery companies, expediting the implementation and wide-scale acceptance of its vehicles.

Opportunities

The field of autonomous delivery holds immense possibilities for future expansion and innovation. Nuro's vehicles could potentially find applications far beyond their current use in food and grocery delivery. Possibilities range from parcel delivery to pharmaceutical logistics or even intra-campus transportation for businesses. As regulations evolve and technology becomes increasingly mature and reliable, Nuro may find significant growth opportunities in new markets or geographic regions.

Conclusion

The advent of autonomous delivery vehicles marks a pivotal turning point in the landscape of logistics and delivery services. Companies like Nuro are spearheading this technological revolution, using cutting-edge technology to address real-world challenges and redefine the future of delivery. Despite facing considerable challenges, including regulatory constraints and public acceptance, the potential benefits of autonomous delivery vehicles are vast, promising substantial economic, environmental, and societal advantages.

INDUSTRY CONTEXT

The global delivery market has seen exponential growth, fueled by the e-commerce boom and changing consumer expectations for speed and convenience. Simultaneously, technology has emerged as a key differentiator in this industry, with innovations in AI, robotics, and autonomous vehicles redefining what's possible. Companies like Nuro are at the forefront of these trends, harnessing autonomous technology to drive efficiency, reduce costs, and meet the ever-growing demand for delivery services.

CHALLENGES

- Regulatory hurdles: Despite advancements in technology, regulations surrounding autonomous vehicles are still in their nascent stages, posing significant challenges.

- Technology reliability and safety: Ensuring the safety and reliability of autonomous vehicles is a monumental task. Any failure could lead to accidents, causing harm and eroding public trust in the technology.
- Public acceptance: Acceptance of autonomous vehicles by the public and traditional businesses is still uncertain. Convincing these stakeholders to trust and use self-driving vehicles is a significant challenge.

LESSONS LEARNED

- A focused approach: Nuro's success illustrates the potential benefits of a focused strategy. By honing in on autonomous delivery, rather than trying to solve all aspects of autonomous driving at once, Nuro has been able to carve out a unique market niche.
- Importance of partnerships: Strategic partnerships can accelerate growth and adoption. Nuro's partnerships with major retail

QUESTIONS

1. What are the key factors contributing to Nuro's success in the autonomous delivery market? How can other companies learn from their approach?
2. How could changes in regulations or public perceptions impact the future of autonomous delivery?
3. Beyond delivery, what other applications might there be for Nuro's autonomous vehicles? How could the company strategically expand into these areas?

UN SDGs: Sustainable cities and communities (11); Responsible consumption and production (12)

RESOURCES

Source: TechCrunch

REFERENCES

1. https://www.nuro.ai/
2. https://www.nuro.ai/technology
3. https://techcrunch.com/2022/01/12/nuro-autonomous-delivery-bot-launch/

Cybersecurity in the IoT Age: Palo Alto Networks' Security Solutions

Themes: Cybersecurity, Application, Technology, IoT

TEACHING OBJECTIVES

The case study is intended to qualify students to:

- Understand the importance of cybersecurity in the IoT age and the role that solutions like those offered by Palo Alto Networks play.
- Analyze the strategies and business models that cybersecurity companies like Palo Alto Networks use to stay ahead of threats.
- Discuss the challenges and opportunities faced by cybersecurity companies in an ever-evolving digital landscape.

SYNOPSIS

The introduction uncovers the significance of Palo Alto Networks, a world leader in providing cybersecurity solutions, in the age where IoT is driving a significant part of our lives. As the count of IoT devices globally continues to surge, the complexity of cybersecurity escalates, making the necessity for comprehensive and advanced security solutions a crucial element in digital operations. Palo Alto Networks, equipped with its extensive assortment of services, is uniquely poised to tackle this surge in cybersecurity threats.

Advantages

Palo Alto Networks' suite of security services offers distinct advantages like instantaneous threat prevention, cloud-native services to ensure scalability and flexibility, and predictive analytics powered by artificial intelligence that aids in detecting threats proactively. Their holistic approach towards cybersecurity goes beyond mere protection; it extends to enabling businesses to proceed with their digital transformation ventures without having to worry about security threats.

Strategies

The company's winning strategy lies in its commitment to providing an integrated, automated security platform aimed at strengthening and simplifying security operations. Innovation is deeply ingrained in the company's culture, enabling them to stay one step ahead of evolving cyber threats continually. Moreover, a deep understanding of the threat landscape, achieved by rigorous research and investment, guides the development of relevant, comprehensive solutions, that benefit businesses across various sectors and sizes.

Opportunities

The interconnected world we live in today presents a wealth of opportunities for cybersecurity solutions. As the need for securing IoT devices and protecting cloud-based services continues to grow, demand for holistic security solutions is expected to skyrocket. Palo Alto Networks, armed with its broad portfolio of security services, is in a prime position to leverage these opportunities and fortify its place in the cybersecurity market.

Conclusion

Despite numerous challenges in the cybersecurity landscape, Palo Alto Networks has carved out a niche as a trailblazer in the industry. Its strategy of blending constant innovation with a profound understanding of the evolving threat landscape offers a blueprint for success to other cybersecurity entities. In conclusion, the case study on Palo Alto Networks delivers valuable insights into the high-stakes world of cybersecurity and the pivotal role it plays in the era of the digital revolution.

INDUSTRY CONTEXT

The cybersecurity industry has become increasingly important as businesses and individuals alike move more of their activities online. This shift, combined with an increasing number of IoT devices, has created a fertile ground for cyber threats. Companies like Palo Alto Networks provide crucial services that protect sensitive data and systems from these threats, allowing businesses to operate securely in the digital world.

CHALLENGES

- Staying ahead of the rapidly evolving cyber threats.
- Securing a vast array of IoT devices, each with its unique security considerations.
- Managing the cybersecurity risks associated with the shift to remote working.

LESSONS LEARNED

- Innovation is key in the cybersecurity industry. The nature of cyber threats means that cybersecurity companies must continually update their services to provide effective protection.
- A comprehensive approach to cybersecurity is more effective than addressing individual threats. By providing an integrated platform, Palo Alto Networks can provide stronger and simpler security solutions.

QUESTIONS

1. How has the rise of IoT devices impacted the cybersecurity landscape?
2. What strategies can cybersecurity companies adopt to stay ahead of the evolving cyber threats?
3. How can companies effectively manage the cybersecurity risks associated with remote working?

UN SDGs: Industry, innovation, and infrastructure (9); Sustainable cities and communities (11)

RESOURCES

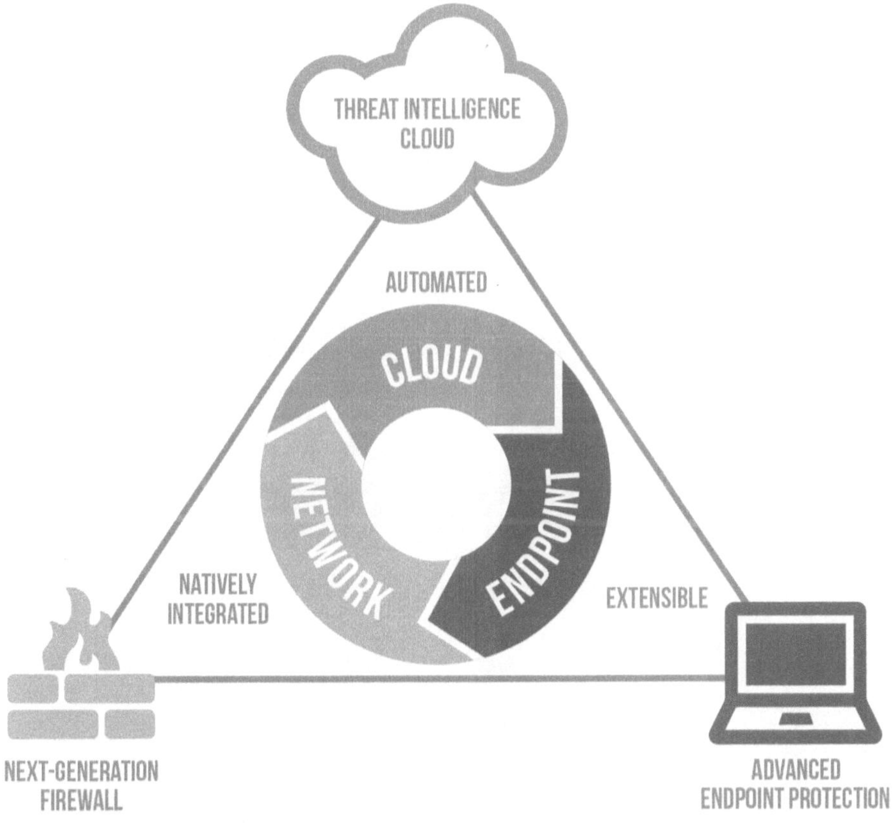

Source: Palo Alto Networks

REFERENCES

1. https://www.paloaltonetworks.com/
2. https://www.paloaltonetworks.com/prisma/cloud
3. https://en.wikipedia.org/wiki/Palo_Alto_Networks

Sustainable Packaging Solutions: Coca-Cola's Ambitious Goals for a Greener Future

Themes: Innovation, Application, Sustainability, Greener, Future

TEACHING OBJECTIVES

The case study is intended to qualify students to:

- Understand the significance of sustainable packaging solutions in the food and beverage industry and how it contributes to overall corporate social responsibility.
- Analyze Coca-Cola's strategies for achieving its sustainable packaging goals and their potential impact on the company's operations and reputation.
- Explore the challenges faced by companies like Coca-Cola in the implementation of sustainable initiatives and how they can overcome these hurdles.

SYNOPSIS

The case study takes a close look at the beverage industry giant, Coca-Cola's ambition to revolutionize its packaging system to align with sustainability standards and the global shift towards environmental conservation. As one of the world's largest contributors to plastic waste, Coca-Cola's move towards a more sustainable packaging approach signals a significant commitment to the environment and its corporate social responsibility.

Advantages

Coca-Cola's journey towards sustainable packaging is an advantageous strategy on multiple fronts. Firstly, the move aligns Coca-Cola with the growing global sentiment favoring eco-friendly practices and products. This environmental stewardship can lead to increased customer loyalty and attract new customers who prioritize sustainability. Furthermore, this alignment with sustainability principles could also provide a competitive edge over other brands that are slower to adapt to eco-friendly practices. In the long term, efficient use of resources in sustainable packaging can translate into cost savings and operational efficiencies.

Strategies

Coca-Cola has committed to several strategic initiatives to realize its sustainability goals. Key among them is the increase in the use of recycled materials in their packaging. The company has also focused on reducing packaging wastage by optimizing the packaging design and encouraging consumers to recycle. On top of this, Coca-Cola is pursuing innovation in the creation of fully recyclable or compostable packaging solutions. These new materials have the potential to significantly reduce the environmental impact of their products. Moreover, Coca-Cola is investing in raising awareness among consumers about the importance of recycling and responsible waste disposal.

Opportunities

The growing global emphasis on sustainability presents vast opportunities for Coca-Cola. The company's initiative towards eco-friendly packaging sets a strong industry precedent and might inspire other businesses to follow suit, leading to an overall reduction in the industry's environmental footprint. As the world continues to grapple with the mounting problem of plastic waste, businesses that take the lead in implementing sustainable practices stand to gain significantly in terms of market reputation and customer preference.

Conclusion

Coca-Cola's pursuit of its sustainability goals is a challenging yet commendable endeavor that puts it at the forefront of environmental stewardship in the beverage industry. Despite the obstacles in the path towards sustainable packaging, the company's commitment stands as a testament to the power and responsibility of corporations in spearheading industry-wide changes. The case serves as a vital reference point for other businesses looking to transition toward more sustainable operations.

INDUSTRY CONTEXT

The beverage industry has been under increasing scrutiny due to its environmental impact, particularly concerning packaging waste. As sustainability becomes a significant factor in consumer purchasing decisions, companies are pressured to implement more eco-friendly practices. This push towards sustainability presents both challenges and opportunities for businesses.

CHALLENGES

- Finding sustainable materials that maintain product quality and safety can be difficult and costly.
- Educating consumers about sustainable practices and encouraging them to recycle can be a daunting task.
- Navigating regulatory landscapes across different regions regarding sustainable packaging and waste disposal can be complex.

LESSONS LEARNED

- Corporate social responsibility, particularly in terms of environmental sustainability, can enhance a company's reputation and drive consumer loyalty.

- Large corporations, due to their considerable influence, can play a pivotal role in driving industry-wide changes toward sustainability.

QUESTIONS

1. What other strategies could Coca-Cola implement to achieve its sustainability goals more efficiently?
2. How can regulatory bodies and governments support corporations in their move toward sustainable practices?
3. How do you see the evolution of consumer behavior toward sustainability impacting the beverage industry in the future?

UN SDGs: Responsible consumption and production (12); Climate action (13); Life on Land (15)

RESOURCES

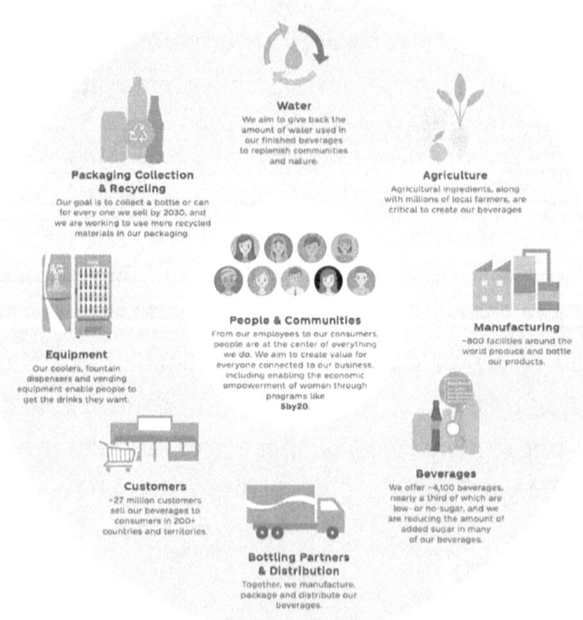

Source: Coca-Cola

REFERENCES

1. https://www.coca-colacompany.com/news/coke-announces-ambitious-sustainability-goal#:~:text=Coca%2DCola%20today%20announced%20an,it%20sells%20globally%20by%202030.
2. https://www.coca-colacompany.com/sustainability
3. https://www.coca-cola.co.uk/sustainability/global-sustainability-vision

The Transition to Sustainable Renewable Energy: Replacing Oil for the Future

Themes: Technology, Safety, Oil & gas, Economy

TEACHING OBJECTIVES

The case study is intended to qualify students to:

- Understand the significance of transitioning from fossil fuels, particularly oil, to renewable energy sources, and the implications for the environment, economy, and society.
- Analyze the strategies and technologies involved in this transition, along with the role of policy and regulatory frameworks.
- Evaluate the challenges and opportunities inherent in this transition, focusing on examples of both successful and unsuccessful efforts in various parts of the world.

SYNOPSIS

The case study provides an in-depth analysis of the global energy sector's shift from dependence on oil to more sustainable renewable energy sources. This transition, driven by factors like climate change, the finite nature of fossil fuels, and technological advancements, is of paramount importance for the sustainability of our planet and economies.

Advantages

The transition to renewable energy offers numerous benefits. It reduces greenhouse gas emissions and air pollution, thus mitigating climate change and improving public health. Economically, it promises energy security and independence while creating jobs and stimulating economic growth. It also offers the potential for universal energy access, contributing to global equity and poverty reduction.

Strategies

Strategies for transitioning to renewable energy involve technological advancements, policy measures, and financial investments. Technological strategies involve the development and deployment of renewable energy technologies like solar, wind, and geothermal. Policy measures include regulatory frameworks, incentives, and carbon pricing to stimulate renewable energy uptake. Financial strategies involve attracting investments and ensuring the economic viability of renewable energy projects.

Opportunities

The transition to renewable energy presents significant opportunities for innovation, economic growth, and societal benefits. It opens up new markets for renewable energy technologies and services. It also offers the potential for countries to achieve energy independence, reducing geopolitical tensions related to oil resources. Furthermore, it presents an opportunity to address social inequalities by providing energy access to disadvantaged communities.

Conclusion

The transition from oil to renewable energy is a complex but necessary endeavor. While the path is fraught with challenges, the opportunities and benefits are immense. This transition is not just about replacing one energy source with another; it is about reshaping our economies and societies toward sustainability and equity. This case study provides valuable insights into the multifaceted nature of this transition, offering lessons for policy-makers, industry players, and society at large.

INDUSTRY CONTEXT

The global energy industry is at a critical juncture as it grapples with the dual challenge of meeting increasing energy demand while reducing its environmental footprint. The sector, historically dominated by fossil fuels like oil, is undergoing a major transformation towards renewable energy sources such as wind, solar, and geothermal power. This transition is driven by a combination of environmental concerns, technological advancements, policy measures, and changing consumer preferences.

CHALLENGES

- Technological barriers: Developing and deploying renewable energy technologies at a large scale is a significant challenge, particularly in areas like energy storage and grid integration.
- Economic hurdles: The transition involves significant capital costs, and many renewable energy technologies struggle to compete with the low costs of fossil fuels, especially in the absence of carbon pricing.
- Regulatory and policy inconsistencies: Policies promoting renewable energy often face opposition from entrenched interests and can be subject to political instability.

LESSONS LEARNED

- Holistic approach: The transition to renewable energy requires a comprehensive approach that addresses technological, economic, and policy aspects simultaneously.
- Stakeholder engagement: The involvement and buy-in of a broad range of stakeholders, including governments, businesses, civil

society, and local communities, is crucial for the success of this transition.

QUESTIONS

1. What strategies can be employed by the automobile industry to overcome the challenges associated with the adoption of biofuels?
2. What are the potential strategies to overcome the technological and economic barriers to renewable energy transition?
3. How can policy measures be designed to effectively promote renewable energy while managing opposition from entrenched interests?
4. What role can businesses, civil society, and local communities play in accelerating the transition to renewable energy?

UN SDGs: Industry, innovation, and infrastructure (9); Responsible consumption and production (12); Climate action (13)

RESOURCES

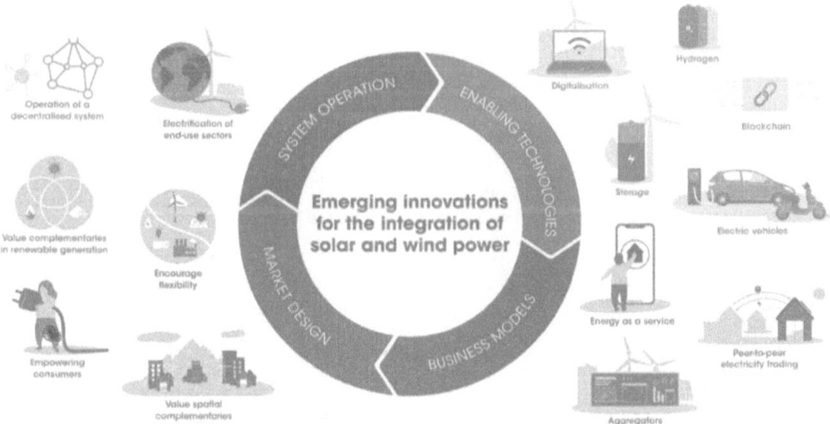

Source: WEF

REFERENCES

1. https://www.spglobal.com/en/research-insights/articles/ what-is-energy-transition#:~:text=Energy%20transition%20 refers%20to%20the,well%20as%20lithium%2Dion%20batteries..

2. https://www.un.org/en/climatechange/raising-ambition/ renewable-energy-transition

3. https://www.frontiersin.org/articles/10.3389/ fenrg.2021.743114/full

Cryptocurrencies: A Catalyst for Small and Medium Firms' Success

Themes: SMEs, e-Commerce, Crypto, Digital, Finance, Bitcoin

TEACHING OBJECTIVES

The case study is intended to qualify students to:

- Understand the basic concept of cryptocurrencies, their functionality, and their impact on financial systems, particularly within the realm of small and medium-sized enterprises (SMEs).
- Explore the advantages and opportunities offered by cryptocurrencies for SMEs, including their potential to catalyze success.
- Discuss and evaluate the strategies SMEs can adopt when integrating cryptocurrencies into their operations while acknowledging the challenges they may face and how to overcome them.

SYNOPSIS

The case study delves into the disruptive world of cryptocurrencies, a digital or virtual form of currency that uses cryptography for security, and their transformative role in the operations of SMEs. It underlines the increasing acceptance and integration of cryptocurrencies like Bitcoin, Ethereum, and more in businesses of all sizes, but with a special focus on SMEs.

Advantages

Cryptocurrencies offer SMEs several advantages. They facilitate speedy, cost-effective, and borderless transactions, enable access to global markets, and offer an alternative to traditional banking systems, which can be especially beneficial for businesses in regions with unstable currencies or limited access to banking. Cryptocurrencies can also foster financial inclusion and help protect against currency inflation.

Strategies

The case study outlines the strategies SMEs can adopt when integrating cryptocurrencies into their operations. These include setting up a digital wallet, choosing the right payment gateway, integrating cryptocurrency payment options into their existing payment systems, educating customers about cryptocurrency payments, and managing cryptocurrency assets effectively.

Opportunities

The rise of cryptocurrencies opens up new opportunities for SMEs. It provides access to a growing global customer base of cryptocurrency users, allows for the introduction of innovative business models, and offers opportunities for differentiation in a competitive market. Furthermore, the ability to carry out micropayments efficiently can unlock new revenue streams for SMEs.

Conclusion

Despite the volatility and regulatory uncertainty surrounding cryptocurrencies, they offer tremendous potential as a catalyst for SMEs' success. Businesses that are open to adopting these new forms of payment can unlock significant opportunities for growth and innovation. Nevertheless, careful and strategic planning is required to navigate the associated challenges and risks.

INDUSTRY CONTEXT

The financial industry is undergoing a paradigm shift with the advent of digital currencies, particularly cryptocurrencies. Initially viewed with skepticism, cryptocurrencies have gradually gained acceptance as a legitimate means of transaction, especially among tech-savvy consumers and innovative businesses. In this evolving landscape, SMEs – known for their adaptability and entrepreneurial spirit – are increasingly exploring and integrating cryptocurrencies into their operations to stay competitive and meet their customers' changing needs.

CHALLENGES

- Volatility: Cryptocurrencies are known for their extreme price volatility, which can pose financial risks.
- Regulatory uncertainty: The regulatory landscape for cryptocurrencies is still evolving and varies by country, creating uncertainty for businesses.
- Acceptance and understanding: While growing, the acceptance of cryptocurrency payments by customers is not universal, and there can be a steep learning curve associated with its use.

LESSONS LEARNED

- Adaptability: The ability to adapt to new technologies and market trends is crucial for the success of SMEs.
- Risk management: While cryptocurrencies offer unique opportunities, it's essential to have strategies in place for managing the associated financial and regulatory risks.

QUESTIONS

1. What are some real-world examples of SMEs successfully integrating cryptocurrency into their operations? What strategies did they use, and what were the outcomes?

2. What specific risks should SMEs consider when deciding whether to accept cryptocurrency and how can they mitigate these risks?

3. How might the role of cryptocurrencies in SMEs evolve in the future, and what implications could this have for the wider economy and society?

UN SDGs: Decent work and Economic Growth (8); Industry, innovation, and infrastructure (9); Sustainable cities and communities (11)

RESOURCES

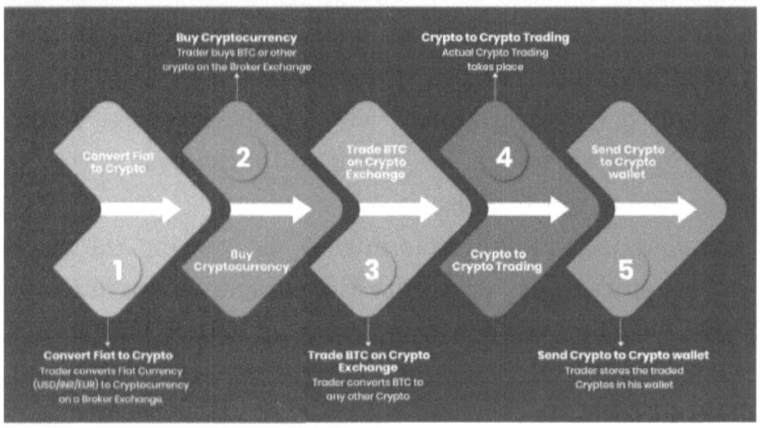

Source: quytech.com

REFERENCES

1. Bracci, E., Tallaki, M., Ievoli, R., & Diplotti, S. (2021). Knowledge, diffusion and interest in blockchain technology in SMEs. *Journal of Knowledge Management.*

2. Cocco, L., Mannaro, K., Tonelli, R., Mariani, L., Lodi, M. B., Melis, A., ... & Fanti, A. (2021). A blockchain-based traceability system in agri-food SME: Case study of a traditional bakery. *IEEE Access,* 9, 62899-62915

The Future of Quantum Computing: Google's Quantum Supremacy

Themes: Quantum, Computing, Google, Technology

TEACHING OBJECTIVES

The case study is intended to qualify students to:

- Introduce the concept of quantum computing, focusing on Google's breakthrough in achieving quantum supremacy.
- Analyze the advantages, challenges, and strategies related to the development and implementation of quantum computing.
- Critically evaluate the opportunities and future implications of quantum computing in various sectors.

SYNOPSIS

This case study explores Google's landmark achievement in quantum computing-the attainment of quantum supremacy. Quantum supremacy is the milestone where a quantum computer successfully performs a computational task that classical computers would find insurmountably difficult or time-consuming. It underlines the commencement of a new era, where quantum computers can solve problems beyond the reach of traditional computers.

Advantages

The shift to quantum computing introduces numerous advantages that extend well beyond those offered by classical computing. Primarily, quantum computers possess unparalleled processing capabilities, making them adept at solving complex problems and conducting simulations at exponentially faster rates. In Google's instance, their 53-qubit quantum computer named Sycamore, demonstrated its remarkable prowess by resolving a specific problem in 200 seconds - a task that would take the world's most powerful supercomputer approximately 10,000 years.

Strategies

The journey toward quantum supremacy required a combination of various strategic initiatives from Google. The company invested significantly in research and development, channeling its resources toward experimenting with and refining quantum technologies. Additionally, Google recognized the value of collaborative efforts, partnering with academic institutions to foster a rich, knowledge-sharing environment.

The company also adopted an open-source approach, launching Cirq, an open-source framework for running algorithms on the noisy intermediate-scale quantum (NISQ) computers of today. Such an approach encourages collective innovation in the field, promoting a faster and more holistic development process.

Opportunities

Quantum computing has the potential to revolutionize industries such as pharmaceuticals, energy, finance, and artificial intelligence by solving problems that are currently considered unattainable by even the most potent classical computers.

In healthcare and pharmaceuticals, quantum computing could enable the design of new drugs and personalized treatments by analyzing and understanding DNA sequences and molecular structures. In finance, it can optimize trading strategies, model financial markets, and manage risk better. In the energy sector, quantum computing can enable efficient energy use and better management of resources.

Conclusion

While Google's attainment of quantum supremacy is a commendable milestone, the journey toward the practical and widespread application of quantum computers is still in its early stages. The technology, while teeming with potential, also presents considerable technical and ethical challenges that must be resolved. The evolution of quantum computing, from its current status to becoming an integral part of technological infrastructure, demands continued research, collaboration, and regulatory oversight.

INDUSTRY CONTEXT

The field of quantum computing, although still in its nascent stage, is transforming the landscape of computing technology. It is capturing the interest of major tech companies like Google, who are investing significantly in this revolutionary technology. Google's achievement of quantum supremacy marks a significant breakthrough, signifying a shift from the theoretical to the practical applicability of quantum computing.

CHALLENGES

- Technical Challenges: Building a stable and scalable quantum computer is technically complex due to issues such as quantum decoherence.
- Lack of Skilled Professionals: The field is so new and specialized that there is a lack of skilled quantum engineers and scientists.
- Ethical and Security Concerns: Quantum computing could potentially break current encryption algorithms, leading to security issues.

LESSONS LEARNED

- Investment in R&D: The pursuit of disruptive technologies like quantum computing requires substantial investment in research and development.
- Collaborative Approach: Success in complex fields like quantum computing requires a collaborative approach, involving academia, industry, and sometimes even open-source communities.

QUESTIONS

1. What are the key factors that have contributed to Google's achievement of quantum supremacy?
2. How might the development of quantum computing impact other sectors like cybersecurity, AI, or healthcare?
3. Given the technical and ethical challenges associated with quantum computing, what strategies can companies like Google adopt to ensure responsible development and use of this technology?

UN SDGs: Quality education (4); Industry, innovation, and infrastructure (9)

RESOURCES

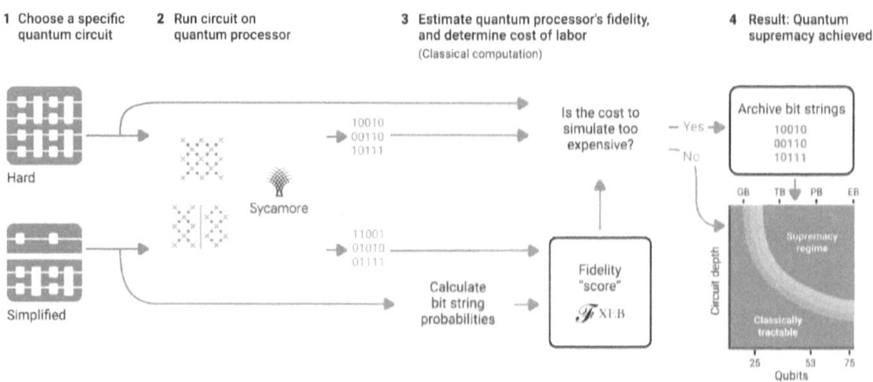

Source: Google Research

REFERENCES

1. https://www.nature.com/articles/d41586-019-03213-z
2. https://techcrunch.com/2022/08/05/googles-quantum-supremacy-usurped-by-researchers-using-ordinary-supercomputer/
3. https://ai.googleblog.com/2019/10/quantum-supremacy-using-programmable.html

Navigating the New Era of Hybrid Instruction

Themes: Hybrid, Learning, Teaching, Blended

TEACHING OBJECTIVES

The case study is intended to qualify students to:

- Understand the concept and importance of hybrid instruction in the context of modern education.
- Explore the benefits, challenges, and strategies associated with implementing hybrid instruction.
- Analyze the opportunities presented by hybrid instruction for the future of learning and teaching.

SYNOPSIS

Hybrid teaching will comprise a fusion of on-campus and digital activities, where learners may have the ability to join on-campus classes, digital classes in the same time frame, or digital classes at diversified time zones. The educational landscape is undergoing rapid transformation due to advancements in technology and recent global events such as the COVID-19 pandemic. One prominent trend is the shift towards hybrid instruction – an educational model that combines traditional face-to-face classroom teaching with online learning. This case study will dissect the components of hybrid instruction and delve into its potential to reshape the future of education.

Advantages

Hybrid instruction offers an array of advantages. It provides flexibility to learners, enabling them to learn at their own pace and time. It also allows for personalized learning experiences, catering to individual students' learning styles and needs. Moreover, it reduces geographical and time constraints, making education more accessible to a wider audience.

Strategies

Successful implementation of hybrid instruction involves various strategies. These include effective course design that integrates in-person and online activities seamlessly, training educators to proficiently use technology and online teaching methodologies, and ensuring learners have the necessary resources and support to engage in online learning. Additionally, maintaining open channels of communication and fostering a sense of community is crucial in a hybrid learning environment.

Opportunities

The rise of hybrid instruction presents numerous opportunities for educational institutions, teachers, and students. It opens avenues for innovative teaching practices, such as flipped classrooms and collaborative online projects. It can also enhance students' digital literacy skills, which are increasingly becoming crucial in the modern workforce.

Conclusion

As we navigate the new era of hybrid instruction, it is essential to embrace the opportunities it offers while tackling its challenges head-on. Hybrid instruction, when executed effectively, can democratize education, enhance learning experiences, and prepare students for a progressively digital world.

INDUSTRY CONTEXT

The education industry is undergoing a significant shift, driven by technology and necessitated by situations like the COVID-19 pandemic. This shift has led to the growing adoption of blended or hybrid learning models that integrate traditional in-person classroom experiences with digital learning platforms. As hybrid learning becomes more prominent, educators and institutions need to understand its intricacies and potential impacts.

CHALLENGES

- Digital divide: The uneven distribution of technology access among students can lead to disparities in learning experiences.
- Maintaining student engagement: Keeping students motivated and engaged in an online learning environment can be difficult.
- Educator training: Teachers may lack the necessary skills or experience to effectively deliver hybrid instruction.

LESSONS LEARNED

- Hybrid instruction can significantly enhance learning flexibility and accessibility but necessitates adequate technological resources and support.
- The success of a hybrid model heavily relies on a well-structured curriculum that effectively integrates online and in-person elements, and the readiness of educators to adapt to this new teaching paradigm.

QUESTIONS

1. What role can educational institutions play in ensuring equitable access to the necessary technology for hybrid instruction?
2. How can teachers maintain student engagement and foster a sense of community in a hybrid learning environment?

3. In what ways can hybrid instruction prepare students for the digital demands of the modern workforce?

UN SDGs: Health and well-being (3); Quality education (4); Sustainable cities and communities (11)

RESOURCES

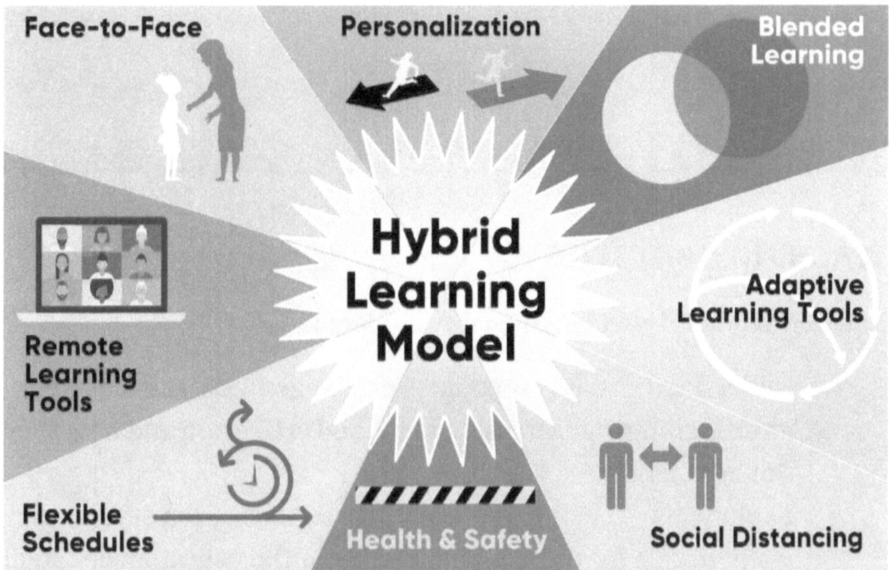

Source: esheninger

REFERENCES

1. Limone, P. (2021). Towards a hybrid ecosystem of blended learning within university contexts. In *CEUR Workshop Proc.*
2. Lockee, B. B. (2021). Online education in the post-COVID era. *Nature Electronics*, 4(1), 5-6.
3. https://feedbackfruits.com/blog/4-tips-to-prepare-for-a-new-phase-of-hybrid-learning

Overcoming the Challenges of Hybrid Teaching: A Solution Guide

Themes: Hybrid, Teaching, Blended, Challenges, Opportunities

TEACHING OBJECTIVES

The case study is intended to qualify students to:

- Understand the specific challenges associated with implementing hybrid teaching in the UAE region and how they can be overcome.
- Explore the benefits and potential strategies for successfully integrating hybrid teaching methods in the educational system of the UAE.
- Critically evaluate the opportunities for future development and growth in the field of hybrid teaching within the UAE's specific cultural and technological context.

SYNOPSIS

This case study delves into the increasingly popular concept of hybrid teaching, focusing on its adoption and implementation in the United Arab Emirates (UAE). Hybrid learning is a teaching approach that combines remote and in-person learning, providing the benefits of both. As global education systems gravitate towards blended learning models, the UAE is also stepping up to adapt to this shift. However, the country's distinct socio-cultural context and technological ecosystem create a unique set of challenges that must be addressed for the successful realization of hybrid instruction.

Advantages

Hybrid teaching holds many benefits, offering a flexible learning environment that merges the best facets of online and in-person teaching. In the context of the UAE, it represents an opportunity to seamlessly embed technology into education and extend high-quality learning opportunities to students across different emirates, even the most remote ones. This format also serves to prepare students for a world increasingly dominated by digital interactions and remote collaborations.

Strategies

Strategic measures are paramount in overcoming the hurdles associated with hybrid teaching in the UAE. One of the foremost steps is enhancing the technological infrastructure to support ubiquitous, reliable internet access and supply the necessary digital devices to all learners. Simultaneously, teachers require robust training programs to develop digital literacy and understand the pedagogical shifts needed for effective hybrid instruction. Curriculum development should also account for hybrid delivery, ensuring the learning objectives can be achieved through a combination of in-person and online methods. Furthermore, fostering a supportive culture that values and encourages digital learning is critical to driving the acceptance and success of the hybrid teaching model.

Opportunities

The adoption of hybrid teaching opens up a realm of opportunities for the UAE. The country stands a chance to be a frontrunner in digital education within the Middle East region, further strengthening its position on the global educational stage. Additionally, the digital competencies that students acquire through this teaching model align well with the UAE's vision of evolving into a knowledge-based economy. The emergence of hybrid teaching could also stimulate the growth of EdTech start-ups and generate new job roles, thereby contributing to economic diversification.

Conclusion

While hybrid teaching presents its unique set of challenges in the UAE context, strategic planning, and determined execution can enable the successful navigation of these hurdles. As the UAE continues its digital transformation journey, the adoption of hybrid teaching will be integral to molding the future of education in the country, positioning it as a pioneer of educational innovation in the region. The transition may be complex, but the potential rewards in terms of student engagement, accessibility of education, and future readiness are vast.

INDUSTRY CONTEXT

With the global shift towards digitalization, the UAE's education industry is increasingly recognizing the potential of hybrid teaching methods. These methods combine online and face-to-face teaching, promising enhanced accessibility, flexibility, and improved learning experiences. However, implementing this approach presents unique challenges due to regional factors, such as technology infrastructure readiness and cultural attitudes toward digital learning.

CHALLENGES

- Inconsistent access to reliable internet and technology resources across the region.
- Lack of familiarity or comfort with digital learning tools among some educators.
- Resistance to change, given the traditional classroom teaching model's cultural dominance.

LESSONS LEARNED

- Technology infrastructure and teacher training are crucial for the successful implementation of hybrid teaching methods.
- The cultural adaptation of hybrid teaching methods is as essential as its technical implementation.

QUESTIONS

1. How can the government and educational institutions collaborate to improve the technological infrastructure necessary for hybrid teaching?
2. What strategies can be adopted to facilitate the transition of teachers and students toward hybrid learning methods?
3. How can the success of hybrid teaching implementation be evaluated and measured in the UAE context?

UN SDGs: Health and well-being (3); Quality education (4); Sustainable cities and communities (11)

RESOURCES

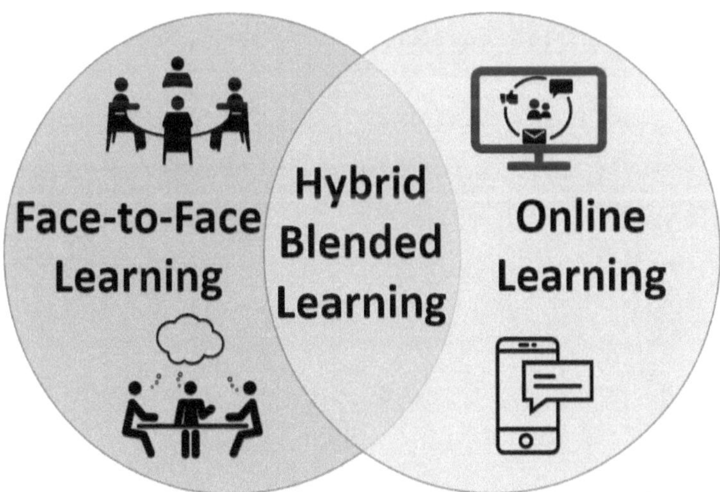

Source: eiu.edu

REFERENCES

1. Adedoyin, O. B., & Soykan, E. (2020). Covid-19 pandemic and online learning: the challenges and opportunities. *Interactive learning environments*, 1-13.

2. Beutner, M., & Pechuel, R. (2020, November). The DISK Online Streaming Concept for Hybrid Learning–Dealing with the challenges of COVID-19 in learning settings. In *Innovate Learning Summit* (pp. 511-519). Association for the Advancement of Computing in Education (AACE).

3. https://myviewboard.com/blog/education/4-challenges-of-hybrid-learning-and-how-to-overcome-them/

Canva's Design Revolution: Democratizing Graphic Design for All

Themes: Technology, Canva, Graphic Design, Accessibility

TEACHING OBJECTIVES

The case study is intended to qualify students to:

- Understand how Canva has revolutionized graphic design by making it accessible and user-friendly.
- Analyze the strategies and business models that have contributed to Canva's success in democratizing design.
- Evaluate the opportunities and challenges that Canva faces in its quest to further expand and enhance its influence in the graphic design industry.

SYNOPSIS

This case study begins by exploring Canva's mission of empowering everyone to design. It unveils the company's inception story and evolution from a humble startup to one of the world's top tech companies. The motive behind Canva's establishment was to fill the market gap for an intuitive and accessible platform for both design novices and professionals.

Advantages

Canva's innovative approach has drastically democratized the domain of graphic design. Its user-friendly platform allows individuals and businesses alike to create professional-grade graphics without the need for extensive design expertise. For businesses, especially small and medium enterprises, this has been transformative, allowing them to develop aesthetically compelling content without a dedicated design team. Individuals too have experienced a new wave of creativity fostered by Canva's accessible tools.

Strategies

Canva's business strategies have played a vital role in its success. Central to this is its freemium business model, allowing users free access to basic features while charging for premium tools and resources. This has enabled the company to monetize its offerings effectively while ensuring widespread access. Canva's emphasis on user-centric design and innovation has kept user engagement high and has fostered loyalty. Strategic partnerships and integrations have also been key to Canva's expansion, adding to its feature set and broadening its global user base.

Opportunities

Canva has leveraged and continues to leverage emerging technologies like AI to enhance the user experience. AI aids in providing personalized design recommendations, saving time, and improving output quality. Simultaneously, Canva has been eyeing opportunities in the realms of 3D design and augmented reality, ensuring it remains ahead of the curve. Moreover, Canva's educational initiatives, such as design courses for students, have become a significant driving force in cultivating a design-savvy user base.

Conclusion

Reflecting on Canva's journey, it's clear how effectively the company has democratized design, harnessing simplicity, user-centric design, and strategic growth to disrupt a traditionally complex, professional-dominated industry. Looking forward, Canva stands as a strong contender in the market with constant innovation and an emphasis on user needs. The story of Canva serves as an inspiring narrative for tech companies aspiring to democratize their services and cater to a diverse user base.

INDUSTRY CONTEXT

In an increasingly digital world, the importance of graphic design has never been more apparent. Businesses and individuals alike rely on quality graphic design to communicate their messages effectively. Canva, a graphic design platform, has revolutionized this space, making professional-level design accessible to all through its user-friendly interface and robust feature set.

CHALLENGES

- Maintaining a balance between simplicity for beginners and providing advanced features for professional designers.
- Ensuring seamless performance and uptime as user base and feature set grow.
- Staying competitive in an increasingly crowded space of online design tools.

LESSONS LEARNED

- A user-centric approach, backed by a robust freemium model, can effectively democratize traditionally complex tasks.
- Continuous innovation and strategic partnerships are critical to maintaining and expanding influence in a rapidly evolving digital industry.

QUESTIONS

1. How has Canva's democratization of design impacted the wider graphic design industry?
2. What further innovations could Canva introduce to continue its growth and maintain its competitive edge?
3. How can Canva continue to cater to both novice and professional designers as it expands its user base and features?

UN SDGS: Industry, innovation, and infrastructure (9); Peace, justice, and strong institutions (16)

RESOURCES

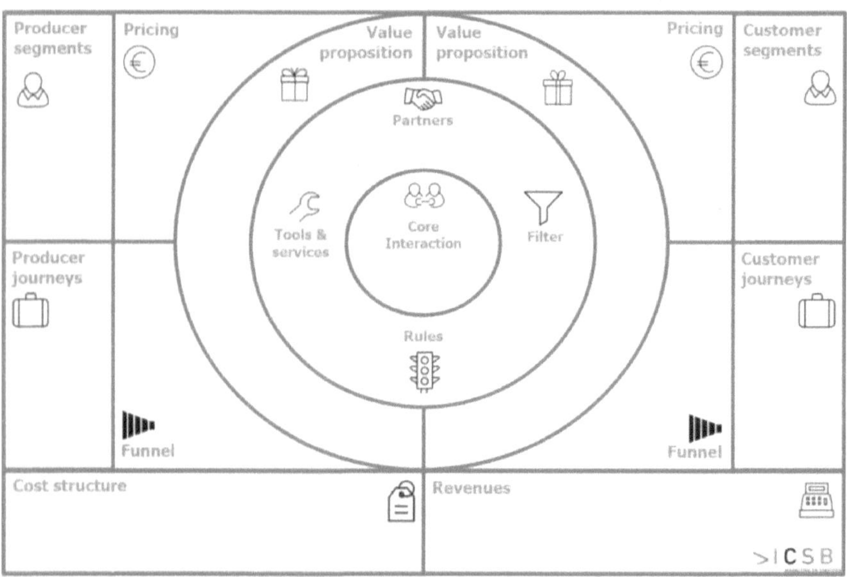

Source: The Canvas Revolution

REFERENCES

1. https://dropoutdudes.com/canva-guide-designing-tools-for-startups/
2. https://www.canva.com/learn/ultimate-guide-history-graphic-design/
3. https://bootcamp.uxdesign.cc/case-study-evolution-of-canva-25d51c37198

Future of Work: Trello's Impact on Project Management

Themes: Project Management, Innovation, Application, Digital Era

TEACHING OBJECTIVES

The case study is intended to qualify students to:

- To understand the role of project management tools like Trello in shaping the future of work.
- To explore how Trello has changed the landscape of project management.
- To discuss the challenges and opportunities involved in implementing Trello in various work environments.

SYNOPSIS

In the age of digital transformation, project management tools like Trello have become crucial components of efficient business operations. Trello's intuitive and visual approach to task organization and team collaboration has positioned it as one of the industry leaders in the realm of project management software. The case study delves into Trello's impact on work dynamics, how its unique design and function have helped businesses overcome traditional project management limitations, and how it's paving the way for future practices.

Advantages

Trello offers numerous benefits that redefine project management paradigms. Its Kanban-style layout promotes easy visualization of work progress and task assignments, fostering a transparent work environment. Further, the flexibility it affords in terms of user roles, card creation, and movement allows projects to be tailored according to specific team needs and changes. Moreover, Trello's integrative capabilities with various apps and platforms make it an even more powerful tool, enhancing its functionality and user experience.

Strategies

Successful integration of Trello into business operations requires strategic implementation. First and foremost, there needs to be an understanding of its capabilities and how they align with the business's needs. Training employees on how to use Trello effectively, not only as individual users but also in terms of team collaboration, is crucial. Further, encouraging a culture of open feedback can help businesses identify any hiccups in the transition process, enabling improvements to be made continuously. Finally, regular usage audits can help ensure that Trello is being used to its full potential and delivering the expected productivity gains.

Opportunities

The increasing trend of remote work and digital collaboration presents abundant opportunities for Trello. As businesses seek more efficient and flexible project management solutions, Trello can continue to evolve its offerings. Innovations in AI and machine learning can also provide opportunities for Trello to improve task automation, predictive capabilities, and more customized user experiences.

Conclusion

Trello's emergence as a powerful tool in the project management space signifies a larger shift towards digital, flexible, and collaborative work environments. While challenges may arise during its implementation, they can be addressed with well-planned strategies and ongoing support. As organizations adapt to the changing world of work, tools like Trello will undoubtedly play a significant role in shaping the future of project management.

INDUSTRY CONTEXT

The project management industry has been revolutionized by digital solutions. In an era where remote and flexible working is becoming the norm, tools like Trello are central to coordinating tasks, improving communication, and ensuring productivity. Amid the digital transformation, organizations are actively seeking out solutions that can help streamline their operations and foster collaboration, making project management tools indispensable in the modern workplace.

CHALLENGES

- Resistance to change: Some employees may resist adopting a new system like Trello, sticking to traditional methods of project management.
- Learning curve: Though Trello is user-friendly, some team members may struggle with understanding and using its features effectively.
- Data security: With important project information being stored and shared on the platform, data security remains a significant concern.

LESSONS LEARNED

- Effective training is crucial to successfully implement a new project management tool like Trello.
- Flexibility and ease of use are key factors in the success of a project management tool.

QUESTIONS

1. How has Trello changed the dynamics of project management?
2. What are some specific challenges that an organization might face when implementing Trello?
3. How can Trello adapt to the changing needs of project management in the future?

UN SDGS: Quality Education (4); Industry, innovation, and Infrastructure (9); Sustainable Cities and Communities (11)

RESOURCES

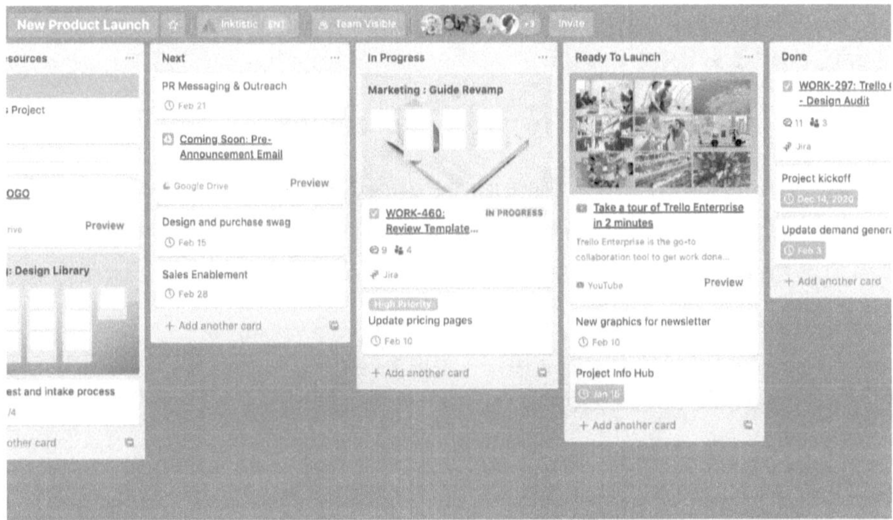

Source: Trello

REFERENCES

1. https://blog.trello.com/future-of-trello
2. https://www.protocol.com/workplace/atlassian-future-work-productivity-expert
3. https://www.theverge.com/2021/2/16/22284873/trello-redesign-new-cards-board-views-remote-work-future

SpaceX's Journey to the Stars: Reimagining Space Travel

Themes: Travel, Innovation, Technology, Tourism

TEACHING OBJECTIVES

The case study is intended to qualify students to:

- Understand SpaceX's unique approach to space travel and the innovation it brought to the industry.
- Analyze the strategic decisions SpaceX made to disrupt the space industry.
- Evaluate the opportunities and challenges that SpaceX faces in its quest to make space travel accessible.

SYNOPSIS

SpaceX, under the leadership of Elon Musk, has emerged as a game-changer in the realm of space travel, revolutionizing the sector that was once the dominion of governmental entities. The company's ambitious vision to make space travel accessible and its commitment to innovation have set it on a trajectory unlike any other in the industry. This case study examines SpaceX's journey, analyzing its innovative strategies, evaluating its advantages, and delving into the challenges it has faced and the opportunities it seeks.

Advantages

SpaceX's primary advantage lies in its groundbreaking reusable rocket technology, which significantly reduces the cost of space missions. This has not only granted it a competitive edge but also enabled the company to disrupt the market and alter the rules of the game. Moreover, its capability to conduct frequent launches allows for more data, enhancing its learning curve and operational efficiency.

Strategies

SpaceX's strategy was two-fold: first, to establish a reliable and cost-effective satellite launch service, and second, to leverage that business to fund the development of more ambitious projects, like Starship. The company's emphasis on vertical integration allowed it to maintain control over its supply chain and reduce costs, while its focus on iterative design enabled rapid testing and improvement of its technologies.

Opportunities

The commercialization of space travel presents an abundance of opportunities for SpaceX. Beyond satellite launches, the company can tap into markets such as space tourism, lunar and Mars missions, and even point-to-point travel on Earth. Additionally, SpaceX's Starlink project, aimed at providing global broadband coverage, opens up a new sector of potential revenue.

Conclusion

SpaceX's journey thus far paints a promising picture of what space travel could become – a viable, accessible venture. The company's innovative approach and daring ambitions have set it apart from its competitors, making it a key player in shaping the future of space exploration. Nevertheless, it must navigate the challenges and uncertainties that come with this largely untapped domain, as it strives to realize its vision.

INDUSTRY CONTEXT

The space industry has been undergoing a significant transformation over the past two decades. Traditionally dominated by government-funded entities, the sector is seeing increased participation from private companies. This change has been propelled by advancements in technology, policy shifts encouraging private sector participation, and declining launch costs. SpaceX is one of the most notable private companies in this sector, having brought substantial innovation and disruption.

CHALLENGES

- Regulatory hurdles: Securing necessary permits for launching rockets and satellites can be a complicated and time-consuming process.
- Technical complexities: Space travel is fraught with technical difficulties and unforeseen challenges that can result in failures and delays.
- Competitive landscape: While SpaceX is a pioneer in many ways, the space industry is becoming increasingly competitive with other private companies making technological advancements.

LESSONS LEARNED

- Innovation as a differentiator: SpaceX's commitment to innovative technologies, such as reusable rockets, demonstrates how innovation can serve as a potent competitive advantage.
- Strategic risk-taking: The company's bold, long-term vision underscores the potential benefits of strategic risk-taking, despite the high-stakes nature of the space industry.

QUESTIONS

1. How has SpaceX's approach to space travel differed from traditional players in the industry, and what has enabled these differences?

2. In what ways has SpaceX's strategy of vertical integration contributed to its successes and challenges?

3. As the space industry becomes increasingly commercialized, what potential new markets could SpaceX tap into, and what obstacles might it face in doing so?

UN SDGS: Industry, innovation, and infrastructure (9); Partnership for goals (17)

RESOURCES

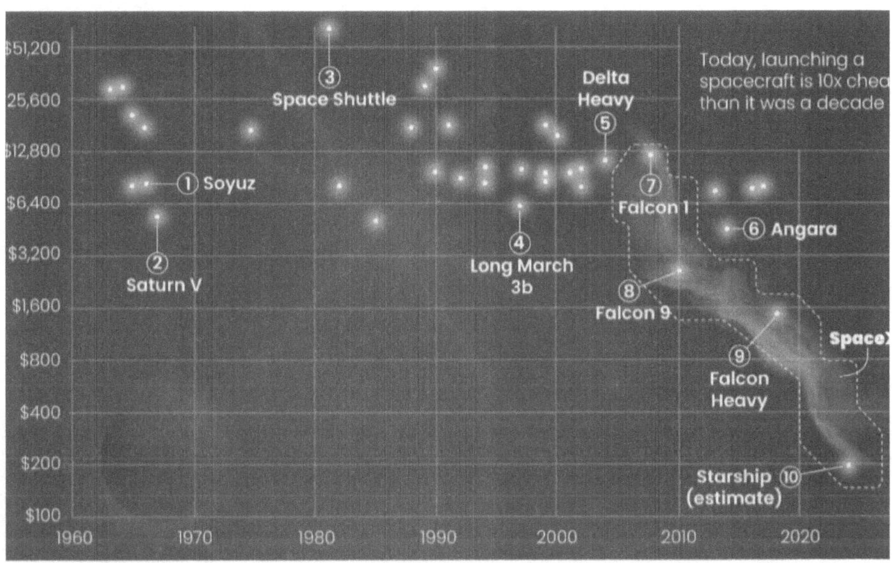

Source: SpaceX

REFERENCES

1. https://www.spacex.com/
2. https://www.visualcapitalist.com/the-cost-of-space-flight/
3. https://www.foxbusiness.com/lifestyle/space-perspective-travel-balloon-liftoff

Case Study **84**

The Role of Biometrics in Security: Apple's Face ID Technology

Themes: Technology, Applications, Facial Recognition, Innovation

TEACHING OBJECTIVES

The case study is intended to qualify students to:

- Understand the role and significance of biometrics in security, focusing on Apple's Face ID technology.
- Analyze the advantages of using biometric technology in enhancing security measures and user experience.
- Evaluate the challenges faced in the implementation and acceptance of biometric technology.
- Synopsis

SYNOPSIS

The utilization of biometrics in security has gained substantial momentum in recent years, with Apple's Face ID technology serving as a pioneering example. Face ID is a facial recognition system designed to replace traditional passcodes, creating a seamless, yet secure, user experience. This case study delves into the introduction of Face ID, the advantages it brought to Apple's product ecosystem, the strategies Apple employed for its adoption, the opportunities it opened, and the conclusion of its impact on the industry.

Advantages

Face ID brought numerous advantages, including an enhanced user experience through quicker and more convenient device access, and improved security by using unique facial features that are hard to replicate. It also strengthened the Apple ecosystem by integrating seamlessly with Apple's suite of services and devices.

Strategies

Apple employed several strategies for the adoption and integration of Face ID. Extensive research and development were conducted to ensure the technology was robust and secure. Apple also prioritized user privacy, ensuring data was encrypted and stored locally on devices. Furthermore, Apple focused on user education to overcome initial resistance and build trust in the new technology.

Opportunities

The successful implementation of Face ID opened various opportunities. It not only set a new standard in device security, but it also paved the way for future applications of biometric technologies in areas like mobile payments and augmented reality.

Conclusion

Face ID marked a significant advancement in the utilization of biometrics for security. Despite initial apprehensions, its successful integration into Apple's product line demonstrated the viability and advantages of biometrics. Moving forward, the continued development of such technologies promises to reshape our interactions with digital devices.

INDUSTRY CONTEXT

The security industry has been consistently evolving, driven by advancements in technology and increasing concerns around data privacy and security. Biometric technology, once a concept confined to science fiction, has now become a significant part of this evolution. It is being used increasingly in various sectors, from mobile devices to airport security, driven by the need for robust, user-friendly security measures.

CHALLENGES

- Privacy concerns: The use of biometric data raises significant privacy concerns, as it involves collecting and processing sensitive personal information.
- Potential for misuse: If biometric data is not properly protected, it can be exploited for identity theft and other malicious activities.
- Technological limitations: While biometric technologies have advanced significantly, they are not foolproof and can have issues with accuracy and reliability.

LESSONS LEARNED

- Importance of user trust: The introduction of Face ID underscores the importance of building user trust when introducing new technologies, particularly those involving sensitive personal data.
- The potential of biometrics: Face ID demonstrates the potential of biometrics in enhancing both security and user experience.

QUESTIONS

1. What were the key factors contributing to the successful adoption of Face ID by Apple's user base?
2. How does Apple manage privacy concerns associated with the use of biometric data in Face ID?
3. What potential future applications and opportunities do you see for biometric technologies, and what challenges might they face?

UN SDGS: Industry, innovation, and infrastructure (9); Partnership for goals (17)

RESOURCES

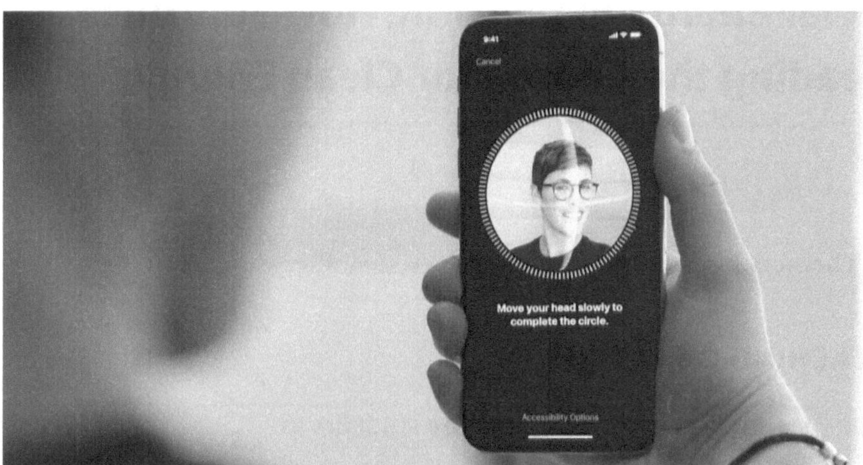

Source: Digital Trends

REFERENCES

1. https://support.apple.com/en-us/HT208108
2. https://blog.passwork.pro/apple-face-id-security/
3. https://www.cnbc.com/2017/09/13/apples-iphone-face-id-security-system-may-prove-unpopular.html

Solar Energy Expansion: How Sunrun is Leading the Charge for Clean Energy

Themes: Innovation, Recycling, Sustainability, Solution

TEACHING OBJECTIVES

The case study is intended to qualify students to:

- Understand the rise and significance of solar energy in the context of global renewable energy initiatives, with a focus on Sunrun's contribution.
- Evaluate the benefits, strategies, and opportunities associated with Sunrun's solar energy expansion.
- Understand the challenges faced by Sunrun and the solar energy sector in the pursuit of clean energy adoption.

SYNOPSIS

The shift towards renewable energy sources is vital to mitigate the escalating impacts of climate change and achieve a sustainable energy future. This case study dives into the journey of Sunrun, a leading provider of residential solar panels, battery storage, and energy services in the United States. The company is at the forefront of the solar energy sector, driving a more sustainable, cost-effective, and reliable energy future.

Advantages

Harnessing solar energy provides significant advantages, ranging from environmental benefits to financial savings. Sunrun, with its customer-centric approach, not only decreases homeowners' carbon footprint but also reduces their electricity bills. Its solar plus storage solution, Brightbox, helps households gain energy independence. During outages, customers can rely on their own solar-powered stored energy, reducing dependence on an often unstable grid.

Strategies

Sunrun's strategies that have contributed to its success and the solar energy sector at large encompass multiple facets. It has championed affordable financing options, eliminating the primary barrier for many households—upfront costs. Their partnerships with utilities and grid operators pave the way for an energy system that's more sustainable, reliable, and cost-effective. Additionally, Sunrun is active in policy advocacy, pushing for reforms that further encourage renewable energy adoption.

Opportunities

Sunrun's pioneering role in the solar industry opens up a world of opportunities. As more people recognize and accept solar energy's potential, it catalyzes job growth in the renewable sector and drives innovative technologies that can further optimize energy use. Sunrun's expansion underscores the potential of solar power in reducing carbon emissions, highlighting its effectiveness in the fight against climate change. Additionally, Sunrun's model provides opportunities for utilities to adapt to the changing energy landscape, moving from being solely energy providers to becoming grid service managers.

Conclusion

Sunrun's influence and progress within the renewable energy sector signify a remarkable advancement in solar energy adoption. As the world continues to seek sustainable energy alternatives, Sunrun's journey offers valuable insights. The company's progress and the subsequent industry growth signify solar power's promising future, suggesting an increasingly vital role in the world's clean energy matrix.

INDUSTRY CONTEXT

The energy industry is experiencing a substantial shift towards renewable resources in response to climate change concerns, government policies, and growing consumer demand for sustainable alternatives. Solar energy, being one of the most abundant and accessible forms of renewable energy, plays a crucial role in this transition, with companies like Sunrun leading the charge.

CHALLENGES

- Regulatory Barriers: Solar companies often face regulatory challenges that can slow adoption and growth.
- High Initial Costs: The high initial costs of solar installations can deter potential customers.
- Grid Integration: Ensuring solar power can be efficiently and effectively integrated into existing power grids is a significant technical challenge.

LESSONS LEARNED

- Accessibility is Key: Offering affordable financing options can significantly boost the adoption of solar energy.
- Advocacy for Policy Support: Actively advocating for favorable policy environments can facilitate the growth of the solar energy industry.

QUESTIONS

1. How has Sunrun contributed to the adoption of solar energy in residential settings?

2. What strategies has Sunrun used to make solar energy more accessible and appealing to consumers?

3. What challenges does Sunrun face, and how might they overcome these to further expand the adoption of solar energy?

UN SDGS: Good health and well-being (3); Climate action (13)

RESOURCES

F-150 Lightning and Ford Intelligent Backup Power

Power your home during an outage with F-150® Lightning™ – and even add a home solar system for carbon-free energy generation. Ford and Sunrun make installing Ford Intelligent Backup Power easy as 1, 2, 3.

1. Place your F-150 Lightning and 80-amp Ford Charge Station Pro order', then contact Sunrun to purchase the Home Integration System and schedule an appointment for installation.

2. Sunrun, America's leading solar company, is the preferred installer of F-150 Lightning home charging solutions and the Home Integration System; interested customers can also have the company install its rooftop solar panels.

3. Plug your F-150 Lightning into Ford Charge Station Pro and enjoy the benefits of bidirectional power delivering the reliability you need, including powering your home with renewable solar energy if you choose that option.

What you need:

 **(A)**
F-150 Lightning

Provides up to 131 kWh of electric energy storage'' with the optional extended-range battery, enough to power the average-size home up to 10 days depending on energy consumption'.

 **(B)**
Ford Charge Station Pro'

Connects the house to the F-150 Lightning charge port to provide up to 80 amps of Level-2 charging and deliver bidirectional power back to the home.

 **(C)**
Home Integration System (Interior)

Acts as a switch to route power where it's needed. That could be from a home solar system to your house or to power the home from your F-150 Lightning.

(D)
Optional Sunrun Solar Energy System

Power your home and charge your F-150 Lightning with zero-carbon solar energy generation.

'80-amp Ford Charge Station Pro is standard on the F-150 Lightning extended-range truck; optional on standard-range. The Home Integration System and related hardware and installation are extra. See Ford.com/trucks/f150/f150-lightning/2022/features/intelligent-backup-power/ for more information.

''Based on manufacturer calculation using computer engineering simulations. Your results may vary.

'When rationing power or in conjunction with solar power and your home is properly equipped and home transfer switch disconnects home from the grid. Based on 30 kilowatt-hours use per day using the F-150 Lightning with the extended-range battery. Your results may vary depending on energy usage. Rationing power assumes limiting the number of devices and turning the truck off when not needed.

Source: Green Car Congress

REFERENCES

1. https://investors.sunrun.com/news-events/press-releases/detail/260/sunrun-celebrates-15-years-leading-the-nations-clean
2. https://cleantechnica.com/2023/02/24/sunrun-installed-almost-a-gigawatt-of-solar-in-2022/
3. https://www.energyjobline.com/company/sunrun-inc

The Intersection of Fashion and Technology: LVMH's Digital Transformation

Themes: Service, Fashion, Market, Transformation, Innovation

TEACHING OBJECTIVES

The case study is intended to qualify students to:

- Understand the significance and challenges of digital transformation in the luxury fashion industry, using LVMH's case.
- Learn about LVMH's digital strategies and how they have revolutionized the brand's global positioning and operations.
- Evaluate the impact and opportunities of digital transformation on the future of the fashion industry.

SYNOPSIS

The luxury fashion industry, once resistant to the digital world, has embraced digital transformation due to changing consumer behaviors and market demands. LVMH, the world's largest luxury goods company, is one such example that has stepped up its digital game. This case study explores the intersections of fashion and technology through the lens of LVMH's digital transformation journey.

Advantages

The digital shift has bestowed LVMH with several advantages. It enabled them to reach a broader audience, personalize customer experiences, and accelerate business processes. Embracing e-commerce platforms has allowed LVMH to mitigate geographical limitations, while social media has enabled them to engage with millennials and Generation Z, a growing customer base.

Strategies

To successfully undergo digital transformation, LVMH implemented various strategies. They heavily invested in their online platforms, optimized their supply chain management through data analytics, and utilized artificial intelligence for better customer service. Furthermore, they created a Chief Digital Officer role, illustrating their commitment to digital progression.

Opportunities

LVMH's digital transformation opened up new opportunities. It led to better brand visibility, consumer connectivity, and insight into consumer behavior. It also paved the way for LVMH to delve into digital innovation, like Virtual Reality (VR) and Augmented Reality (AR), offering unique and immersive shopping experiences.

Conclusion

LVMH's digital transformation journey demonstrates how a luxury brand can embrace technology to enhance its brand value and customer experience. While it has faced its share of challenges, its willingness to adapt has made LVMH a digital pioneer in the luxury fashion industry, indicating a promising future for digital luxury fashion.

INDUSTRY CONTEXT

The fashion industry, especially luxury fashion, has been known for its in-store experiences and personal customer relations. However, with the proliferation of technology and changes in consumer behavior, digital transformation has become an inevitable step for brands to stay relevant. As more customers shift towards online shopping, and social media, and demand personalized experiences, brands must adapt accordingly. The digital transformation journey of brands like LVMH is reshaping the landscape of the luxury fashion industry.

CHALLENGES

- Balancing the exclusivity of luxury fashion while making the brand more accessible digitally.
- Maintaining the same level of personalized customer service online as in physical stores.
- Adapting to the rapidly changing digital landscape and evolving consumer behaviors.

LESSONS LEARNED

- Embracing change is crucial for survival. LVMH's willingness to adapt to the digital world has been a significant factor in its sustained success.
- Digital transformation should be an integral part of a brand's strategy, not just an afterthought or a mere trend to follow.

QUESTIONS

1. How has LVMH's digital transformation influenced its global positioning and customer engagement?
2. How can luxury brands maintain their exclusivity while expanding their digital presence?
3. What future trends can we anticipate in the intersection of fashion and technology?

UN SDGS: Good health and well-being (3); Industry, innovation, and infrastructure (9); Sustainable cities and communities (11)

RESOURCES

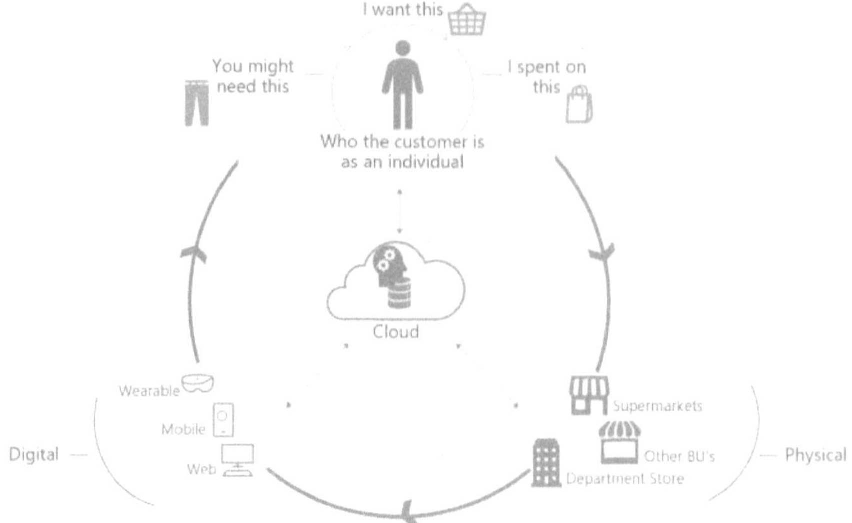

Source: Business Process Incubator

REFERENCES

1. https://www.intelligentautomation.network/transformation/articles/lvmhs-bespoke-approach-to-digital-transformation
2. https://www.heuritech.com/fashion-industry-digital-transformation-innovation/
3. https://www.lvmh.com/news-documents/news/viva-technology-rendezvous-with-the-digital-transformation/

The Impact of Smart Cities on Urban Development: The Case of Songdo, South Korea

Themes: Innovation, Technology, Urban Development, Smart Cities

TEACHING OBJECTIVES

The case study is intended to qualify students to:

- Explore the concept of smart cities and their impact on urban development using Songdo, South Korea as a case study.
- Understand the advantages, strategies, and opportunities presented by the adoption of smart city technologies.
- Analyze the challenges and lessons learned in the development and implementation of a smart city from scratch.

SYNOPSIS

Songdo, South Korea, represents one of the earliest and most ambitious attempts to create a smart city from scratch. The city's design and infrastructure incorporate various digital technologies intended to optimize resource use, improve urban services, and enhance residents' quality of life.

Advantages

The smart city initiative has offered Songdo numerous benefits. The city has one of the most advanced urban infrastructures globally, leading to more efficient resource management, reduced environmental footprint, and improved public services. Furthermore, technologies incorporated into Songdo's design enhance security, transportation, and communication, significantly improving residents' living standards.

Strategies

Songdo's development relied on a comprehensive, technology-centered urban planning approach. The city was designed with a ubiquitous technology network, embedding sensors throughout the city to collect data for managing urban systems effectively. Partnerships with tech companies, innovative urban planning, and investment in sustainable infrastructure have been key strategies in Songdo's smart city evolution.

Opportunities

Songdo's smart city model presents several opportunities. It has become a blueprint for other cities looking to incorporate smart technologies. The data-driven management approach can be leveraged for future urban planning insights. The city's eco-friendly design also aligns with global sustainability efforts, providing a model for sustainable urban development.

Conclusion

The development of Songdo demonstrates the transformative potential of smart cities for urban development. While not without challenges, its accomplishments offer valuable lessons for other cities aiming to integrate smart technologies into their urban planning and management.

INDUSTRY CONTEXT

The concept of smart cities has gained momentum in the context of rapid urbanization and technological advancement. As cities worldwide grapple with population growth, resource management, and sustainability issues, smart technologies offer potential solutions. By embedding digital technology into urban infrastructure, smart cities aim to enhance the efficiency and quality of urban services and improve residents' quality of life.

CHALLENGES

- Overcoming the high costs associated with developing a smart city from scratch.
- Ensuring data privacy and security in a city where data collection is pervasive.
- Achieving sustainable development in a new city while maintaining technological advancement.

LESSONS LEARNED

- Strong partnerships between the public sector, private tech companies, and urban planners are crucial for successful smart city development.
- Technology alone isn't enough; creating a smart city also requires considering sustainability, livability, and citizens' needs.

QUESTIONS

1. What key strategies contributed to Songdo's success as a smart city?
2. How can the model of Songdo be adapted or improved for future smart city projects?
3. How can smart cities balance the need for extensive data collection with ensuring residents' privacy and security?

UN SDGS: Good health and well-being (3); Industry, innovation, and infrastructure (9); Partnership for goals (17)

RESOURCES

Source: Development Education

REFERENCES

1. https://www.rbcwealthmanagement.com/en-ca/insights/how-are-smart-cities-meeting-the-challenges-of-urbanization-in-the-21st-century#:~:text=Smart%20City%20solutions%20span%20a,buildings%2C%20and%20safer%20public%20spaces.

2. https://earth.org/urban-planning-and-smart-cities/

3. https://www.twi-global.com/technical-knowledge/faqs/what-is-a-smart-city

Smart Weather Forecasting: The Power of Machine Learning

Themes: Forecasting, Machine learning, Prediction, Algorithms

TEACHING OBJECTIVES

The case study is intended to qualify students to:

- Understand the role of machine learning in weather forecasting and its advantages over traditional methods.
- Analyze the strategies used in developing and applying machine learning models for weather prediction.
- Evaluate the opportunities, challenges, and lessons learned in the implementation of machine learning in weather forecasting.

SYNOPSIS

The rapid evolution of technology has greatly influenced weather forecasting, with machine learning (ML) emerging as a particularly transformative force. As a subset of artificial intelligence, ML is being used to predict weather patterns with an impressive degree of accuracy. By processing vast amounts of meteorological data and identifying hidden patterns, ML is enabling more reliable and efficient weather forecasting than ever before.

Advantages

Machine learning offers numerous advantages over traditional weather forecasting methods. One such benefit is its ability to process and analyze large datasets in a short time frame, improving forecast speed and accuracy. Unlike traditional models, ML can account for a wide range of factors and their interrelationships, yielding more comprehensive and precise predictions. Furthermore, machine learning is adaptive; it can learn from new data, improving its predictions over time without explicit programming.

Strategies

A variety of strategies are employed in the application of machine learning to weather forecasting. These include meticulous data collection and preprocessing, which involves cleaning the data and handling missing or irrelevant data points. This is followed by the selection of suitable ML algorithms based on the data and forecasting goals. After the model is trained using historical weather data, it undergoes rigorous validation and testing to ensure accuracy and reliability. Lastly, model optimization techniques are employed to enhance the performance and efficiency of the predictive model.

Opportunities

Machine learning's application in weather forecasting offers a myriad of opportunities. It can transform industries heavily reliant on accurate weather predictions, such as agriculture, where it can aid in determining the best times for planting and harvesting, and aviation, where it can help in flight planning. Additionally, it holds great potential in the field of climate research, aiding scientists in understanding the complex dynamics of climate change and forecasting its future impact with greater precision.

Conclusion

Despite facing challenges related to data complexity, reliability, and computational requirements, machine learning's potential in transforming weather forecasting is undeniable. Its successful implementation offers a blueprint for integrating ML in other complex, data-rich fields. As advancements in AI and ML continue to progress, they promise to revolutionize our approach to understanding and predicting weather patterns.

INDUSTRY CONTEXT

The meteorological industry has been keen to adopt technological advancements to improve weather forecasting accuracy and efficiency. Machine learning, with its ability to learn patterns from complex and large-scale datasets, offers a powerful tool for the industry. It has the potential to improve not only weather forecasting but also our understanding of climate patterns and change.

CHALLENGES

- Dealing with the complexity and diversity of weather data, which can be challenging for ML models to process and learn from.
- Ensuring the reliability of ML-based weather forecasts, especially in predicting severe weather events.
- Overcoming computational challenges associated with training ML models on vast and complex weather datasets.

LESSONS LEARNED

- A careful and systematic approach to data preprocessing and model training is crucial for successful ML implementation in weather forecasting.

- Cross-disciplinary collaboration between meteorologists and data scientists can significantly enhance the development and application of ML models in this field.

QUESTIONS

1. How does machine learning contribute to improving the accuracy of weather forecasting?
2. What challenges might arise in applying machine learning models for weather prediction, and how might they be addressed?
3. What sectors stand to benefit most from the improvement in weather forecasting due to machine learning, and why?

UN SDGS: Quality education (4); Decent work and economic growth (8); Industry, innovation, and infrastructure (9)

RESOURCES

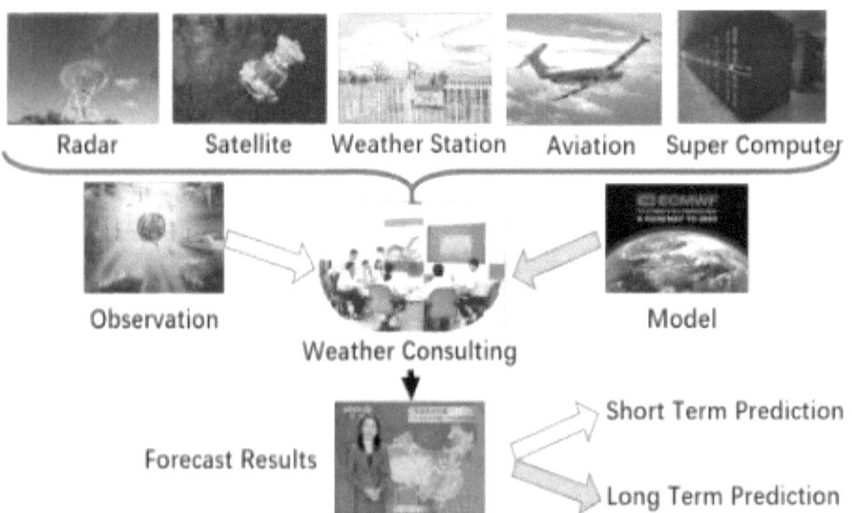

Source: english.cas.cn

REFERENCES

1. Fathi, M., Haghi Kashani, M., Jameii, S. M., & Mahdipour, E. (2021). Big data analytics in weather forecasting: A systematic review. *Archives of Computational Methods in Engineering*, 1-29.
2. Islam, S., Akter, M., & Uddin, M. S. (2021). Design and implementation of an internet of things based low-cost smart weather prediction system. *International Journal of Information Technology, 13*(5), 2001-2010.
3. https://www.researchgate.net/publication/360365118_Smart_Weather_Prediction_Using_Machine_Learning

Artificial Intelligence: Integrating Everyday Technology for a Better Future

Themes: Artificial Intelligence, Routines, Knowledge, Creativity

TEACHING OBJECTIVES

The case study is intended to qualify students to:

- Understand the role of Artificial Intelligence (AI) in enhancing and simplifying everyday technologies.
- Learn about the strategies and tools used in integrating AI into everyday technologies.
- Evaluate the advantages, challenges, and future opportunities associated with the application of AI in everyday technologies.

SYNOPSIS

Today, AI is present in every aspect of our professional and personal virtual lives. International interconnectivity and communication in business are critical domains. It is essential to take advantage of AI and data science, and its possible progress path is not limited. Human knowledge, innovation, intelligence, experience, and creativity are the key drivers for the growth of current and future machine intelligence technologies. Artificial Intelligence (AI) has transitioned from being a high-concept scientific notion to an integral part of everyday technologies. From smartphones and home automation systems to advanced healthcare services and transportation, AI now forms the backbone of numerous daily functionalities. This case study will delve into how AI continues to reshape everyday technology, paving the way for a smarter future.

Advantages

AI brings several advantages to everyday technology. It enhances user experience through personalization, reduces human effort by automating routine tasks, and improves decision-making with data-driven insights. The convenience and efficiency provided by AI-integrated technologies greatly improve productivity and quality of life for users worldwide.

Strategies

The strategies for integrating AI into everyday technology involve careful data management, employing suitable machine learning models, and continuously improving these models based on user feedback and changing demands. Ethics and privacy are crucial considerations in AI implementation, requiring robust security measures and transparency with users about data usage.

Opportunities

The opportunities for AI in everyday technology are expansive. AI holds the potential to further advance areas such as autonomous vehicles, smart homes, intelligent personal assistants, and e-health services. Additionally, AI can contribute to solving complex societal challenges, including climate change, healthcare, and accessibility issues.

Conclusion

While integrating AI into everyday technologies comes with its challenges, such as data privacy concerns and the risk of dependence on automated systems, its advantages, and opportunities outweigh these hurdles. As AI continues to evolve, it holds promise for further enhancing the capabilities of everyday technologies and contributing to a smarter and more convenient future.

INDUSTRY CONTEXT

The era of AI has introduced unprecedented changes in the technology industry. The consumer electronics segment, healthcare, transportation, and home automation are some sectors witnessing the significant impact of AI. As AI's potential continues to be harnessed, it is expected to bring even more revolutionary changes to various industries.

CHALLENGES

- Ensuring data privacy and security in the era of AI-powered technologies.
- Overcoming the technical challenges associated with integrating complex AI systems into small, user-friendly devices.
- Addressing the ethical implications and potential societal impacts of widespread AI integration, including job displacement due to automation.

LESSONS LEARNED

- Privacy and security must be prioritized when implementing AI into everyday technologies to ensure user trust and acceptance.
- Continued advancements in AI call for the need for regulations and ethical guidelines to mitigate potential negative societal impacts.

QUESTIONS

1. How has the integration of AI into everyday technologies influenced our lives, and what future changes can we anticipate?
2. What measures can be taken to address the data privacy concerns associated with AI-powered technologies?
3. How can industries prepare for the ethical and societal implications of AI integration into everyday technologies?

UN SDGS: Good health and well-being (3); Quality education (4); Sustainable cities and communities (11)

RESOURCES

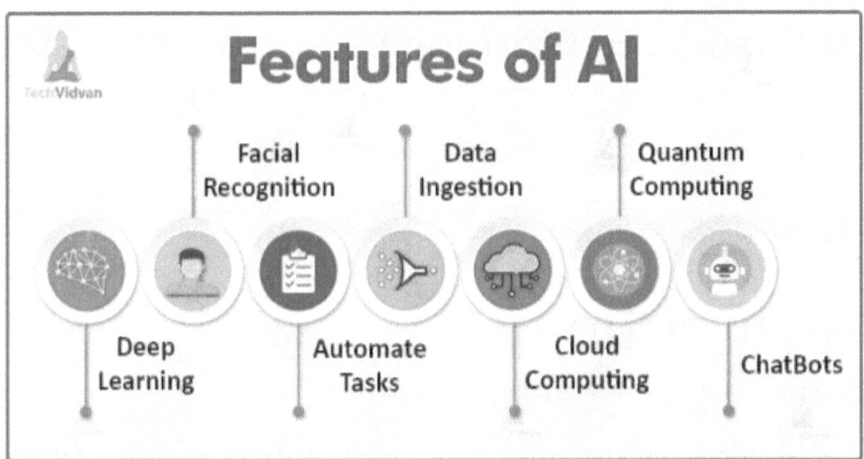

Source: techvidvan.com

REFERENCES

1. Rust, R. T., & Huang, M. H. (2021). The feeling economy: *How artificial intelligence is creating the era of empathy*. Cham, Switzerland: Palgrave Macmillan.

2. Zaman, S., Alhazmi, K., Aseeri, M. A., Ahmed, M. R., Khan, R. T., Kaiser, M. S., & Mahmud, M. (2021). Security threats and artificial intelligence based countermeasures for internet of things networks: a comprehensive survey. *Ieee Access, 9*, 94668-94690.

3. https://builtin.com/artificial-intelligence/artificial-intelligence-future

Drone Delivery: Amazon Prime Air's Quest for Speed and Efficiency

Themes: Prime, Drone Delivery, Customer service, Logistics

TEACHING OBJECTIVES

The case study is intended to qualify students to:

- Understand the concept of drone delivery and its practical applications in the e-commerce industry, focusing on Amazon Prime Air.
- Learn about the strategies, technological requirements, and regulatory hurdles in implementing a drone delivery system.
- Analyze the potential advantages, challenges, and future opportunities for drone delivery in the global e-commerce sector.

SYNOPSIS

The Camera Shield is a novel product that uses a magnetic lock and is compatible with all types of mobile devices. It is easy to use and highly secure, and can be removed with a single master key. The value proposition of the product is that hotels and event organizers can offer greater privacy to their guests, which can lead to more bookings and reduce the risk of legal liability. The company offers two extra camera shields per contract, and in the event of any issues, the client can inform the company through social media or customer service. The staff will then record the client's name, date, time, location, and the number of camera shields required. The company has worked to develop a camera shield that is suitable for all mobile devices, easy to use, highly secure, and can be removed with a single master key.

INDUSTRY CONTEXT

The integration of drone technology in the delivery sector has been a trending topic within the logistics and e-commerce industries. By my knowledge cutoff in September 2021, Amazon was one of the leading players working to make drone delivery a reality. Their Prime Air project was a bold move to redefine the e-commerce delivery landscape and increase their competitive edge in the market.

CHALLENGES

- Meeting strict regulatory and safety requirements for operating drones in various jurisdictions.
- Ensuring security and preventing theft during drone deliveries.
- Overcoming technical challenges such as limited battery life, payload capacity, and navigation in varied weather conditions.

LESSONS LEARNED

- Innovation and technological advancement are key to staying competitive in the rapidly evolving e-commerce industry.
- Collaboration with regulatory authorities is essential for pioneering initiatives like drone delivery, ensuring safety and compliance with laws.

QUESTIONS

1. How might the widespread use of drone delivery reshape the e-commerce industry?
2. What measures could be taken to ensure the security and reliability of drone deliveries?

3. How can companies and regulators collaborate to address the challenges and maximize the benefits of drone delivery technology?

UN SDGS: Good health and well-being (3); Sustainable cities and communities (11)

RESOURCES

Source: USA Today

REFERENCES

1. https://www.aboutamazon.com/news/transportation/a-drone-program-taking-flight
2. https://depts.washington.edu/sctlctr/news-events/in-the-news/amazon-drone-delivery-really-all-environmentally-friendly
3. https://www.thenationalnews.com/business/technology/2022/11/11/amazon-to-start-drone-deliveries-in-california-and-texas-this-year/

The Growth of Telehealth: Amwell's Telemedicine Services

Themes: Telehealth, Telemedicine, Technology, Virtual

TEACHING OBJECTIVES

The case study is intended to qualify students to:

- Understand the rise and development of telehealth, focusing on the services offered by Amwell.
- Analyze the strategic considerations, technological underpinnings, and regulatory compliance necessary to deliver telemedicine services.
- Evaluate the potential benefits, challenges, and future opportunities in telehealth from both healthcare providers and patients' perspectives.

SYNOPSIS

The introduction of telehealth has drastically transformed the dynamics of healthcare, offering unprecedented accessibility and efficiency. This case study probes into the journey of Amwell, a global leader in telehealth. This sector's growth has been fueled by technological innovation and a changing healthcare landscape where patients seek convenience and safety. With Amwell at the epicenter of this digital transformation, the case study explores the company's vision, its value proposition, and how it leverages technology to redefine healthcare.

Advantages

The advent of telehealth brings significant benefits to the healthcare ecosystem. It ushers in a new era of accessibility, especially for individuals in remote areas or those with limitations that hinder mobility. Further, telehealth allows more efficient use of medical resources, potential cost savings, and enhanced patient engagement. It makes healthcare a matter of a few clicks, eliminating geographic boundaries. Amwell's platform stands as a testament to these benefits, providing a conduit for patients to connect with a broad range of healthcare professionals. It efficiently removes the need for travel and slashes wait times, making healthcare more patient-friendly.

Strategies

Amwell's success in the telehealth space can be traced back to its strategic and operational maneuvers. To ensure a secure and reliable telemedicine service, Amwell has developed robust digital platforms that adhere to patient privacy norms and regulatory requirements. Simultaneously, the company forges strategic partnerships with traditional healthcare providers. The integration of Amwell's technology with these providers' existing systems broadens their outreach while ensuring a seamless patient experience, which is a crucial factor in healthcare delivery today.

Opportunities

As technology continues to evolve at breakneck speed, the realm of possibilities for telehealth is continually expanding. The potential integration of advanced technologies, such as artificial intelligence, could lead to improved predictive healthcare, making preventive care more feasible and efficient. Further, there is room for the extension of telehealth services into new medical specialties, including psychiatry and dermatology. Moreover, the utilization of telehealth services for continuous patient monitoring and routine follow-ups has the potential to revolutionize long-term care.

Conclusion

While the journey of telehealth does have its share of roadblocks, such as ensuring equal access for all and dealing with regulatory inconsistencies across regions, the benefits are too significant to overlook. The domain of telehealth is brimming with potential, and companies like Amwell, driving this change, continue to push boundaries. As they forge the path, their work is setting the stage for the next evolution in healthcare, one where technology and healthcare converge to provide superior care.

INDUSTRY CONTEXT

Telehealth, an innovative intersection of healthcare and technology, has been steadily growing over the past decade. However, the COVID-19 pandemic greatly accelerated its adoption as it became a crucial tool for maintaining healthcare provision while minimizing virus exposure. Companies like Amwell have played a pivotal role in enabling this shift and continuing to shape the telehealth landscape.

CHALLENGES

- Ensuring reliable and equitable access to the internet and technology for all patients to benefit from telehealth.
- Navigating regulatory and licensing complexities that vary across states and countries.
- Maintaining the quality of care and patient-doctor relationship in a virtual setting.

LESSONS LEARNED

- The integration of technology in healthcare can greatly enhance access to medical services and improve efficiency.
- Adapting to and meeting regulatory requirements in a rapidly evolving field is crucial for the sustainable growth of telehealth services.

QUESTIONS

1. How can telehealth services bridge the gap in healthcare access for remote and underserved communities?
2. What measures can be taken to ensure that the quality of care is not compromised in a virtual healthcare setting?
3. How might the integration of artificial intelligence and other advanced technologies further enhance telehealth services?

UN SDGS: Good health and well-being (3); Sustainable cities and communities (11); Partnership for goals (17)

RESOURCES

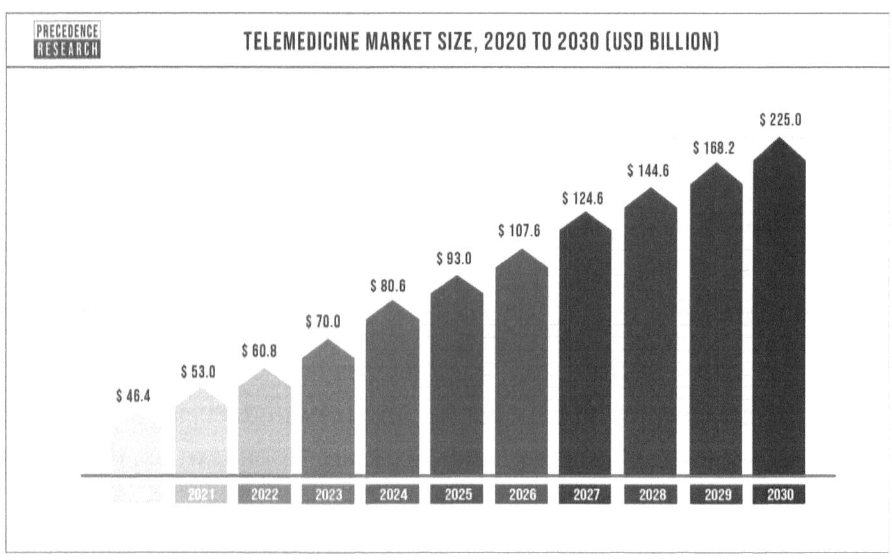

Source: Precedene Research

REFERENCES

1. https://business.amwell.com/about-us/news/press-releases/2020/new-amwell-research-finds-telehealth-use-will-accelerate-post-pandemic

2. https://www.fiercehealthcare.com/health-tech/amwell-sees-strong-demand-telehealth-visits-losses-deepen-q1
3. https://www.pymnts.com/healthcare/2023/amwell-says-re-platforming-is-driving-increased-use-of-its-telehealth-tools/

Digital Twins in Industry 4.0: The Case of GE Digital

Themes: Digital, Technology, Customers, Operations, Innovation

TEACHING OBJECTIVES

The case study is intended to qualify students to:

- Understand the concept of Digital Twins in the context of Industry 4.0 and its significance in the modern industrial setup.
- Analyze how GE Digital leverages Digital Twins technology to optimize its operations and offer innovative solutions.
- Discuss the potential challenges and opportunities presented by Digital Twins technology and its future implications.

SYNOPSIS

Digital Twins, the revolutionary technology that enables the creation of real-time digital counterparts of physical entities, have found a pivotal role in shaping Industry 4.0 and leading the charge is GE Digital. As a leading subsidiary of General Electric, GE Digital has successfully utilized Digital Twins to enhance its operational capabilities and offer superior services. This case study commences with an overview of GE Digital's foray into Digital Twins technology, detailing its integration into its existing framework, thereby signifying the start of a new chapter in industrial optimization.

Advantages

Digital Twins provide a host of advantages that serve to streamline operations and enhance efficiency. By creating an accurate virtual representation of its machinery and systems, GE Digital has been able to facilitate real-time monitoring and analysis, significantly augmenting predictive maintenance protocols. This capability has not only minimized equipment downtime but also optimized performance, resulting in cost reductions and improvements in service quality. This section of the study delves deeper into how GE Digital has harnessed these advantages to redefine its operational metrics and offer innovative solutions.

Strategies

Building upon its existing technological prowess, GE Digital has employed a strategic approach to unlock the full potential of Digital Twins. By incorporating advanced analytics and Artificial Intelligence (AI) within its digital models, the company has boosted its predictive power, thereby enabling improved foresight and risk management. Further, GE Digital continues to invest in refining these digital models to reflect changes in their physical counterparts more accurately. This section explores the strategic approach adopted by GE Digital in its journey toward technological advancement and industry leadership.

Opportunities

The advent of Digital Twins and their successful integration into GE Digital's operations opens up an array of future opportunities. Looking beyond the immediate benefits, the case study expands on the potential of Digital Twins when coupled with emerging technologies like the Internet of Things (IoT) and blockchain. It also elaborates on the broader scope of Digital Twins in other sectors such as healthcare, urban planning, and infrastructure, setting the stage for a future where digitization and simulation go hand-in-hand.

Conclusion

While acknowledging the challenges that come with the territory, the case study concludes on the note that the benefits of Digital Twins outweigh the obstacles. With strategic planning and foresight, these hurdles can be successfully navigated, as exemplified by GE Digital. The conclusion serves as a forward-looking statement on how the convergence of advanced technologies will shape the future of industries, paving the way for an era characterized by innovation, efficiency, and interconnectivity.

INDUSTRY CONTEXT

The concept of Digital Twins is one of the key enablers of the fourth industrial revolution or Industry 4.0. As industries around the world increasingly adopt digitization and automation, the relevance of technologies such as Digital Twins, IoT, AI, and blockchain is magnified. In this rapidly evolving context, Digital Twins stand out as a revolutionary technology that can help businesses create more value, improve efficiency, and innovate faster. Companies like GE Digital are at the forefront of harnessing this technology to create competitive advantages and drive future growth.

CHALLENGES

- Ensuring data privacy and security, given the massive amount of data used in creating and maintaining Digital Twins.
- Achieving accurate and timely synchronization between the physical entity and its digital twin.
- Overcoming technological complexities and skill gaps associated with developing and managing Digital Twins.

LESSONS LEARNED

- Digital Twins technology, when properly implemented and leveraged, can yield significant benefits such as improved efficiency, reduced costs, and enhanced decision-making.

- Continuous refinement and updates are necessary to ensure the Digital Twin accurately represents its physical counterpart, ensuring the reliability of the insights derived.

QUESTIONS

1. How has the implementation of Digital Twins technology impacted GE Digital's operational efficiency and decision-making process?
2. How might the challenges associated with Digital Twins be addressed to ensure the secure and effective use of this technology?
3. In which other sectors or industries do you see the potential for a significant impact of Digital Twins technology, and why?

UN SDGS: Decent work and economic growth (8); Industry, innovation, and infrastructure (9)

RESOURCES

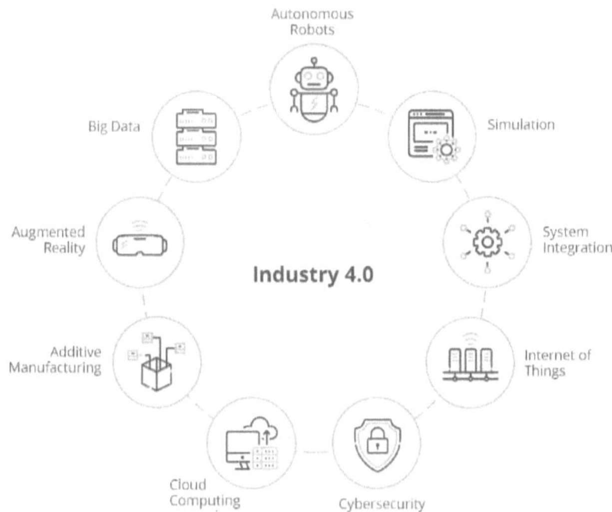

Source: Intellias

REFERENCES

1. Bhatti, G., Mohan, H., & Singh, R. R. (2021). Towards the future of smart electric vehicles: Digital twin technology. *Renewable and Sustainable Energy Reviews, 141*, 110801.
2. https://www.ge.com/digital/applications/digital-twin
3. https://www.ge.com/digital/blog/digital-twins-bridge-between-industrial-assets-and-digital-world

The Future of Sustainable Fashion: Patagonia's Circular Economy Model

Themes: Sustainability, Fashion, Economy, Risk, Model

TEACHING OBJECTIVES

The case study is intended to qualify students to:

- Understand the principles and implications of the circular economy model in the fashion industry.
- Analyze Patagonia's strategic approach to sustainable fashion and its implementation of a circular economy model.
- Identify the challenges, opportunities, and lessons from Patagonia's experience and discuss their applicability to other businesses and industries.

SYNOPSIS

The world is gradually shifting towards sustainable models of production, and the fashion industry is no exception. Patagonia, a renowned outdoor clothing company, has been at the forefront of this change, transforming its business operations to align with the principles of the circular economy. This shift involves a move away from the traditional linear economy of "take-make-waste" towards a circular system of "reduce-reuse-recycle." This case study provides an overview of Patagonia's journey to integrate the circular economy model into its business operations.

Advantages

Adopting a circular economy model has provided Patagonia with multiple advantages. It has helped the company reduce its environmental footprint, align its operations with sustainability goals, and create a brand image as a responsible and ethical business. Moreover, by investing in long-lasting, high-quality products and promoting repair, reuse, and recycling, Patagonia has been able to build strong customer loyalty and differentiate itself in a highly competitive market.

Strategies

Patagonia's strategy for integrating a circular economy model has been multifaceted. It involves designing durable products, encouraging customers to buy used items, offering repair services, and taking back products at the end of their life for recycling. The company has also been transparent about its supply chain and sustainability efforts, educating consumers about the impact of their purchases and advocating for systematic change in the fashion industry.

Opportunities

Patagonia's commitment to the circular economy model opens up significant opportunities for innovation and growth. By focusing on sustainable practices, the company can explore new materials, technologies, and business models that contribute to a circular economy. It also sets the company apart as a leader in sustainable fashion, providing opportunities to influence industry practices and consumer behavior toward more sustainable choices.

Conclusion

Despite the challenges, Patagonia's journey towards a circular economy model demonstrates that businesses can be successful while also being environmentally responsible. The case study concludes by emphasizing the crucial role of companies like Patagonia in transforming the fashion industry and highlighting the need for more businesses to adopt sustainable practices.

INDUSTRY CONTEXT

In recent years, the fashion industry has been under increasing scrutiny for its environmental and social impacts. The industry is one of the largest polluters globally and is known for practices like fast fashion, which contribute to massive waste. Moreover, labor issues in the industry have also been a cause for concern. However, consumer awareness about these issues is growing, and there is a rising demand for more sustainable and ethically produced fashion. Companies like Patagonia that prioritize sustainability in their operations are helping to drive this change in the industry.

CHALLENGES

- Shifting consumer behavior away from fast fashion and encouraging them to buy less, repair, and recycle.
- Sourcing sustainable materials and ensuring ethical labor practices in all stages of the supply chain.
- Balancing the need for profitability with the costs associated with implementing sustainable practices.

LESSONS LEARNED

- Transparent communication with consumers about sustainability efforts and supply chain practices can build trust and loyalty.
- Companies can be drivers of change in consumer behavior and industry practices through their commitment to sustainability.

QUESTIONS

1. How can other businesses in the fashion industry adopt and benefit from a circular economy model?

2. What role can regulatory bodies and governments play in promoting the circular economy in the fashion industry?

3. How might emerging technologies aid in the transition toward a more sustainable fashion industry?

UN SDGS: Quality education (4); Industry, innovation, and infrastructure (9); Sustainable cities and communities (11)

RESOURCES

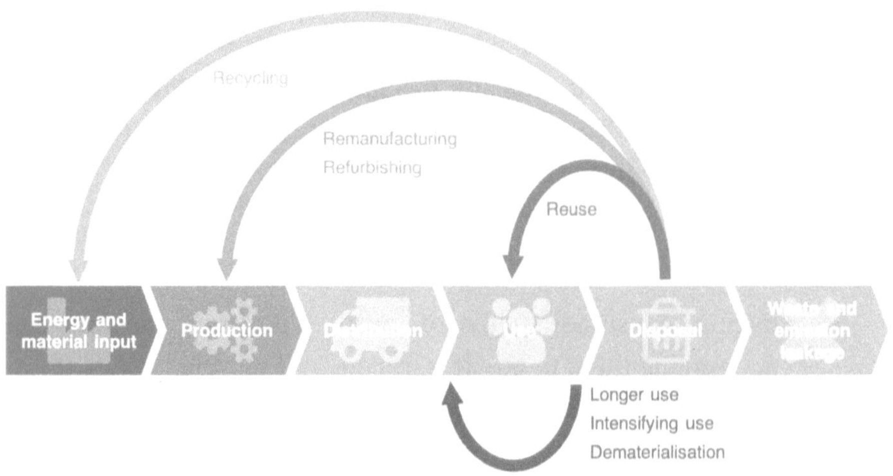

Source: Wikipedia

REFERENCES

1. https://eu.patagonia.com/lt/en/stories/our-quest-for-circularity/story-96496.html

2. https://www.consultancy.uk/news/31228/kearney-finds-patagonia-to-be-worlds-most-circular-brand

3. https://www.businessoffashion.com/articles/sustainability/how-patagonia-transformed-the-circular-economy/

Cloud-based Video Conferencing: Zoom's Rise to Prominence During the Pandemic

Themes: Video Conferencing, Zoom, Technology, Information

TEACHING OBJECTIVES

The case study is intended to qualify students to:

- Understand the importance of using the e-card to get information retrieval services.
- Examine probable challenges faced by developers in preparing the Marhaba Al Saa card.
- Explore strategies used by developers to propose an efficient e-card solution for information retrieval.

SYNOPSIS

The onset of the COVID-19 pandemic marked an unprecedented global shift towards remote work, virtual learning, and online social interaction. Amid this massive change, cloud-based video conferencing platforms became indispensable tools for sustaining business operations, educational continuity, and social connectivity. Among such platforms, Zoom, a relatively under-the-radar entity before the pandemic, catapulted to the forefront, serving as the communication lifeline for millions around the globe.

Advantages

Zoom provides a comprehensive, user-friendly, and high-quality video conferencing solution. It allows users to host multi-participant meetings and offers a suite of features such as screen sharing, recording capabilities, virtual backgrounds, and breakout rooms, setting it apart from many competitors. These features, combined with its compatibility with various devices and operating systems, made Zoom the go-to choice for businesses, educational institutions, and individual users alike. The platform's remarkable scalability also played a crucial role in supporting its swift growth during the pandemic.

Strategies

The unexpected surge in demand presented a unique set of challenges and opportunities. Zoom had to strategize quickly to meet the escalating requirements. The company scaled its infrastructure rapidly, managing a delicate balance between the demand surge and maintaining seamless service. Additionally, Zoom confronted several security and privacy concerns head-on, updating its encryption standards, introducing more user controls, and consistently communicating these changes to its users. This proactive and responsive approach significantly contributed to preserving user trust and satisfaction during a critical period.

Opportunities

The accelerated trend towards remote work and online communication created vast opportunities for Zoom. Despite the intense competition in the digital communication space, Zoom's robust platform offered a launchpad for expansion into other sectors. The company has begun venturing into areas such as webinars, large-scale virtual events, and telehealth services. With the emergence of hybrid working models, Zoom's continued relevance in the post-pandemic world appears promising.

Conclusion

Zoom's meteoric rise during the pandemic underscores the transformative potential of cloud-based video conferencing tools across numerous sectors. It emphasizes the power of a user-centric approach, highlighting the importance of simplicity, reliability, and quality in digital tool adoption. Furthermore, Zoom's journey exemplifies the significance of agility, scalability, and trust in navigating dynamic business landscapes, delivering valuable insights for tech companies operating in a rapidly changing world. The lessons drawn from Zoom's growth trajectory are applicable beyond the realm of video conferencing, resonating with any digital enterprise striving to flourish in the face of rapid change and uncertainty.

INDUSTRY CONTEXT

Before the pandemic, video conferencing tools were largely used in a corporate setting, with occasional use in the personal realm. The sudden onset of COVID-19 necessitated physical distancing, accelerating the adoption of these tools across various sectors, from education and healthcare to entertainment and social interactions. This transformation has led to a rethinking of work models and communication norms, signifying a fundamental change in the industry.

CHALLENGES

- Handling the sudden surge in demand while maintaining service quality.
- Addressing security and privacy concerns arising from the wider usage.
- Navigating competition and differentiation in a rapidly saturating market.

LESSONS LEARNED

- Rapid scalability and agility are crucial in responding to sudden changes in demand.
- Trust and transparency are paramount when dealing with issues of privacy and security.

QUESTIONS

1. How has the rise of platforms like Zoom changed the dynamics of work and communication?
2. What strategies can Zoom implement to maintain its growth post-pandemic?
3. How can Zoom further improve its services to address the evolving needs of remote and hybrid working models?

UN SDGS: Quality education (4); Industry, innovation, and infrastructure (9); Sustainable cities and communities (11)

RESOURCES

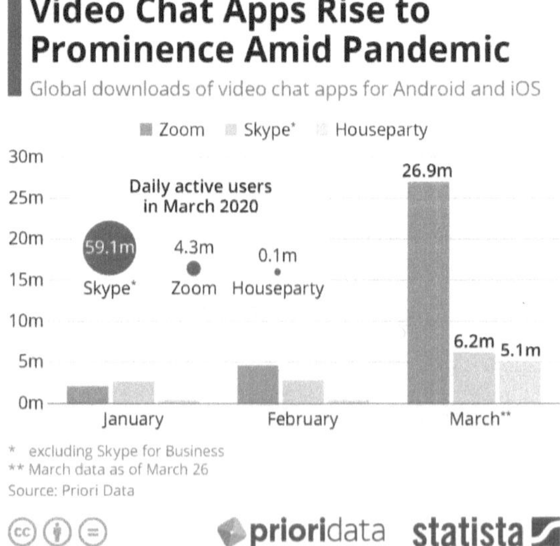

Source: Statista

REFERENCES

1. https://www.bbc.com/news/business-52884782
2. https://www.statista.com/chart/21906/zoom-revenue/
3. https://www.businessofapps.com/data/zoom-statistics/

Case Study **95**

The Power of Esports: Riot Games and the Success of League of Legends

Themes: Games, Gen Z, Media, Growth, Esports

TEACHING OBJECTIVES

The case study is intended to qualify students to:

- Understand the growth and impact of esports within the entertainment industry, focusing on the success story of Riot Games and their flagship product, "League of Legends."
- Analyze the strategies employed by Riot Games in developing, marketing, and maintaining the relevance of "League of Legends" in an ever-evolving digital environment.
- Explore the challenges and opportunities in the esports industry, encouraging students and professionals to identify future trends and potential business opportunities.

SYNOPSIS

In the fast-paced world of digital entertainment, the esports segment has rapidly emerged as a potent force. The case study underscores this evolution, with a particular focus on Riot Games and its flagship product, "League of Legends." Once considered a niche hobby, gaming has evolved into a multi-billion-dollar industry with professional competitions and an audience spanning the globe. As one of the most successful games in this realm, "League of Legends" serves as a fascinating lens to explore the growth and impact of esports.

Advantages

"League of Legends" brings to the fore several unique advantages that have led to its meteoric rise. The game's free-to-play model democratizes access, reducing barriers for new players. However, it's the intricate and strategic gameplay that provides a stimulating challenge and helps to retain those players over time. Riot Games' regular updates keep the game fresh and engaging, while their conscious efforts to foster a vibrant and inclusive community make players feel heard and valued. Their push to professionalize esports, by staging regular, high-stakes tournaments, also draws a growing audience of spectators, boosting the game's visibility and cultural relevance.

Strategies

The strategic decisions made by Riot Games are instrumental in "League of Legends" maintaining its dominant position in the esports arena. The game developers give considerable weight to player feedback, creating a two-way communication channel that fosters community trust and leads to game improvements. Their investment in the esports ecosystem, from organizing large-scale tournaments to setting up regional leagues, has helped validate esports as a professional sport. This commitment to esports has not only elevated the status of "League of Legends" but has also built a sustainable revenue stream through sponsorships, media rights, and in-game purchases.

Opportunities

With the burgeoning growth of esports, there's a raft of opportunities ahead for Riot Games and "League of Legends." One of the most promising is the potential for geographical expansion, particularly into emerging markets with a fast-growing gamer base. The use of advanced technologies like Virtual and Augmented Reality could enhance the spectator experience and bring a new dimension to the game. Furthermore, the game's rich lore and character base offer the potential for diversification into other media formats, such as films or merchandise, offering new avenues for revenue and brand expansion.

Conclusion

Riot Games and its premier offering, "League of Legends," exemplify the incredible success achievable within the esports industry. By marrying a complex, engaging game with a robust community focus and a commitment to professionalizing esports, they've created a powerful, multifaceted entertainment platform. This case study lays bare the strategic decisions and actions that led to this success, offering invaluable insights for those interested in gaming, digital entertainment, and the fascinating world of esports.

INDUSTRY CONTEXT

The esports industry has grown exponentially in recent years, driven by advances in internet technology, the widespread availability of gaming devices, and the rise of online streaming platforms. It has transformed video games into a spectator sport, with professional players, leagues, and tournaments that draw millions of viewers. Riot Games' "League of Legends" is a key player in this sector, demonstrating the possibilities and potential of esports in the entertainment industry.

CHALLENGES

- Ensuring fair play and dealing with toxic behavior within the community.
- Keeping the game continually engaging and relevant in a rapidly evolving gaming market.
- Navigating the regulatory complexities of operating in multiple international markets.

LESSONS LEARNED

- Emphasizing community engagement and user feedback can significantly enhance game development and player retention.
- Esports has immense potential as a form of entertainment, and investing in the infrastructure for competitive events can provide a sustainable revenue model.

QUESTIONS

1. What key factors contributed to the success of "League of Legends" as a standout esports game?
2. How can Riot Games further enhance its community engagement strategies?
3. What potential opportunities and challenges might arise with the increasing mainstream acceptance of esports?

UN SDGS: Good health and well-being (3); Partnership for goals (17)

RESOURCES

Source: OneShot

REFERENCES

1. https://www.riotgames.com/en/news/building-the-future-of-sport-at-riot-games
2. https://www.gamesindustry.biz/league-of-legends-understanding-the-success-of-an-unprofitable-esport
3. https://www.nytimes.com/2014/10/12/technology/riot-games-league-of-legends-main-attraction-esports.html

Case Study **96**

From DNA Sequencing to Healthcare: AncestryDNA's Genetic Testing Services

Themes: Genetics, DNA, Healthcare, Testing services

TEACHING OBJECTIVES

The case study is intended to qualify students to:

- Understand the integration of genomics and healthcare services, specifically through the lens of AncestryDNA's genetic testing services.
- Analyze the advantages, strategies, and opportunities that AncestryDNA offers to customers, the healthcare industry, and scientific research.
- Examine the challenges faced in genetic testing services, including privacy, accuracy, and ethical issues, and how AncestryDNA is addressing them.

SYNOPSIS

The era of personalized healthcare has dawned, driven by advancements in genomics and the rise of direct-to-consumer genetic testing services. A standout in this evolving landscape is AncestryDNA, a division of Ancestry, the largest for-profit genealogy company in the world. By providing individuals access to their genetic data in an easily comprehensible format, AncestryDNA has empowered individuals to discover their heritage and understand potential genetic health risks. Their business model and innovative offerings have set new standards in the industry and fueled a surge in consumer interest in genetic testing and its implications for healthcare.

Advantages

AncestryDNA has opened the door to an array of advantages for both individuals and the broader medical and scientific community. For consumers, AncestryDNA's genetic testing service provides fascinating insights into their ethnic backgrounds, enabling a deeper understanding of their heritage. On the health front, the service provides valuable information on potential genetic health risks, paving the way for preventive healthcare measures. The immense database of genetic information that AncestryDNA has amassed also serves as a vital resource for the broader scientific community. Researchers can leverage this extensive pool of data to drive breakthroughs in our understanding of human genetics, contributing to the broader field of personalized medicine.

Strategies

AncestryDNA's growth and influence in the genetic testing market can be attributed to a series of well-executed strategies. First, they have committed to making their services accessible and user-friendly. Their online platform is designed to be intuitive and informative, ensuring that users of varying age groups and digital literacy levels can easily navigate their results. Second, AncestryDNA places a high emphasis on data privacy. They have set up robust security measures and provide clear, transparent information about their data use policy to build trust with their users. Lastly, AncestryDNA's collaborations with scientific research institutions not only bolster the credibility of their services but also ensure that their vast collection of genetic data contributes to advancements in genetic research and personalized medicine.

Opportunities

AncestryDNA, like other players in the direct-to-consumer genetic testing space, stands on the precipice of numerous opportunities. As scientific understanding of the human genome continues to evolve, the potential for detailed, actionable health insights based on a person's genetic profile is immense. By partnering with healthcare providers, AncestryDNA could facilitate more personalized healthcare based on an individual's genetic predispositions. Furthermore, as artificial intelligence and machine learning continue to develop, there is an increasing potential to glean even more insights from their vast repository of genetic data.

Conclusion

In conclusion, AncestryDNA stands at a unique crossroads of genomics, consumer technology, and healthcare. The company has shown that personalized genetic information can be made accessible and meaningful to the public while also contributing to the broader scientific community. However, as with any rapidly growing industry, challenges persist, particularly around data privacy and ethical considerations. By dissecting AncestryDNA's journey, one can gain valuable insights into how to navigate the evolving landscape of direct-to-consumer genetic testing and the intersection of genomics and personalized healthcare.

INDUSTRY CONTEXT

The era of personalized healthcare has dawned, driven by advancements in genomics and the rise of direct-to-consumer genetic testing services. A standout in this evolving landscape is AncestryDNA, a division of Ancestry, the largest for-profit genealogy company in the world. By providing individuals access to their genetic data in an easily comprehensible format, AncestryDNA has empowered individuals to discover their heritage and understand potential genetic health risks. Their business model and innovative offerings have set new standards in the industry and fueled a surge in consumer interest in genetic testing and its implications for healthcare.

Advantages

AncestryDNA has opened the door to an array of advantages for both individuals and the broader medical and scientific community. For consumers, AncestryDNA's genetic testing service provides fascinating insights into their ethnic backgrounds, enabling a deeper understanding of their heritage. On the health front, the service provides valuable information on potential genetic health risks, paving the way for preventive healthcare measures. The immense database of genetic information that AncestryDNA has amassed also serves as a vital resource for the broader scientific community. Researchers can leverage this extensive pool of data to drive breakthroughs in our understanding of human genetics, contributing to the broader field of personalized medicine.

Strategies

AncestryDNA's growth and influence in the genetic testing market can be attributed to a series of well-executed strategies. First, they have committed to making their services accessible and user-friendly. Their online platform is designed to be intuitive and informative, ensuring that users of varying age groups and digital literacy levels can easily navigate their results. Second, AncestryDNA places a high emphasis on data privacy. They have set up robust security measures and provide clear, transparent information about their data use policy to build trust with their users. Lastly, AncestryDNA's collaborations with scientific research institutions not only bolster the credibility of their services but also ensure that their vast collection of genetic data contributes to advancements in genetic research and personalized medicine.

Opportunities

AncestryDNA, like other players in the direct-to-consumer genetic testing space, stands on the precipice of numerous opportunities. As scientific understanding of the human genome continues to evolve, the potential for detailed, actionable health insights based on a person's genetic profile is immense. By partnering with healthcare providers, AncestryDNA could facilitate more personalized healthcare based on an individual's genetic predispositions. Furthermore, as artificial intelligence and machine learning continue to develop, there is an increasing potential to glean even more insights from their vast repository of genetic data.

Conclusion

In conclusion, AncestryDNA stands at a unique crossroads of genomics, consumer technology, and healthcare. The company has shown that personalized genetic information can be made accessible and meaningful to the public while also contributing to the broader scientific community. However, as with any rapidly growing industry, challenges persist, particularly around data privacy and ethical considerations. By dissecting AncestryDNA's journey, one can gain valuable insights into how to navigate the evolving landscape of direct-to-consumer genetic testing and the intersection of genomics and personalized healthcare.

CHALLENGES

- Ensuring data privacy: With sensitive genetic data at stake, ensuring robust data security and privacy is a significant challenge.
- Accuracy and interpretation of results: Providing accurate results and helping consumers understand the implications of their genetic data is a complex task.
- Ethical considerations: Balancing the potential benefits of genetic testing with the ethical implications of such data collection and use presents ongoing challenges.

LESSONS LEARNED

- Trust is paramount: AncestryDNA has shown that earning and maintaining customer trust, particularly concerning data privacy, is crucial in this sensitive field.
- Education is key: The company's efforts to educate consumers about the value and limitations of its services have been vital in managing customer expectations and promoting the responsible use of genetic data.

QUESTIONS

1. How can AncestryDNA further enhance the privacy and security of the genetic data they handle?
2. How might advances in AI and machine learning impact the services AncestryDNA can offer?
3. What role should regulatory bodies play in overseeing the direct-to-consumer genetic testing industry, and how might this impact companies like AncestryDNA?

UN SDGS: Good health and well-being (3); Gender equality (5); Partnership for goals (17)

RESOURCES

Source: AncestryDNA

REFERENCES

1. https://www.23andme.com/en-eu
2. https://sequencing.com/ancestry-dna-test
3. https://www.bu.edu/sph/news/articles/2018/at-home-genetic-testing-leads-to-misinterpretations-of-results/

Renewable Energy Storage: Sonnen's Residential Battery Systems

Themes: Technology, Renewable, Storage, Battery, System

TEACHING OBJECTIVES

The case study is intended to qualify students to:

- Understand the role and importance of energy storage systems in the context of renewable energy, using Sonnen's residential battery systems as a case study.
- Analyze Sonnen's strategies in promoting and distributing its residential battery systems, and the advantages it has offered to consumers and the energy market.
- Identify and discuss the challenges faced by Sonnen and the renewable energy storage industry, and contemplate the potential opportunities and future developments in the field.

SYNOPSIS

The renewable energy industry has seen an unprecedented surge, propelling the need for efficient energy storage systems to the forefront. One key player answering this call is Sonnen, a German company specializing in residential battery systems. Sonnen's journey to providing solar battery solutions for homes worldwide is a masterclass in meeting consumer needs and tackling inherent industry challenges, ultimately contributing significantly to the renewable energy landscape.

Advantages

Sonnen's residential battery systems offer distinct advantages by tackling two of the primary concerns around renewable energy - continuity of supply and grid stability. As these systems store excess solar energy produced during daylight hours, they assure power availability during the night or periods of cloud cover, essentially enabling homeowners to be less dependent on the grid. The stored power can also be fed back into the grid during peak demand, thereby aiding in maintaining grid stability. Such capabilities enhance the overall appeal of renewable energy installations, which subsequently could lead to more widespread adoption of renewable energy.

Strategies

Key to Sonnen's successful growth in the energy storage sector has been its persistent focus on technological innovation paired with astute business strategy. Their residential battery systems offer reliability, efficiency, and ease of use, significantly enhancing customer value. Furthermore, Sonnen has developed unique energy service models like the SonnenCommunity and SonnenFlat, which allow energy sharing among community members and provide fixed-rate electricity plans respectively. Such customer-centric approaches have played a substantial role in Sonnen's market growth.

Opportunities

The current momentum towards a greener planet provides a fertile environment for businesses like Sonnen. With increasing climate change awareness and endeavors to reduce carbon footprints, the demand for renewable energy storage will likely continue to grow. This presents numerous opportunities for Sonnen to diversify its product range, venture into new markets, and form strategic alliances to push energy storage systems' integration into the renewable energy industry. One promising concept is the "virtual power plant" (VPP) that combines multiple distributed energy storage systems into a network that can be centrally managed, potentially offering grid services and creating a shared energy economy.

Conclusion

Sonnen's story in the renewable energy storage industry demonstrates the vital role and significant potential of energy storage systems in the renewable energy era. Despite the hurdles, such as the need for technological advancements and regulatory support, the path forged by companies like Sonnen provides optimism for a sustainable and resilient energy future, underscoring the power of innovation and strategic planning in overcoming challenges and capitalizing on opportunities.

INDUSTRY CONTEXT

The energy storage industry has become increasingly important with the rise of renewable energy sources like solar and wind, which are intermittent by nature. Batteries that can store excess energy produced during peak production times are a key solution to this problem. Among the leading firms in this industry is Sonnen, known for its home energy storage solutions. These battery systems are designed to store energy generated by home solar power systems, ensuring that the power is available when needed, regardless of whether the sun is shining.

CHALLENGES

- High upfront costs of energy storage systems can be a barrier to widespread adoption.
- Technological limitations around energy density and battery life span.
- Regulatory and policy issues can affect the growth and viability of energy storage solutions.

LESSONS LEARNED

- Technological innovation paired with attractive business models can drive the adoption of new energy technologies.
- The importance of regulatory support and policy frameworks in shaping the energy landscape.

QUESTIONS

1. How does energy storage contribute to the value of renewable energy installations, and how has Sonnen capitalized on this?
2. What are the key factors influencing consumer decisions to adopt residential energy storage systems?
3. Looking ahead, what technological or market developments could further enhance the value proposition of energy storage systems?

UN SDGS: Good health and well-being (3); Industry, innovation, and infrastructure (9); Partnership for goals (17)

RESOURCES

Source: Sonnen

REFERENCES

1. https://sonnengroup.com/
2. https://sonnen.com.au/product/
3. https://www.cleanenergyreviews.info/blog/sonnen-battery-review

5G and the Automotive Industry: BMW's V2X Communication Initiatives

Themes: Application, Platform, 5G, Automotive, Communication

TEACHING OBJECTIVES

The case study is intended to qualify students to:

- Understand the implications of 5G technology in the automotive industry, particularly its role in vehicle-to-everything (V2X) communication.
- Analyze BMW's V2X communication initiatives, their strategies, benefits, and the challenges encountered.
- Discuss the potential opportunities, future scenarios, and the transformative impact of 5G and V2X communication in the automotive industry and beyond.

SYNOPSIS

The fifth generation of wireless communication technology, commonly known as 5G, is revolutionizing industries and reshaping our everyday interaction with technology. In the heart of this transformation is the automobile industry. This case study centers on BMW's pioneering efforts in harnessing the potential of 5G for Vehicle-to-Everything (V2X) communications, a technology enabling vehicles to interact with any entity that may affect it and vice versa. The case focuses on the role of 5G in the evolution of the automotive industry and BMW's robust implementation of this technology.

Advantages

5G delivers several advantages over its predecessor technologies, including exceptional speed, increased capacity, and low latency. These features make V2X communication viable, significantly enhancing traffic flow and vehicle safety. As an early adopter, BMW benefits from these advancements, leading to a superior customer experience and differentiation from competitors. This section highlights these benefits and explores how the transition to 5G V2X communication revolutionizes BMW's offerings and positions them as an industry leader.

Strategies

The case study delves into BMW's strategies for implementing V2X communication powered by 5G. It provides an extensive overview of BMW's partnerships with pivotal players in the telecommunications and automotive industries, considerable investments in research and development, and the company's push for V2X technology standardization to ensure maximum interoperability and reliability. The case also underscores BMW's role in the 5G Automotive Association (5GAA), demonstrating the company's commitment to this transformative cause.

Opportunities

5G technology unveils a plethora of opportunities for the automotive industry, paving the way for autonomous vehicles, remote vehicle diagnostics, over-the-air updates, and enhanced infotainment. Furthermore, it supports the broader concept of smart city infrastructure, contributing to a more sustainable environment and improving quality of life. This segment of the case study explores these prospective scenarios, discussing the transformative potential of 5G in the context of BMW and the broader automotive industry.

Conclusion

In conclusion, the case study encapsulates the revolutionary role of 5G in the automotive industry, emphasizing BMW's groundbreaking efforts in V2X communication and acknowledging the hurdles that lie ahead. Despite these challenges, BMW's strategic measures and the potential of 5G in sculpting the future of automotive transportation send an optimistic message. The case study concludes by emphasizing that BMW's journey serves as a model for the entire industry, illustrating the possibilities of leveraging 5G technology to drive safer, more efficient, and more intelligent transportation.

Benefits of the Car Platform application:

1. The Car Platform application helps to handle all the vehicle disruption operations for car owners and garage management.
2. Users can log in to their accounts and then proceed to share the present status of their cars or vehicles.
3. The garage will efficiently solve the issue as soon as possible.
4. Once the service is done, the client can share feedback and suggestions. For any further support, clients can contact the customer support team.

INDUSTRY CONTEXT

The automotive industry is amidst a significant shift with the advent of 5G technology. As vehicles become increasingly connected, 5G, with its high-speed and low-latency characteristics, is set to redefine vehicular communication, creating safer and more efficient roads. In particular, V2X communication, where vehicles can communicate with various elements of the traffic system, is emerging as a crucial application of 5G in the automotive industry. With industry leaders like BMW pioneering the implementation of these technologies, the sector is on the brink of a transformative change.

CHALLENGES

- Technological challenges related to ensuring consistent 5G coverage and addressing interoperability issues across various regions and devices.
- Regulatory and standardization issues around the use of 5G in V2X communication.
- Privacy and security concerns related to the handling of large volumes of data generated and shared through V2X communication.

LESSONS LEARNED

- Collaboration is key: BMW's initiatives underline the importance of collaboration with telecommunication partners, tech companies, and regulators in achieving the successful implementation of 5G V2X communication.
- Innovation leads the way: Staying ahead in the digital curve

QUESTIONS

1. What are the implications of 5G-powered V2X communication on road safety and traffic efficiency?
2. How might BMW's V2X initiatives shape the future of autonomous vehicles?
3. How can the automotive industry address the challenges related to privacy, security, and standardization in implementing 5G V2X communication?

UN SDGS: Good health and well-being (3); Sustainable cities and communities (11)

RESOURCES

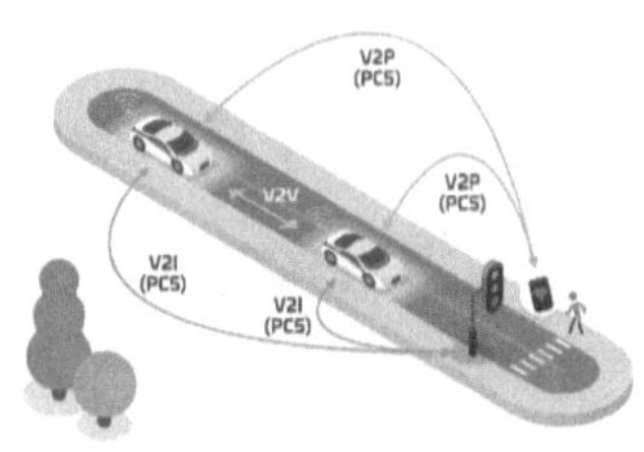

Source: Cloud Flight

REFERENCES

1. https://www.press.bmwgroup.com/global/article/detail/T0264148EN/telecommunications-and-automotive-players-form-global-cross-industry-5g-automotive-association?language=en

2. https://www.audi-mediacenter.com/en/press-releases/telecommunications-and-automotive-players-form-global-cross-industry-5g-automotive-association-6817

3. https://www.thebusinessresearchcompany.com/report/automotive-v2x-market

Green Finance and Sustainable Investment: Accelerating the Transition to a Low-Carbon Economy

Themes: Finance, Sustainability, Transition, Low-Carbon

TEACHING OBJECTIVES

The case study is intended to qualify students to:

- Understand the concept and importance of green finance and sustainable investment in achieving a low-carbon economy.
- Analyze the strategies and instruments used in promoting sustainable investments.
- Explore the opportunities and challenges in the sector of green finance and how they can be addressed.

SYNOPSIS

This case study delves into the importance and role of green finance and sustainable investment in steering the global economy toward environmentally sustainable practices. It presents the driving forces behind the rising importance of sustainability in the financial sector, the role of the finance industry in combating climate change, and the rationale for moving towards a low-carbon economy.

Advantages

The benefits of green finance and sustainable investment are multifold. Primarily, they promote environmentally sustainable practices while potentially offering competitive financial returns. By investing in sustainable businesses and projects, investors contribute to efforts towards reducing carbon emissions and mitigating climate change. Moreover, green investments often involve fewer risks than traditional investments since they consider environmental, social, and governance (ESG) factors, which are increasingly affecting the financial performance of companies. This section offers an in-depth view of the benefits of green finance and sustainable investments, backed by examples and data illustrating their potential for both profitability and positive environmental impact.

Strategies

There are a variety of strategies employed to promote sustainable investments. This includes green bonds, climate-aligned bonds, and ESG investing. Such instruments help in redirecting capital toward sustainable businesses and initiatives. Additionally, the advent of financial technology has made sustainable investing more accessible to a wider range of investors. This section delves into each of these strategies in detail, providing real-life examples and outcomes.

Opportunities

With a growing consciousness about climate change and its dire consequences, there is an increasing demand for green finance and sustainable investment options. This has opened up a wealth of opportunities in the sector, from the potential for innovative financial products to job creation and improved financial stability and resilience. This part of the case study delves into these opportunities, providing analysis and evidence on how sustainable finance can be a key driver for growth and stability in the economy.

Conclusion

The study concludes by asserting that while there are challenges in the path toward green finance and sustainable investment, the benefits and opportunities they bring are immense and far outweigh the obstacles. The role of sustainable finance in achieving a low-carbon economy is critical. Despite barriers such as a lack of universal standards and the risk of greenwashing, with the right strategies and regulatory support, green finance can pave the way for sustainable economic growth, job creation, and risk mitigation.

INDUSTRY CONTEXT

The finance industry plays a significant role in society's transformation towards sustainability. It has the power to guide capital toward sustainable business practices and innovations, enabling the transition to a low-carbon economy. As global awareness and concern over climate change increase, so too does the demand for investments that consider environmental, social, and governance (ESG) factors. Green finance and sustainable investment have emerged as essential components in this transition, redefining the landscape of the finance industry.

CHALLENGES

- Lack of universally accepted standards and definitions of what constitutes 'green' or 'sustainable' investment.
- Difficulty in measuring and reporting the environmental impact of investments.
- Greenwashing, where investments are misrepresented as more environmentally friendly than they are.

LESSONS LEARNED

- Integration of ESG factors into investment decisions can lead to better financial performance and reduced risk.

- Collaboration between governments, regulators, and the financial sector is essential in developing and promoting green finance.

QUESTIONS

1. What role can regulatory bodies play in promoting green finance and sustainable investment?
2. How can greenwashing be effectively addressed in the finance industry?
3. In what ways can technology contribute to the advancement of green finance?

UN SDGS: Quality education (4); Decent work and economic growth (8); Industry, innovation, and infrastructure (9)

RESOURCES

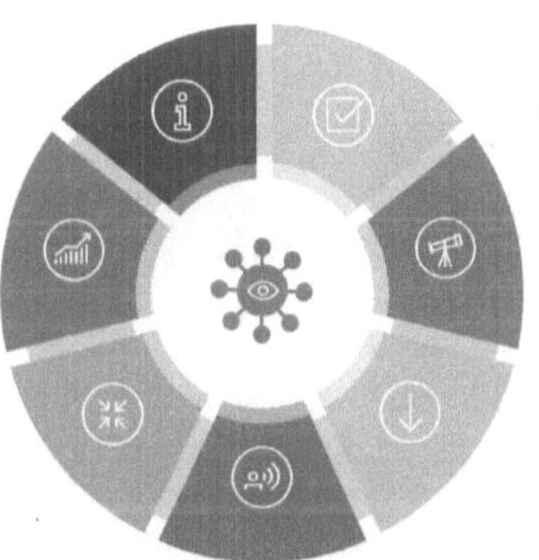

Source: Deloitte

REFERENCES

1. https://www.iso.org/files/live/sites/isoorg/files/store/en/PUB100458.pdf
2. https://www.amf.org.ae/en/financial-sector/sustainable-finance
3. https://finance.ec.europa.eu/sustainable-finance/overview-sustainable-finance_en

Augmented Reality: A Game-changing Innovation for Business

Themes: Augmented reality, Consumer, Technology, Mobile

TEACHING OBJECTIVES

The case study is intended to qualify students to:

- Understand the fundamental principles of augmented reality (AR) and its application in business.
- Analyze the advantages and challenges that AR presents for businesses in different industries.
- Examine real-world case studies of companies successfully implementing AR and discuss strategies for integrating AR into existing business models.

SYNOPSIS

Augmented reality in an online environment considerably affects consumer engagement, behavior, and sales. Augmented Reality (AR) technology is transforming industries by overlaying digital information in the real world, creating immersive and interactive experiences. This section introduces the readers to AR, explaining its working mechanism and applications across different industries. It mentions businesses like IKEA, Snapchat, and Pokémon Go that have used AR for enhancing customer experiences, and discusses the scope of AR in fields like real estate, manufacturing, and healthcare.

Advantages

This section elaborates on the significant advantages of AR in business operations. AR enhances the customer experience by providing them with virtual try-on or product visualization experiences, leading to informed decision-making. It discusses how AR aids in efficient training methods, providing interactive and immersive learning experiences. The advantages section also provides examples of how AR has helped streamline processes in sectors such as manufacturing and healthcare, increasing accuracy and efficiency. The advantages are further illustrated with case studies of businesses reaping the benefits of AR.

Strategies

Implementing AR into business operations requires careful planning and strategic execution. This section outlines strategies for successful AR integration, starting from the selection of appropriate AR tools that align with the business needs to the training of staff in using and managing AR systems. The segment also discusses the importance of ensuring hardware compatibility and scalability for future technological advancements. It emphasizes the need for businesses to address privacy and security concerns proactively while deploying AR solutions.

Opportunities

As AR technology continues to advance rapidly, new opportunities are arising for businesses willing to innovate. This section explores these potential future applications, including advanced data visualization, remote collaboration, and personalized marketing. The discussion also expands on the prospective growth of the AR market and how different industries can contribute to and benefit from this expansion. Future trends, like AR combined with AI and IoT, are also touched upon in this part, providing a glimpse into the exciting future of AR in business.

Conclusion

This section concludes the study by reinforcing the transformative potential of AR in the business world. It emphasizes that despite the challenges, the advantages and future opportunities of AR are significant. It argues that businesses that are willing to invest in AR, adapt to its challenges, and innovate their offerings will likely gain a significant competitive advantage in their respective markets.

INDUSTRY CONTEXT

The rise of augmented reality comes at a time when businesses are seeking innovative ways to engage with customers, improve operational efficiency, and stand out in increasingly competitive markets. With the digital transformation sweeping across industries, businesses are exploring technologies like AR to enhance their services, products, and internal processes. As such, understanding AR is critical in the current business landscape.

CHALLENGES

- High implementation and maintenance costs.
- Technical issues such as software compatibility and latency.
- Privacy and security concerns related to AR data.

LESSONS LEARNED

- AR technology, while advantageous, needs careful planning and implementation to be beneficial.
- Businesses need to invest in regular training and system upgrades to effectively use AR.

QUESTIONS

1. In what ways can your chosen industry benefit from the implementation of AR technology?

2. How might businesses overcome the high costs and technical challenges associated with implementing AR?

3. How can businesses ensure data privacy and security when using AR technology?

UN SDGS: Quality education (4); Decent work and economic growth (8); Industry, innovation, and infrastructure (9)

RESOURCES

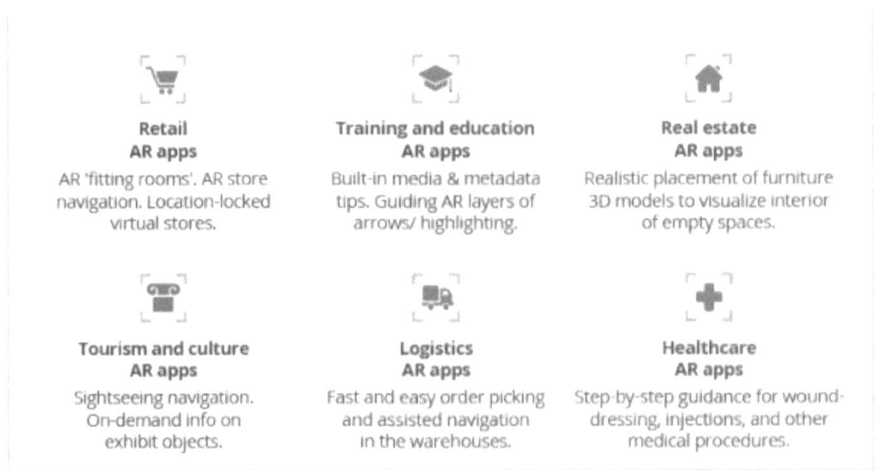

Source: softwaretestinghelp.com

REFERENCES

1. https://insightssuccess.com/augmented-reality-a-game-changer-for-modern-business-success/

2. https://kiber.tech/why-augmented-reality-for-business-game-changer-2021/

3. https://designhubz.com/the-future-of-advertising-how-ar-is-changing-the-game/

Talent Management and Learning and Development: Emirates NBD's Programs During the Outbreak

Themes: Talent Management, Learning, Development, Pandemic

TEACHING OBJECTIVES

The case study is intended to qualify students to:

- Examine how Emirates NBD continued learning and development for its employees amid the COVID-19 pandemic
- Discuss the key roles that Emirates NBD's talent management programs play in contributing to the success and resilience of the company
- Provide recommendations on how Emirates NBD can further improve its talent management programs.

SYNOPSIS

The world has seen a major transformation in technology over the past decades, with better and more robust internet connectivity and information technology systems. Several organizations have been exploring new ways to do work and engage with their talents. Some have been implementing remote work, while many others were still reluctant to adopt that setup. It is only after the pandemic has paralyzed the whole world that many organizations considered and implemented new ways of human resource management, such as remote work, to keep their companies afloat and navigate the negative effects of the COVID-19 outbreak. It is interesting to take a look at how organizations implemented talent management programs during the coronavirus outbreak and how they contributed to the company's resilience and success despite the crisis. This study takes the case of Emirates NBD. Emirates NBD is No. 2 among the banks in the United Arab Emirates (UAE) in terms of assets. It is based in Dubai, with a workforce of about 9,243 full-time employees and a net profit of AED 7 billion. Emirates NBD has 915 branches and 4,029 ATMs and SDMs in the country and abroad. The bank deals with different financial business segments, such as retail and wholesale banking, wealth management, and Islamic banking. Emirates NBD considers its people as its most important assets, and its values are built around them: integrity, passion for performance, and teamwork.

Emirates NBD's COVID-19 Precautionary Measures

The coronavirus posed incredible risks to people, and companies needed to protect their employees more than ensure that their businesses continue to operate. At Emirates NBD, people's safety and well-being were prioritized and the bank implemented bank-wide precautionary measures following the directives from the UAE government. The bank immediately put into action its business resilience and continuity plan.

Talent Management Practices Amid the Pandemic

Despite the crisis, it is important for organizations to continuously provide learning and development opportunities for their talents. They must be able to adapt to changing circumstances because the business landscape is constantly shifting and evolving fast. Employees' development helps the company improve outcomes and gain a competitive advantage in the market. 6 However, the COVID-19 pandemic has posed new challenges in retaining talents and helping them realize their potential.

Opportunities

Emirates NBD recognized the importance of implementing recognition programs during the pandemic to show its employees that they are extremely appreciated. 7 It is an essential element of effective talent management, which will help position the company for long-term growth because it has a workforce that performs excellently. An organization that offers attractive compensation and benefits and a supportive work environment tends to increase employee retention. 8 In today's competitive business landscape, retention of top talents is crucial and more cost-effective than hiring new people.

Conclusion

Even when an organization is going through a crisis, it must continue to ensure that its people are getting the training and development that they need. Emirates NBD was able to fulfill that and provided learning and growth opportunities for its employees despite the pandemic. The shift to remote work setup actually speeded up the company's adoption of digital learning tools. Emirates NBD recognizes the value that its people bring to the organization and that all its efforts during the pandemic would not be possible without them. Being able to see and unlock human potential and identify the best role for each employee is a crucial aspect of running an excellent team. 16 Meanwhile, remote training and digital learning created new challenges for employees and it is not easy to measure the success rates of training and development programs in this setup. A lot of Emirates NBD's training involves taking online courses. While they are good at increasing knowledge, the company needs to find innovative ways that employees can immediately apply their learnings. Otherwise, they might simply lose it. Nevertheless, Emirates NBD was proud to say that its employees demonstrated that they are resilient and solution-oriented during the COVID-19 pandemic.

INDUSTRY CONTEXT

The banking industry is characterized by constant changes due to digital transformation, regulatory shifts, and varying customer expectations. The COVID-19 pandemic added another layer of complexity, forcing banks to rethink their operations, particularly in managing their human resources. With many employees working from home, traditional talent management and L&D practices have been challenged, necessitating a shift towards more flexible and digital-centric solutions.

CHALLENGES

- The sudden switch to remote work due to the pandemic posed logistical and technical challenges.
- Maintaining employee engagement and ensuring effective communication in a remote work environment proved challenging.
- Adapting L&D programs to cater to the diverse needs of employees in a virtual setting was a considerable task.

LESSONS LEARNED

- The importance of proactive planning and investment in digital learning infrastructure is evident in the swift transition to remote work and continued L&D.
- The crisis underscored the significance of continuous learning and adaptability, which are crucial for organizational resilience in the face of uncertainties.

QUESTIONS

1. How did Emirates NBD's focus on talent management and L&D contribute to its resilience during the pandemic?
2. What strategies did Emirates NBD use to overcome the challenges posed by the shift to remote work and learning?

3. How can other organizations learn from Emirates NBD's experience in maintaining effective talent management and L&D practices during a crisis?

UN SDGS: Sustainable cities and communities (11); Peace, justice, and strong institutions (16)

RESOURCES

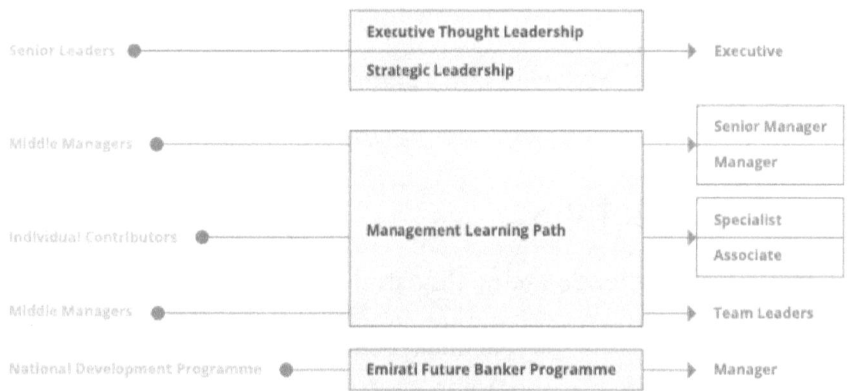

Source: Emirates NBD Sustainability Report – 2020

REFERENCES

1. Corporate Finance Institute, "Top Banks in UAE," https://corporatefinanceinstitute.com/resources/careers/companies/top-banks-in-uae/.

2. Emirates NBD, "Emirates NBD COVID-19 Coronavirus Precautionary Measures," https://www.emiratesnbd.com/en/media-centre/media-centre-info/?mcid_en=856, March 2020.

3. Becky Frankiewicz & Thomas Chamorro-Premuzic, "The Post-Pandemic Rules of Talent Management," Harvard Business Review, https://hbr.org/2020/10/the-post-pandemic-rules-of-talent-management, October 13, 2020.

People Management at Jollibee: Adapting to the Trying Times

Themes: People Management, Time Management, Flexibility, Pandemic

TEACHING OBJECTIVES

The case study is intended to qualify students to:

- Understand the people management strategies employed by Jollibee during trying times, such as the COVID-19 pandemic.
- Analyze the impact of these strategies on the company's operations and overall business performance.
- Assess the value of flexible and adaptable people management strategies in navigating business challenges and uncertainties.

SYNOPSIS

As Jollibee, a major fast-food chain from the Philippines, confronts the disruptive effects of the COVID-19 pandemic, its long-standing success in the fast-food industry is put to the test. Jollibee has always thrived due to its deep-rooted culture of customer satisfaction and employee engagement. However, the challenge now is to maintain that record while the world grapples with an unprecedented crisis.

Advantages

Jollibee's ability to swiftly respond to changing circumstances is proving to be beneficial during this challenging period. The company's people-first philosophy, centered on employee well-being and engagement, has helped it to maintain a robust operational structure, ensuring continued service to its loyal customer base. This focus on employee safety not only bolsters the company's reputation as a responsible employer but also bolsters its position for future recruitment and retention strategies.

Strategies

Adapting to the global crisis, Jollibee has put into action various strategic measures to support its employees and ensure the continuity of operations. The company transitioned to flexible working arrangements swiftly, aiding employees in managing their professional responsibilities alongside personal ones in a work-from-home setup. Rigorous health and safety measures were enacted in line with government guidelines to ensure the safety of both the employees and customers. In addition to physical health, Jollibee showed a deep understanding of the importance of mental health by providing necessary resources and support in these trying times. Financial aid was offered to the employees most affected by the pandemic, reinforcing the company's commitment to its people.

Opportunities

Jollibee's crisis response has not been merely reactive; it has also been proactive in identifying and capitalizing on opportunities. The necessity of innovative people management strategies has driven the company towards developing a more resilient organizational structure that could serve the company well beyond the immediate crisis. These initiatives, including a more significant focus on mental health, may pave the way for a more empathetic and supportive corporate culture that could become a permanent part of the company's ethos.

Conclusion

Jollibee's journey through the challenges of the pandemic highlights how an organization can implement effective people management strategies in a crisis. It reflects a commitment to its people that extends beyond mere words, ensuring that employees feel valued, supported, and cared for during this difficult time. This case is an exemplar for other organizations on how to adapt and lead with compassion and resilience during a global crisis, further underlining the importance of placing people at the heart of the business.

INDUSTRY CONTEXT

The fast-food industry is highly competitive and customer-centric, requiring companies to maintain high levels of efficiency and service. The COVID-19 pandemic severely disrupted this industry, leading to significant challenges, such as implementing safety protocols, managing the workforce, and ensuring operational continuity. Organizations like Jollibee had to reinvent their people management strategies to navigate this crisis effectively.

CHALLENGES

- Ensuring the health and safety of both employees and customers in the face of a global pandemic.
- Maintaining operational continuity and customer service levels despite disrupted supply chains and new safety protocols.
- Keeping employee morale high and preventing burnout amid increased work pressure and uncertainties.

LESSONS LEARNED

- The importance of flexible and adaptable people management strategies in ensuring business continuity and employee well-being during crises.

- The crisis underscored the significance of employee engagement and well-being as key components of organizational resilience.

QUESTIONS

1. How did Jollibee's people management strategies contribute to its resilience during the pandemic?
2. How did the company maintain employee morale and engagement during such trying times?
3. What lessons can other organizations in the fast-food industry learn from Jollibee's approach to people management during the pandemic?

UN SDGS: Sustainable cities and communities (11); Peace, justice, and strong institutions (16)

RESOURCES

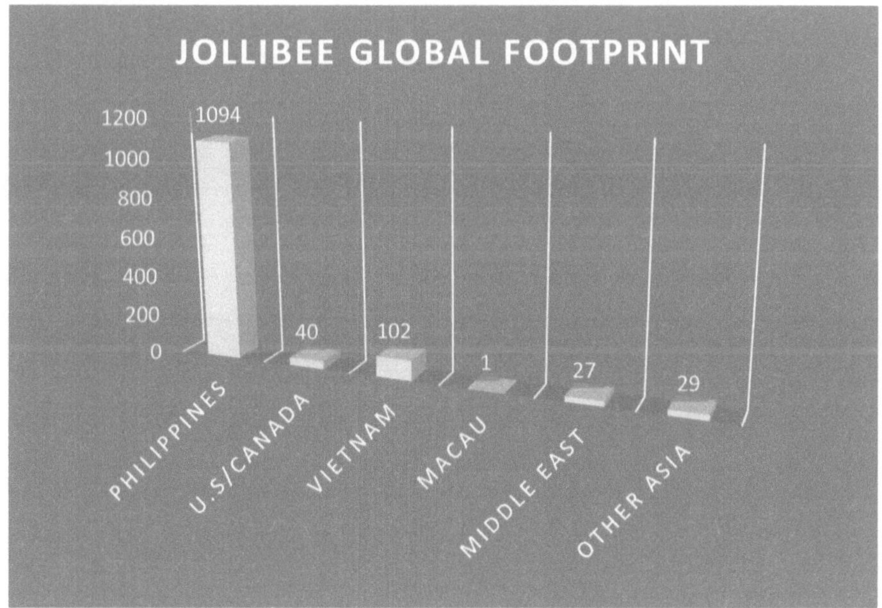

Source: Ardvin et al. 2022

REFERENCES

1. Miñana, J. A. (2020). *Jollibee Foods Corp. (JFC) SEC Sustainability Report. https://bucketeer-9d45a0bc-28bd-439b-9619-e2bfda478d44.s3.amazonaws.com/public/uploads/ETnPKOuI-FINAL-JFC-2020-SEC-Sustainability-Report-with-Audited-Figures.pdf*

2. Reyes, J. P. (2020, March 30). *Best practices of Jollibee Foods Corporation.* Employers Confederation of the Philippines. https://ecop.org.ph/best-practices-of-jollibee-foods-corporation/

3. Dumlao-Abadilla, D. (2020, March 19). Jollibee sets P1B employee COVID-19 support fund. *Inquirer.net.* https://business.inquirer.net/292964/jollibee-sets-p1b-employee-covid-19-support-fund

Roads and Transport Authority's People Happiness and Leading Sustainability Efforts: Traces of the COVID-19 Experience

Themes: Transportation, Road Management, Development, Pandemic, Health and Safety

TEACHING OBJECTIVES

The case study is intended to qualify students to:

- Evaluate how RTA promotes employee happiness
- Discuss how RTA ensures employee health and safety
- Examine RTA's leading sustainability efforts

SYNOPSIS

The Roads and Transport Authority (RTA) of Dubai is a major force in the transportation infrastructure of the United Arab Emirates. When COVID-19 stormed the world, the RTA had to reimagine its operational strategies to ensure service continuity and maintain its commitment to employee happiness and sustainability. In the face of this adversity, the RTA illustrated its resiliency, developing strategies that took into account not only the exigencies of the situation but also the welfare of its people and its mandate to promote sustainability.

Advantages

Long before the pandemic, the RTA had always put its people first, fostering an environment that values employee well-being. This advantage was even more apparent when the COVID-19 crisis struck. The organization was able to maintain high levels of morale and productivity, thanks to a well-established culture that cared for the employees and prioritized their happiness. In addition, the RTA's ongoing commitment to sustainability ensured that the organization remained operationally efficient and environmentally conscious, even during a crisis, helping to reduce the environmental impact and paving the way for sustainable practices that can be a model for other transportation entities.

Strategies

Given the challenges of the pandemic, the RTA rolled out various strategies to ensure employee safety and maintain a strong line of communication with its staff. Recognizing the dangers posed by the virus, the organization introduced remote work arrangements to reduce infection risks. Essential workers, who were needed to keep the transport system running, were provided with protective equipment, and stringent health protocols were enforced. But more than these, the RTA made sure that every member of the organization understood its COVID-19 response initiatives, utilizing transparency and open communication to maintain trust and engagement within its ranks.

Opportunities

While the COVID-19 pandemic brought significant disruption, it also opened doors for the RTA to rethink its operations and adapt to the rapidly evolving business environment. With digital transformation trends accelerating across the globe, the RTA saw an opportunity to leverage technology more extensively to enhance its services, ensure smooth operations, and maintain high levels of employee satisfaction. Moreover, the pandemic underscored the role of sustainability in organizational resilience, providing the RTA with an opportunity to amplify its commitment to environmentally friendly practices, and potentially lead the transportation sector towards a more sustainable future.

Conclusion

The RTA's experience during the COVID-19 pandemic demonstrates the crucial role of prioritizing people's happiness and sustainability in the face of crises. Despite the significant challenges posed by the pandemic, the RTA's strategic approach, grounded on its organizational values, has proven effective in maintaining operations, supporting its people, and sustaining a high level of service. This case study highlights how an organization's core values can serve as a guiding principle during crisis management and become a foundation for continued growth and resilience in the post-pandemic world.

INDUSTRY CONTEXT

The global transportation industry faced significant challenges during the COVID-19 pandemic, with lockdown measures and travel restrictions affecting all facets of the sector. Amidst the industry's turmoil, the Roads and Transport Authority (RTA) in Dubai, a major hub in global logistics and travel, had to navigate unprecedented disruptions to its operations. The RTA's approach to these challenges, focusing on people's happiness and sustainability, offers valuable insights into crisis management in this critical industry.

CHALLENGES

- Adapting to new safety regulations and procedures to protect both the employees and the public.
- Ensuring the continuity of services in the face of reduced mobility and increased remote working.
- Maintaining employee happiness and morale amidst the stress and uncertainty of the pandemic.

LESSONS LEARNED

- The importance of proactive planning and investment in digital learning infrastructure is
- A strong organizational culture that prioritizes employee happiness can significantly contribute to resilience during a crisis.
- A commitment to sustainability can provide a guiding principle for decision-making during challenging times, promoting both operational efficiency and environmental responsibility.

QUESTIONS

1. How did the RTA's pre-existing focus on people's happiness and sustainability shape its response to the COVID-19 pandemic?
2. How can the RTA leverage the digital transformation accelerated by the pandemic to improve its services and operations in the future?
3. In what ways can other organizations in the transportation industry learn from the RTA's response to the COVID-19 crisis?

UN SDGS: Sustainable cities and communities (11); Peace, justice, and strong institutions (16)

RESOURCES

Human Resources

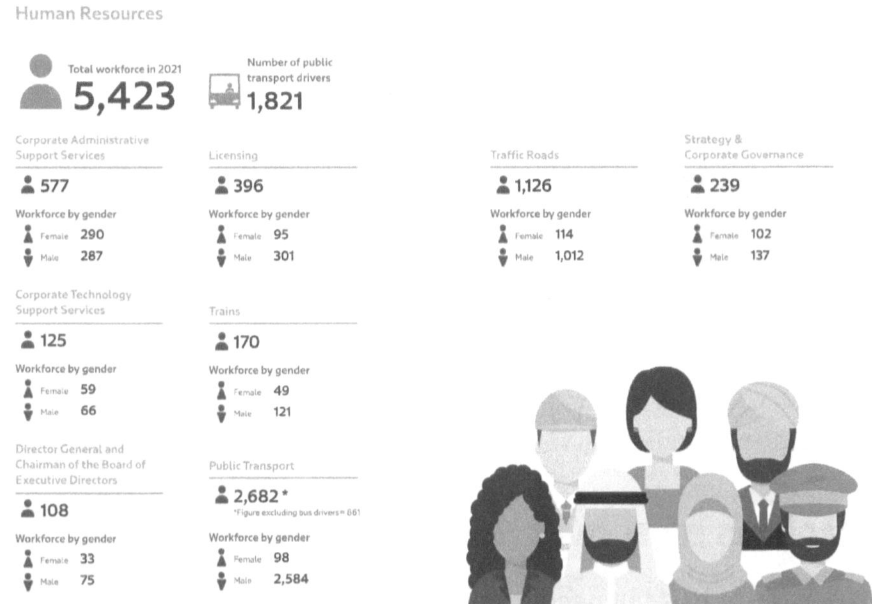

Source: RTA Annual Report 2021

REFERENCES

1. Qureshi, S. (2015, February 18). RTA takes initiative to enhance welfare for employess and customers. CustomerService.ae. https://www.customerservice.ae/resources/news/rta-takes-initiative-to-enhance-welfare-for-employees-and-customers/

2. Bedirian, R. (2016, February 12). RTA seeks to drive up workforce positivity. Gulf News. https://gulfnews.com/uae/government/rta-seeks-to-drive-up-workforce-positivity-1.1670969

3. RTA. (2018, March 17). Initiatives to thrill employees, clients on International Day of Happiness. https://www.rta.ae/wps/portal/rta/ae/home/news-and-media/all-news/NewsDetails/initiatives+to+thrill+employees%2C+clients+on+international+day+of+happiness

Sustainable Innovation: Universal Robina Corporation's Initiatives during the COVID-19 Pandemic

Themes: Sustainability, Learning, Pandemic, Innovation

TEACHING OBJECTIVES

The case study is intended to qualify students to:

- Understand the concept of sustainable innovation and how it can be incorporated into business models.
- Explore the strategies and initiatives that Universal Robina Corporation (URC) employed to maintain sustainability during the COVID-19 pandemic.
- Assess the impact and effectiveness of sustainable innovation practices in addressing business challenges, particularly in times of crisis.

SYNOPSIS

In this study, we delve into the transformative actions taken by Universal Robina Corporation (URC), a leading branded consumer food and beverage product company in the Philippines, in the wake of the COVID-19 pandemic. We discover how URC's commitment to sustainable innovation played a pivotal role in its reaction to the unprecedented crisis. The company had to rapidly adapt, redesign its business processes, maintain operational continuity, and ensure the safety and well-being of its workforce during these challenging times.

Advantages of Sustainable Innovation

Sustainable innovation offers a plethora of advantages to URC. It is paramount in minimizing the company's environmental footprint and ensuring a consistent flow of value to society. Sustainable innovation not only enhances the company's resilience to withstand crises but also bolsters its reputation among its consumers and stakeholders. The commitment to sustainability contributes to the long-term viability of the business, facilitating growth and expansion in an era where sustainable practices are of paramount importance to consumers.

Strategies Adopted by URC

URC's response to the pandemic was characterized by a diverse set of strategies. First, the company prioritized enhancing its supply chain resilience, recognizing the significance of uninterrupted supply in times of crisis. Second, the health and safety of URC's employees were held in the highest regard. The company invested heavily in measures to protect its workforce, demonstrating the value it places on its human resources. Third, the company leveraged digital technologies, facilitating remote work and virtual collaboration. Fourth, the company focused on redesigning its packaging solutions to be more eco-friendly. Lastly, URC intensified its efforts in providing community support and relief donations, reinforcing its commitment to corporate social responsibility even in challenging times.

Opportunities

The ongoing pandemic has underscored the role of sustainable innovation in times of crisis, unveiling numerous opportunities. For URC, the crisis serves as a period of introspection and reinforces its commitment to sustainable practices. It presents an opportunity to review and strengthen its existing sustainability initiatives and further innovate its product line, solidifying its commitment to its customers, employees, and the communities it serves.

Conclusion

URC's actions throughout the pandemic underpin the crucial role of sustainable innovation in navigating through unprecedented challenges. The company's commitment to sustainability not only guides its journey through the pandemic but also sets an example for other businesses to emulate. It emphasizes the crucial role of sustainable innovation in building a resilient business that can withstand not just the current crisis but future ones as well.

INDUSTRY CONTEXT

The food and beverage industry has been heavily impacted by the COVID-19 pandemic. Supply chain disruptions, changes in consumer behavior, and the imposition of safety protocols posed significant challenges. Despite these adversities, companies like URC leveraged the crisis as an opportunity to reevaluate and transform their business models towards more sustainable practices, reflecting an industry-wide shift towards sustainability.

CHALLENGES

- Navigating supply chain disruptions caused by the pandemic and ensuring a steady supply of products.
- Maintaining the health and safety of the workforce while sustaining operations.
- Adapting to changes in consumer behavior and preferences brought about by the crisis.

LESSONS LEARNED

- Sustainable innovation is not merely an optional strategy; it is crucial for business resilience and longevity, especially in times of crisis.
- Organizations that embed sustainability in their operations and corporate strategies can better navigate challenges and are

more likely to earn the trust and loyalty of their customers and stakeholders.

QUESTIONS

1. What makes sustainable innovation a critical business strategy, especially during crises like the COVID-19 pandemic?
2. How did URC's commitment to sustainability contribute to its response to the pandemic?
3. How can other companies in the food and beverage industry learn from URC's sustainable innovation practices during the pandemic?

UN SDGS: Good health and well-being (3); Sustainable cities and communities (11)

RESOURCES

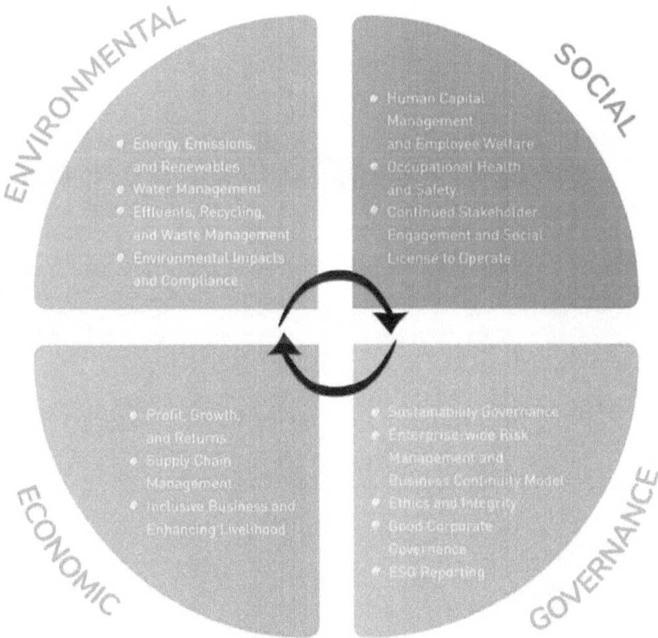

Source: Universal Robina Corporation Sustainability Report - 2016

REFERENCES

1. Universal Robina Corporation, "Company Profile," https://www.urc.com.ph/about-us/profile?ref=menu
2. Universal Robina Corporation, "URC weathers challenging times with people-first approach," https://www.urc.com.ph/stories/corporate-news/urc-weathers-challenging-times-with-people-first-approach?ref=stories_feed_1
3. International Trade Centre, "SME COMPETITIVENESS OUTLOOK 2020, page 10" https://www.intracen.org/uploadedFiles/intracenorg/Content/Publications/ITCSMECO2020.pdf

Corporate Social Responsibility and Business Ethics in a Post-Pandemic World

Themes: Pandemic, CSR, Business, Ethics

TEACHING OBJECTIVES

The case study is intended to qualify students to:

- Understand the importance of corporate social responsibility (CSR) and business ethics in the modern business environment, specifically in a post-pandemic context.
- Explore how CSR and business ethics can shape a company's strategy, public image, and relations with its stakeholders.
- Discuss the challenges and opportunities for businesses when implementing CSR initiatives and maintaining high ethical standards in a post-pandemic world.

SYNOPSIS

The pandemic has intensified numerous existing societal and economic challenges, thereby accentuating the need for businesses to operate ethically and contribute positively to society. The transformative nature of the pandemic has undeniably reshaped the business landscape, making CSR and ethical business conduct a cornerstone of any organization's resilience and long-term survival.

Advantages

In the face of adversities triggered by the pandemic, companies that invest in CSR and ethical business conduct experience several advantages. They distinguish themselves competitively by cultivating a positive reputation, heightening consumer loyalty, and fostering trust among their stakeholders. Additionally, businesses that commit to social responsibility and ethical practices engender a productive and dedicated workforce, thereby ensuring business continuity and sustainability. Such businesses also tend to attract and retain talent more effectively and can reap financial rewards in the form of higher profitability and stock performance.

Strategies

Organizations are adopting diverse strategies to integrate CSR and uphold business ethics in the wake of the pandemic. The focus ranges from employee well-being, transparent stakeholder communication, sustainability in business operations, and active community support initiatives, to adaptability to the ever-evolving societal expectations. Depending on the organization's size, industry type, and geographical location, these strategies vary and often require customization. Companies have demonstrated their flexibility by expanding sick leave policies, supporting remote work, focusing on reducing environmental impact and aiding local communities through donations and other means.

Opportunities

The post-pandemic period unveils a myriad of opportunities for organizations to showcase their commitment to CSR and business ethics. Amidst the pandemic-induced challenges such as social distancing, economic instability, and disruptions to supply chains, businesses have had the chance to display their adaptability, resilience, and dedication to societal welfare. Further, the increasing demand for sustainable and ethical products and practices presents businesses with the opportunity to distinguish themselves in the market and appeal to a more conscientious consumer base.

Conclusion

The case study concludes that CSR and business ethics are fundamental for businesses as they traverse the post-pandemic landscape. The understanding is that these principles need to be an integral part of the company's strategy rather than standalone initiatives. Organizations that successfully integrate socially responsible and ethical business practices into their corporate identity are the ones that thrive in the new era.

INDUSTRY CONTEXT

In the post-pandemic era, businesses are facing a transformative period that requires a reevaluation of their priorities and practices. Consumers, employees, and stakeholders are increasingly looking toward businesses that actively consider the societal and environmental impact of their operations. Therefore, the integration of CSR and business ethics into core business strategies has become essential.

CHALLENGES

- Balancing profitability with ethical considerations and social responsibility.
- Ensuring transparent communication with stakeholders about the company's CSR and ethical efforts, especially in times of crisis.
- Adapting to evolving societal expectations and norms in the post-pandemic world.

LESSONS LEARNED

- CSR and business ethics are not just moral imperatives but can significantly contribute to a company's competitive advantage, resilience, and sustainability.

- A commitment to CSR and business ethics requires consistent effort and should be integrated into every facet of a business's operations.

QUESTIONS

1. How has the COVID-19 pandemic changed the way companies view and approach CSR and business ethics?
2. How can businesses balance the need for profitability with their ethical responsibilities and societal expectations?
3. What examples have you seen of businesses successfully integrating CSR and ethics into their response to the pandemic, and what can we learn from them?

UN SDGS: Quality education (4); Sustainable cities and communities (11)

RESOURCES

Source: Embroker

REFERENCES

1. He, H., & Harris, L. (2020). The impact of Covid-19 pandemic on corporate social responsibility and marketing philosophy. *Journal of business research, 116*, 176-182.
2. Karagiannopoulou, S., Sariannidis, N., Ragazou, K., Passas, I., & Garefalakis, A. (2023). Corporate Social Responsibility: A Business Strategy That Promotes Energy Environmental Transition and Combats Volatility in the Post-Pandemic World. *Energies, 16*(3), 1102.
3. Lee, S. (2022). Corporate social responsibility and COVID-19: Research implications. *Tourism Economics, 28*(4), 863-869.

AI in Customer Service: The Use of Chatbots by Zendesk

Themes: Chatbots, Learning, Artificial Intelligence, Customer Service

TEACHING OBJECTIVES

The case study is intended to qualify students to:

- Understand the role and implementation of AI, particularly chatbots, in customer service, using Zendesk as a prime example.
- Analyze the impact of chatbots on customer engagement, satisfaction, and overall business efficiency.
- Assess the challenges and opportunities involved in integrating AI-driven solutions into traditional customer service models.

SYNOPSIS

In the bustling landscape of customer service software, Zendesk emerges as a crucial player. With a pioneering approach, Zendesk introduces artificial intelligence (AI) to its customer service suite by leveraging chatbots. This strategic shift showcases how crucial AI's role is in the continuously evolving digital realm. By integrating chatbots, Zendesk heightens its ability to provide instantaneous, efficient, and reliable customer service, setting new industry benchmarks.

Advantages

Chatbot integration brings a host of advantages. Zendesk's chatbots instantly respond to customer inquiries, drastically improving service delivery speed and efficiency. They manage a high volume of customer interactions, thereby bolstering customer satisfaction. Additionally, they act as a data collection hub, offering invaluable insights into customer behavior, needs, and service optimization opportunities.

Strategies

A critical aspect of the transformation involves Zendesk's strategic approach to integrating AI. Through heavy investment in AI research and development and a gradual, phased approach to chatbot incorporation, Zendesk ensures the harmonious coexistence of human agents and chatbots. Moreover, a user-centric design philosophy forms the core of chatbot development, guaranteeing customer interactions that not only meet but exceed customer expectations.

Opportunities

With AI and chatbots, an array of opportunities emerges in the customer service realm. The potential extends to chatbots handling complex customer queries, offering personalized experiences, and predicting customer need based on past interactions. This shift transcends the bounds of efficiency and opens avenues for deepened customer relationships and loyalty, alongside a responsive, dynamic customer service framework.

Conclusion

The case study ends with a summation of Zendesk's transformation journey, brought about by AI's integration into its operations. It reiterates that AI isn't an auxiliary component but a crucial part of their customer service model. It highlights the company's innovative spirit and commitment to continuous improvement, ensuring a superior, efficient, and future-forward customer experience.

CHALLENGES

- Convincing customers to trust and engage with AI-powered chatbots can be challenging.
- Maintaining a balance between AI-powered and human-operated customer service to ensure that complex issues are resolved efficiently.
- Ensuring privacy and security of customer data while leveraging AI for customer service.

LESSONS LEARNED

- Implementing AI in customer service can greatly enhance efficiency and customer satisfaction when done strategically and thoughtfully.
- It is essential to maintain a human element in customer service while integrating AI, to ensure complex issues are aptly addressed.

QUESTIONS

1. What other applications of AI can be explored in the customer service industry apart from chatbots?
2. How can companies ensure the security and privacy of customer data when implementing AI-driven customer service?
3. How can companies balance AI-powered and human-operated customer service to ensure maximum efficiency and customer satisfaction?

UN SDGS: Quality Education (4); Sustainable Cities and Communities (11)

RESOURCES

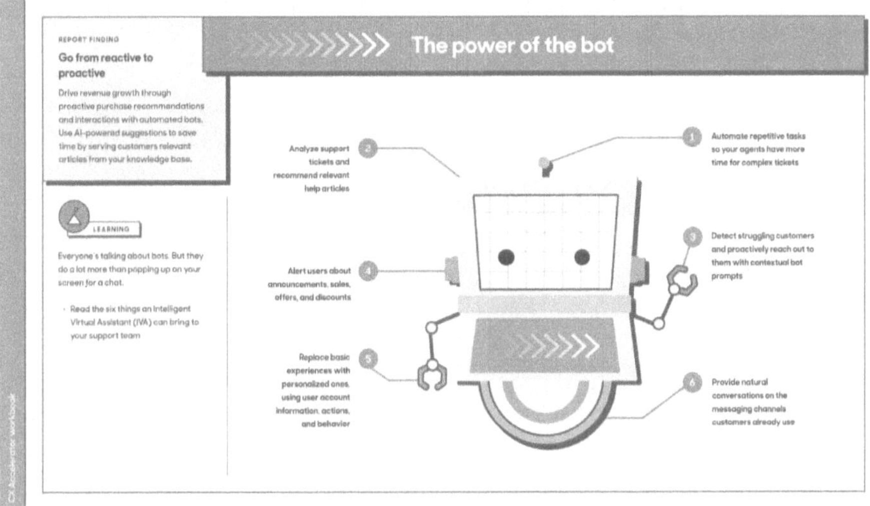

Source: Zendesk

REFERENCES

1. https://www.zendesk.com/service/ai/#:~:text=With%20Zendesk%20bots%2C%20AI%20feels,instant%20answers%20to%20every%20customer.&text=%22The%20bot%20is%20perfect%20for,bot%20to%20get%20answers%20quickly.
2. https://www.zendesk.com/blog/5-benefits-using-ai-bots-customer-service/
3. https://www.zendesk.com/blog/chatbots-for-business/

The Growth of Subscription Services: Exploring Netflix's Business Model

Themes: Business Model, Subscriptions, Online Streaming

TEACHING OBJECTIVES

The case study is intended to qualify students to:

- Understand the business model and growth strategy of Netflix in the context of the global subscription service market.
- Analyze the advantages and potential challenges facing subscription-based businesses in the digital age.
- Investigate opportunities for innovation and customer retention within the subscription service model, particularly in the entertainment sector.

SYNOPSIS

The introduction sets the stage by providing a snapshot of Netflix's business model evolution and its instrumental role in the subscription-based entertainment industry. Starting from its humble beginnings as a DVD rental business, Netflix disrupts the traditional video rental market with its innovative subscription model. The adoption of streaming technology positions Netflix as a pioneer in on-demand entertainment, providing viewers unlimited access to a vast library of content.

Advantages

The subscription model offers numerous advantages to Netflix. It ensures predictable and consistent revenue streams, facilitating long-term budget planning and investment in original content. The model also strengthens Netflix's customer relationships by fostering regular interaction and building customer loyalty. The analysis further delves into how Netflix leverages its extensive data on viewer preferences to inform its content strategy and personalize user experiences. Netflix's continual innovation, from introducing mobile streaming to developing interactive content, further solidifies its leadership position.

Strategies

The strategic maneuvers of Netflix are highlighted. The company invests heavily in original content, mitigating reliance on external content providers and differentiating its offerings from competitors. Its data-driven decision-making process allows it to cater to the diverse tastes of a global audience and deliver personalized recommendations, increasing viewer engagement and reducing churn rates. Moreover, Netflix's aggressive global expansion strategy has not only extended its market reach but also diversifies its content portfolio by incorporating international films and series.

Opportunities

Amid a highly competitive landscape, numerous opportunities await Netflix. These include diversifying content types and formats, enhancing its recommendation algorithm, and incorporating cutting-edge technology like virtual reality. Additionally, by collaborating with international content creators, Netflix can continue to offer culturally diverse content, thereby catering to the global audience's varied preferences.

Conclusion

The conclusion paints a comprehensive picture of Netflix's success as a global subscription service. Its pioneering efforts in redefining how content is consumed, its continual pursuit of innovation, and its unwavering focus on customer satisfaction are key takeaways. While recognizing the challenges posed by an intensely competitive environment and ever-evolving customer preferences, the case study affirms Netflix's resilience and adaptability in maintaining its reign in the world of entertainment.

INDUSTRY CONTEXT

In the contemporary digital landscape, subscription services have gained significant momentum across various sectors, from entertainment and software to retail and personal care. As consumers prefer access over ownership, businesses like Netflix have capitalized on this trend to offer a wide range of services under a recurring payment model. This trend has been particularly noticeable in the media and entertainment industry, with video streaming platforms becoming a popular choice for global audiences.

CHALLENGES

- Maintaining a unique content library amidst intensifying competition and the rising costs of content production and acquisition.
- Balancing global expansion with local content preferences and regulatory challenges.
- Managing the risk of subscriber churn due to price sensitivity and availability of alternative platforms.

LESSONS LEARNED

- Innovation is crucial for survival in the digital entertainment industry. By investing in original content and personalized recommendations, Netflix stays ahead of its competitors.
- A strong focus on customer retention alongside acquisition helps ensure steady growth in subscription-based models.

QUESTIONS

1. How has Netflix's subscription model contributed to its success and how can it influence the future of the entertainment industry?
2. What are the key challenges Netflix might face in the future, and how could they be addressed?
3. How does Netflix's strategy reflect the balance between global expansion and localization, and why is this important for subscription services?

UN SDGS: Industry, innovation, and infrastructure (9); Sustainable cities and communities (11)

RESOURCES

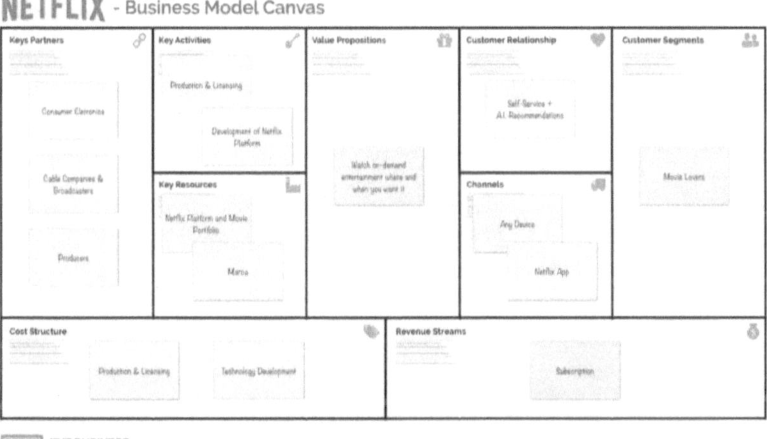

Source: The business Model Analyst

REFERENCES

1. https://blog.gitnux.com/business-guides/netflix-business-model/
2. https://www.alphansotech.com/blog/netflix-business-model-how-netflix-makes-money/
3. https://valueinvestorscentral.com/what-is-the-netflix-business-model-revolutionizing-the-entertainment-industry/

The Future of Digital Identity: Estonia's e-Residency Program

TEACHING OBJECTIVES

The case study is intended to qualify students to:

- Understand the concept of e-Residency and its implications for the future of digital identity and citizenship.
- Analyze the strategies employed by Estonia in implementing and managing its e-Residency program.
- Discuss the challenges and opportunities faced by Estonia's e-Residency initiative in an increasingly digitized world.

SYNOPSIS

The journey of Estonia's innovative e-Residency program commences with a comprehensive introduction. Initiated by the government of Estonia, the program empowers global citizens, allowing them to start and manage an online business within Estonia's regulatory framework. This revolutionary step in digitization takes governmental interaction with individuals and businesses to an entirely new level, forging a path toward a future where digital identities become a norm.

Advantages

The e-Residency program harbors an array of advantages for global entrepreneurs. A chief characteristic of this section is the exploration of the program's ability to facilitate the effortless establishment and management of a business based in the European Union. The program is known for its stable and efficient business environment, acceleration of administrative processes, minimizing red tape, and granting global accessibility. It has proven invaluable for digital nomads and international entrepreneurs, significantly altering their business operations for the better.

Strategies

This portion of the case study focuses on the strategic blueprint Estonia adhered to breathe life into this groundbreaking initiative. Starting from considerable investment in a secure digital infrastructure and stringent cybersecurity measures, to implementing legislation favorable for digital growth, the country's strategies converge on a single point: creating an environment that's not only efficient and secure but also user-friendly for its digital residents.

Opportunities

Estonia's e-Residency program promises an abundance of opportunities, as elaborated in this section. The program fosters a climate conducive to digital entrepreneurship and is a magnet for foreign investments, effectively bolstering Estonia's digital leadership. The scope for expansion and enhancement is substantial and the e-Residency model stands as a template for nations seeking to digitize their services for citizens.

Conclusion

The study culminates in a conclusion summarizing the e-Residency program's impact on digital citizenship and identity. It underlines Estonia's progressiveness and adaptability in the face of digital transformation. While the road to this revolutionary change comes with its share of hurdles, Estonia's unwavering dedication to digital innovation shapes a brighter future for its citizens, e-residents, and the global digital community.

INDUSTRY CONTEXT

The concept of digital identity has gained momentum with the advent of technology and the digitalization of various services. Governments worldwide are exploring ways to improve their public services, reduce administrative burdens, and foster innovation. Estonia stands at the forefront of these efforts, with its e-Residency program representing a significant leap in the realm of digital governance.

CHALLENGES

- Managing the security and privacy concerns associated with digital identities and online transactions.
- Ensuring the legal and regulatory framework keeps pace with the rapid evolution of digital technology.
- Expanding the program and maintaining user-friendly services while addressing issues of scalability.

LESSONS LEARNED

- Digital transformation in public services can significantly enhance efficiency and global accessibility, offering a considerable advantage in a highly digitized global economy.
- Careful planning, robust infrastructure, comprehensive legislation, and a strong emphasis on security are essential for successfully implementing digital identity programs.

QUESTIONS

1. What are the implications of e-Residency and similar programs for global entrepreneurship and digital nomadism?
2. How does Estonia's e-Residency program handle potential security and privacy concerns?
3. How could other nations implement similar programs, and what factors should they consider in doing so?

UN SDGS: Sustainable cities and communities (11); Peace, justice, and strong institutions (16)

RESOURCES

Source: e-Estonia

REFERENCES

1. https://e-estonia.com/weekly-press-review-e-residency-and-the-future-of-digital-identities/
2. https://www.xolo.io/zz-en/e-residency
3. https://www.zdnet.com/article/estonias-new-e-residency-security-focus-you-cant-launder-money-with-a-digital-id/

Neobanks Disrupting Traditional Banking: A Look at Revolut's Rapid Expansion

Themes: Banking, Disruption, Expansion, Evolution

TEACHING OBJECTIVES

The case study is intended to qualify students to:

- Understand the concept of neo-banking and how it is disrupting the traditional banking sector.
- Evaluate the strategies implemented by Revolut in achieving rapid expansion and handling regulatory and competitive challenges.
- Discuss the opportunities presented by the digital banking landscape for neo-banks and the future implications for traditional banking institutions.

SYNOPSIS

The case study begins with a focus on Revolut's inception and its pivotal role in disrupting traditional banking paradigms. As one of the prominent figures in the emerging neo-banks landscape, Revolut exemplifies a digital banking alternative that prioritizes speed, simplicity, and customer convenience. Utilizing cutting-edge technologies and banking innovations, Revolut is rapidly transforming how customers interact with financial institutions.

Advantages

Revolut's core advantages in the market, which are drawn from its digital-native approach, form the crux of this section. The platform's ease of use, expansive features, and focus on seamless international transactions all contribute to its appeal. Moreover, its capacity to provide real-time notifications, budgeting tools, cryptocurrency support, and other novel services puts it a notch above the traditional banking system.

Strategies

The discussion then delves into the strategies that drive Revolut's rapid expansion. The company's innovative digital solutions, focus on customer-centricity, aggressive global expansion strategy, and adaptation to local markets are highlighted. This strategy section also covers Revolut's robust compliance framework to adapt to the diverse financial regulations of the countries they operate in.

Opportunities

This segment explores the manifold opportunities that Revolut's digital banking platform brings to the forefront. Besides setting a new benchmark for customer experience, Revolut is enabling easier access to financial services and fostering financial inclusion. Furthermore, as traditional banking customers increasingly shift toward digital solutions, a considerable growth opportunity lies ahead for neo-banks like Revolut.

Conclusion

The case study concludes with a thorough assessment of Revolut's role in transforming the banking sector. Revolut's successful model of providing enhanced convenience, coupled with diverse financial services, exemplifies the disruptive potential of neo-banks. Though the path is fraught with regulatory challenges and stiff competition,

Revolut's strategy of incessant innovation and customer focus makes it a formidable force in the evolving financial landscape.

INDUSTRY CONTEXT

The banking industry has been undergoing a significant transformation with the advent of digital technologies. Traditional banking models have been challenged by the rise of neo-banks - digital-only banks that operate without physical branches. Neobanks, like Revolut, offer a user-friendly, seamless, and efficient banking experience, which has attracted a large number of customers, especially among the younger demographics. With a focus on convenience, customization, and customer-centricity, these digital-first banks are changing the competitive landscape of the industry and forcing traditional banks to rethink their strategies.

CHALLENGES

- Regulatory Hurdles: Compliance with diverse financial regulations in different markets is a substantial challenge for neo-banks like Revolut.
- Scalability: Rapidly scaling operations while maintaining service quality and security can be daunting.
- Market Penetration: Gaining customer trust and penetrating markets dominated by established traditional banks poses a significant challenge.

LESSONS LEARNED

- Customer-Centricity: Revolut's success underlines the importance of putting the customer at the forefront of business strategy. By offering superior customer experience and personalized services, neobanks can gain a competitive edge.
- Embracing Technology: Leveraging cutting-edge technologies to provide innovative features can significantly differentiate a neo-bank in the crowded banking landscape.

QUESTIONS

1. How have neo-banks like Revolut managed to disrupt the traditional banking sector? What are some key features that distinguish them from conventional banks?
2. What are the challenges Revolut might face in maintaining its rapid growth? How can it overcome these obstacles?
3. Considering the rise of neo-banks, what strategies should traditional banks adopt to retain their customer base and remain competitive in the market?

UN SDGS: Industry, innovation, and infrastructure (9); Sustainable cities and communities (11)

RESOURCES

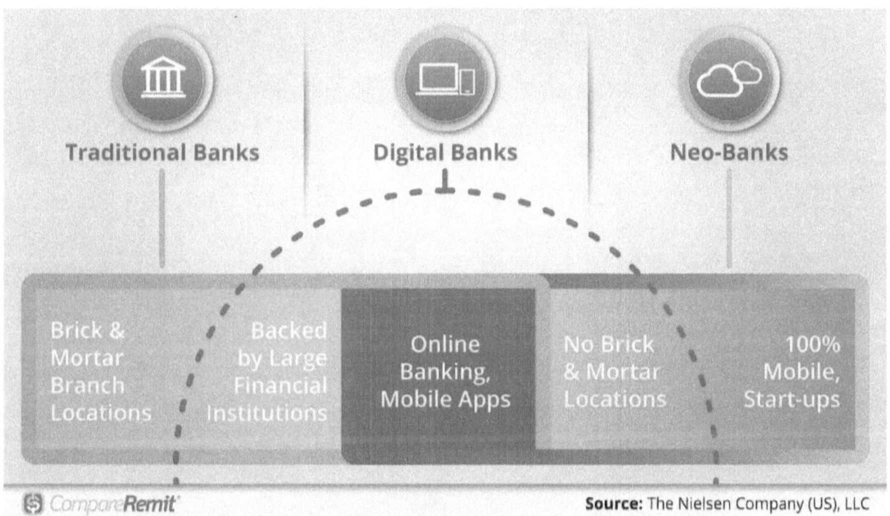

Source: The Nielsen Company

REFERENCES

1. https://sdk.finance/top-neobanks-of-2023-revolutionizing-the-banking-industry/
2. https://www.digipay.guru/blog/neobanking-future-trends-opportunities/
3. https://www.finextra.com/blogposting/21843/how-neobanks-are-defining-the-future-of-banking

The Use of Drones in Humanitarian Efforts: DJI's Disaster Relief Efforts

Themes: Drones, Humanitarian, Disaster, Community service

TEACHING OBJECTIVES

The case study is intended to qualify students to:

- Understand the application and impact of drone technology in humanitarian efforts and disaster relief.
- Analyze DJI's strategies in implementing drone technology in various disaster relief missions.
- Explore the challenges and opportunities in the application of drone technology in the humanitarian sector.

SYNOPSIS

In the realm of disaster relief and humanitarian efforts, DJI, a world-leading drone manufacturer, has played a pivotal role by effectively deploying its drone technology. This case study examines the real-world application of DJI's drones in disaster relief and showcases their impact on enhancing traditional response measures.

Advantages

DJI's drones offer several advantages in disaster relief operations:

1. Rapid Response: DJI's drones enable swift deployment and provide an immediate aerial assessment of disaster-stricken areas, allowing authorities to quickly gather critical information.
2. Remote Monitoring: The drones offer real-time situational awareness, allowing responders to monitor disaster areas, identify potential hazards, and track the movement of personnel.
3. Access to Inaccessible Areas: DJI's drones can access difficult-to-reach or hazardous locations, such as collapsed buildings or flooded areas, facilitating search and rescue operations and saving valuable time.

Strategies

DJI has employed strategic approaches to maximize the effectiveness of its drones in disaster relief:

1. Collaborative Partnerships: The company has established partnerships with local government bodies, non-profit organizations, and humanitarian agencies to ensure seamless coordination during disaster response efforts.
2. Operator Training Programs: DJI provides comprehensive training programs to operators, equipping them with the necessary skills to navigate drones effectively, capture high-quality aerial footage, and carry out specific tasks in disaster scenarios.
3. Ongoing Innovation: DJI consistently invests in research and development to enhance the capabilities of its drone technology, making them more robust, adaptable, and suitable for a wide range of disaster response applications.

Opportunities

1. Enhanced Payload Capabilities: Continual advancements in drone design can lead to increased payload capacities, allowing drones to transport larger supplies, and medical equipment, or even perform aerial deliveries to remote disaster areas.
2. Extended Flight Durations: Improvements in battery technology and energy efficiency can extend the flight durations of drones, enabling longer missions and more extensive coverage of disaster zones.
3. Integration with Artificial Intelligence: Integrating AI capabilities with drones can enhance their capabilities for autonomous flight, object recognition, and data analysis, enabling faster and more accurate decision-making in disaster response scenarios.

Conclusion

DJI's drones have proven to be instrumental in disaster relief operations by providing rapid response, remote monitoring, and access to inaccessible areas. The strategic partnerships, operator training programs, and ongoing innovation by DJI have further amplified the impact of their drones. As advancements continue and regulatory support for drone usage in humanitarian aid grows, the future holds immense potential for the expanded use of drone technology in disaster management strategies, improving the efficiency and effectiveness of humanitarian efforts.

INDUSTRY CONTEXT

The rise of drone technology has revolutionized various industries, with its impact being significantly felt in the humanitarian sector. Drones have been deployed for disaster relief operations, including search and rescue missions, damage assessments, and delivery of medical supplies. Companies like DJI have led this transformation, showcasing the potential of drones to enhance the efficiency, safety, and effectiveness of disaster response efforts.

CHALLENGES

- Regulatory Hurdles: Compliance with different countries' aviation regulations and obtaining necessary permissions can be challenging.
- Operational Issues: Issues like battery life, range, and payload capacity can limit the effectiveness of drones in disaster relief.
- Privacy and Security Concerns: The use of drones raises concerns about privacy and data security, which need to be addressed responsibly.

LESSONS LEARNED

- Innovation for Impact: DJI's success in disaster relief efforts demonstrates how innovative technology can have a profound social impact when applied thoughtfully and strategically.
- Collaboration is Key: Effective collaboration with local authorities, relief organizations, and the community is crucial for successful implementation and maximizing the potential of drone technology.

QUESTIONS

1. What advantages does drone technology offer in disaster relief efforts, and how has DJI capitalized on these?
2. What are the key challenges in using drones for disaster relief, and how can these be addressed?
3. Given the success of DJI's drones in disaster relief, how might the future landscape of disaster response change with further advancements in drone technology?

UN SDGS: Sustainable cities and communities (11); Peace, justice, and strong institutions (16)

RESOURCES

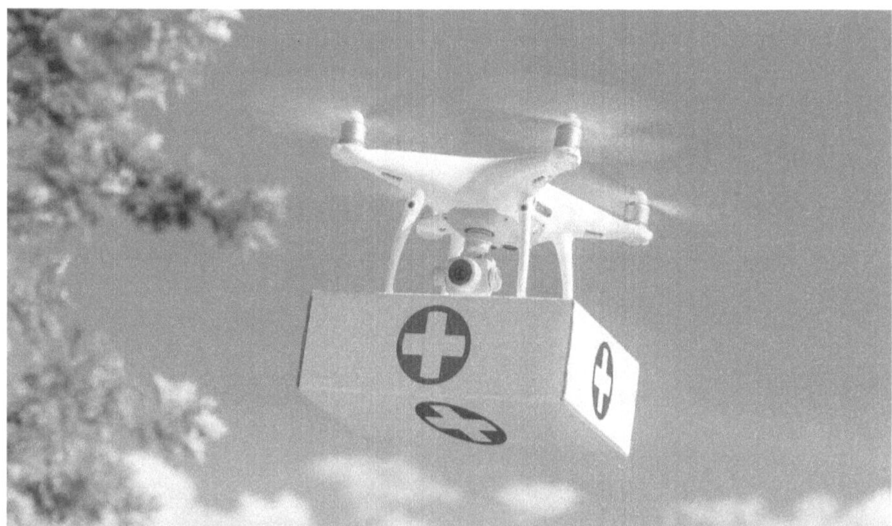

Source: Aeromotus

REFERENCES

1. https://drones.wfp.org/updates/using-drones-deliver-critical-humanitarian-aid
2. https://ts2.shop/en/posts/the-role-of-drones-in-humanitarian-aid-and-disaster-relief
3. https://ts2.space/en/the-benefits-of-military-drones-for-humanitarian-and-peacekeeping-operations/

Veganism and Food Tech: Impossible Foods' Meat Alternatives

Themes: Technology, Food industry, Alternatives, Business Model

TEACHING OBJECTIVES

The case study is intended to qualify students to:

- Understand the rise of veganism as a dietary choice and its impact on the food industry.
- Explore the advantages and benefits of meat alternatives in terms of sustainability, health, and animal welfare.
- Analyze the strategies and opportunities for companies like Impossible Foods in the food tech industry.

SYNOPSIS

This case study focuses on Impossible Foods, a leading player in the food tech industry that has revolutionized the concept of meat alternatives. It examines the rise of veganism as a dietary choice and the increasing demand for plant-based alternatives to meat products.

Advantages

Impossible Foods' meat alternatives offer several advantages:

1. Sustainability: Plant-based alternatives have a significantly lower environmental impact compared to traditional animal

farming, reducing greenhouse gas emissions, land use, and water consumption.

2. Health Benefits: Meat alternatives are cholesterol-free, lower in saturated fat, and often rich in protein and essential nutrients, offering a healthier alternative for individuals.

3. Animal Welfare: By eliminating the need for animal slaughter, meat alternatives contribute to improved animal welfare and ethical considerations.

Strategies

Impossible Foods has employed strategic approaches to promote and establish its meat alternatives in the market:

1. Product Development: The company focuses on creating meat alternatives that mimic the taste, texture, and aroma of animal-based products, appealing to both vegans and meat-eaters.

2. Marketing and Branding: Impossible Foods utilizes effective marketing campaigns to raise awareness about the environmental and ethical benefits of its products, targeting health-conscious consumers and partnering with restaurants and food service providers.

3. Innovation and Research: The company invests in research and development to continuously improve its products, exploring new ingredients and technologies to enhance the taste, nutritional profile, and sustainability of its meat alternatives.

Opportunities

Market Expansion: As consumer demand for plant-based alternatives grows, there is an opportunity for companies to expand their product lines and cater to diverse dietary preferences and cultural tastes.

1. Collaboration with Foodservice Industry: Partnering with restaurants, fast-food chains, and other food service providers can increase the availability and accessibility of meat alternatives to a wider audience.

2. Global Reach: The global market for meat alternatives is expanding, providing opportunities for companies to enter new markets and adapt their products to local preferences and cuisines.

Conclusion

Impossible Foods' meat alternatives have disrupted the food industry by offering sustainable, healthy, and delicious alternatives to traditional meat products. Through strategic product development, marketing efforts, and ongoing innovation, the company has successfully positioned itself as a leader in the food tech industry. As the demand for plant-based alternatives continues to rise, there are significant opportunities for companies like Impossible Foods to drive further innovation, expand market reach, and contribute to a more sustainable and ethical food system.

INDUSTRY CONTEXT

The food industry is undergoing a significant transformation with the rise of veganism and the increasing demand for sustainable and ethical food options. The global shift towards plant-based diets is driven by concerns over the environmental impact of animal agriculture, health considerations, and ethical concerns regarding animal welfare. This has created a growing market for meat alternatives, offering opportunities for companies like Impossible Foods to disrupt the traditional food industry and cater to evolving consumer preferences.

CHALLENGES

- Consumer Acceptance: One of the challenges faced by Impossible Foods and other meat alternative companies is gaining widespread consumer acceptance. Convincing meat-eaters to adopt plant-based alternatives requires addressing taste, texture, and perceived barriers associated with traditional meat products.

- Scalability and Production Capacity: As the demand for meat alternatives increases, ensuring sufficient production capacity and scalability to meet market demands can be a significant challenge. Expanding production facilities and securing reliable ingredient sourcing is crucial for scaling operations effectively.
- Regulatory and Labeling Requirements: The meat alternative industry faces challenges related to regulatory frameworks and labeling requirements. Ensuring compliance with existing regulations and establishing clear labeling standards for plant-based products can be complex and vary across different markets.

LESSONS LEARNED

- Product Innovation is Key: Impossible Foods' success highlights the importance of continuous product innovation to create meat alternatives that not only mimic the taste and texture of traditional meat but also offer additional benefits such as sustainability and health.
- Strategic Partnerships Drive Market Reach: Collaborating with food service providers and establishing partnerships with restaurants and fast-food chains is crucial for expanding market reach and making meat alternatives more accessible to a wider consumer base.

QUESTIONS

1. How can meat alternative companies address the taste and perception barriers associated with traditional meat products to encourage wider consumer acceptance?
2. What are the key factors for successful scaling of production capacity in the meat alternative industry?
3. What are the potential regulatory and labeling challenges faced by companies like Impossible Foods, and how can they navigate these challenges to ensure compliance and transparency?

UN SDGS: Good health and well-being; Sustainable cities and communities (11)

RESOURCES

Source: The Counter

REFERENCES

1. https://unfccc.int/climate-action/momentum-for-change/planetary-health/impossible-foods
2. https://impossiblefoods.com/
3. https://www.bloomberg.com/news/features/2023-01-19/beyond-meat-bynd-impossible-foods-burgers-are-just-another-food-fad

Contributors

We are thankful to our contributors for supporting this initiative.

Dr. Kiran Nair, Abu Dhabi University, Abu Dhabi, UAE

1. Al Ain's Winning Formula: Promoting Vitamin D Water in the Middle East
2. Abu Dhabi Uncovered: A New Tourist Hotspot on the Horizon

Dr. Lakshmi C Radhakrishnan, Universiti Brunei Darussalam, Brunei

1. Recycling Initiatives: Shaping the Future of Plastic Industry in UAE and Brunei
2. Career Reinvention for the Post-pandemic Workplace: Insights from UAE and Brunei
3. Public Sector Entrepreneurship: Unlocking Public-Private Partnership Models in UAE and Brunei
4. Public-Private Partnership (PPP) Models Driving Corporate Entrepreneurial Outcomes: Nigeria's Lekki-Epe Expressway Project

Mary Rose F. Becodo and John Rey P. Tarraja

1. Sustainable Innovation: Universal Robina Corporation's Initiatives during the COVID-19 Pandemic